D1431774

ALSO BY JIM SQUIRES

Horse of a Different Color:
A Tale of Breeding Geniuses, Dominant Females,
and the Fastest Derby Winner Since Secretariat

The Secrets of the Hopewell Box:
Stolen Elections, Southern Politics, and a City's Coming of Age

Read All About It!:
The Corporate Takeover of America's Newspapers

HEADLESS HORSEMEN

HEADLESS HORSEMEN

A TALE OF CHEMICAL COLTS,
SUBPRIME SALES AGENTS, AND THE
LAST KENTUCKY DERBY ON STEROIDS

JIM SQUIRES

TIMES BOOKS | HENRY HOLT AND COMPANY | NEW YORK

Times Books
Henry Holt and Company, LLC
Publishers since 1866
175 Fifth Avenue
New York, New York 10010
www.henryholt.com

Henry Holt® is a registered trademark of
Henry Holt and Company, LLC.

Library of Congress Cataloging-in-Publication Data
Squires, James D., 1943—
  Headless horsemen : a tale of chemical colts, subprime sales agents, and
the last Kentucky Derby on steroids / James D. Squires. — 1st ed.
    p.   cm.
  ISBN-13: 978-0-8050-9060-4
  ISBN-10: 0-8050-9060-6
  1. Horse racing—United States.   2. Doping in horse racing—United States.
3. Race horses—Breeding —United States.   I. Title.
  SF335.U5S73 2009
  798.400973'0905—dc22   2009001147

Henry Holt books are available for special promotions and
premiums. For details contact: Director, Special Markets.

First Edition 2009

Designed by Kelly Too

Printed in the United States of America
3   5   7   9   10   8   6   4   2

For the people a horse will come to

It was just part of the game, ever since I can remember. Everybody was looking for an edge. I don't care who it was. A trainer would say, "Don't get me caught, but keep me worried."

—DR. ALEXANDER HARTHILL

CONTENTS

HEADLESS HORSEMEN

INTRODUCTION

Betty Jo Stewart and her son Rob were among those horse-racing fans who always knew to "bet on the grays." So for the 2001 Kentucky Derby they placed a modest wager on Monarchos, the colt born and raised on our Two Bucks Farm in Kentucky. When Monarchos won that year, they hugged each other and rushed to the off-track betting parlor window as if they'd won a million.

The Stewarts lived in Wyoming, which is a long way from Kentucky, but they had been trying for years to get seats at the Derby through a mail-order lottery. In the euphoria of the winning moment, the son promised his mother, "Next year, somehow, I'm going to take you to the Kentucky Derby."

That would never happen, at least not the way twenty-four-year-old Rob Stewart intended. Eight months later, he died from injuries suffered in a traffic accident. But the dream lived on in the mind of his cousin Sandy Swanson. Inspired by a 2002 television commercial showing Monarchos frolicking in his paddock at historic Claiborne Farm in his new role as a breeding stallion, she wrote to Churchill Downs asking for seats at the 2003 Derby, citing the tragedy as a special cause for her quest.

Once the tickets had been secured, she began searching for a way to visit Claiborne Farm, eighty miles east of Louisville, so her aunt could see Monarchos in the flesh.

Swanson had never heard of Two Bucks Farm, where the Kentucky Derby champion had been born and raised. And she had no idea that the owner of the tour company, Kentucky Horse Tours, that she had telephoned at random was also co-owner of Two Bucks and had danced among the swells in the good seats under the Twin Spires the day he won.

"Can your company take us to see Monarchos at Claiborne Farm?" she asked.

"I'll see if I can arrange that," said the tour company owner, never one to promise anything she might not be able to deliver.

But there is hardly a stallion that my wife of twenty-five years cannot arrange for a visitor to Kentucky to see. A breeder of good racehorses herself, she is a recognizable and welcome tour guide on almost every farm. She is also well known in the Bluegrass as the "dominant female" at Two Bucks who figured prominently in the story of Monarchos.

The day she took Betty Jo Stewart and her family to finally meet the Derby winner is now a poignant memory for everyone present.

Charismatic and friendly, Monarchos had quickly become a fan favorite at Claiborne, gentle enough to be touched, fed peppermints, and have his picture made with visitors. On the way up to his barn, Sandy Swanson related the story of her cousin's death and how much seeing the horse meant to the family. Her voice began to quiver with the telling. This of course brought tears to the eyes of Betty Jo and her sister Peggy, Sandy's mother. It also touched a nerve in the stallion handler as well.

There were tears in the man's eyes as he pulled a handful of mane from Monarchos and handed it to Betty Jo. She grasped the hairs like they were gold and announced that they would be placed in her son's gravestone repository in Utah, where he had been laid to rest beside his grandfather. This prompted another round of sniffling.

The scene is testament to the way horses touch the lives of people who love them. Even their stories have lasting emotional impact. The "dominant female" gets wet-eyed every time she recalls how another tour guide once brought a female customer over for an introduction.

The tourist, who was wheelchair bound, said, "You're the dominant female people talk about. I used to be you."

Sandy, Betty Jo, and Peggy return regularly to Kentucky now, usually bringing beautiful equine photographs of horses they follow and bet on and never failing to visit Monarchos. Upon learning that his mother, Regal Band, had died, they sent a floral wreath for her grave.

Nearly all white now, their favorite Derby winner has moved from Claiborne Farm to the Versailles farm of the Charles Nuckols family, having been repurchased by John and Debbie Oxley, who owned him when he won the Derby, and who own the farm next door where most of their mares reside.

Once back on the Woodford County soil where he was raised, Monarchos has begun to flourish as a breeding stallion, having his best year in 2008. The sire of twenty-four stakes horses now, he will likely go down in history as a sire of productive mares, which is his genetic blueprint.

Monarchos was the only real male star among the many fine racehorses produced by his sire, Maria's Mon, now deceased, who in turn was the most outstanding son of his sire, Wavering Monarch. Both were products of a breeding theory grounded in mating the offspring of outstanding broodmare sires to each other.

Secretariat, the only horse other than Monarchos to run the Kentucky Derby's mile-and-a-quarter distance in less than two minutes, made his mark as a sire of broodmares who then produced great runners who went on to become great breeding stallions.

The source of Monarchos's royal blood strain came from Regal Band. When she died on Easter Sunday in 2007, the same year as his sire, it was like a death in the family for Two Bucks. A great loss but—as in the case of Maria's Mon—a blessing that halted the suffering of a noble animal who had profoundly affected our lives.

The unlikely, almost unimaginable, success of their Derby champion son sunk my roots deep into the magic loam soil of the picturesque farm where Monarchos grew up and where Regal Band is now buried, halting forever three decades of migratory wandering through the nation's concrete jungles.

It also plunged me hopelessly into an addictive and difficult endeavor to which the word *business* can only be flagrantly and loosely applied. Raising horses for a living is in fact the biggest gamble of all in what is essentially a gambling enterprise, the rewards as uncertain as those of the old game of chance native to the rural South known as "Rooster Bingo," in which a chicken walks aimlessly about in a wire cage suspended from a roadhouse ceiling, while below otherwise seemingly intelligent human beings wait unreasonable amounts of time for a plop of excrement to fall on a numbered board. The experience has made my years in the rough-and-tumble worlds of big-city newspapers and politics seem like a picnic in short pants. Exceedingly difficult even for those in it just for the money, it is even harder for those in it "just for the horses."

My first thoroughbred mare, a stakes winner from Chile named Lichi, was purchased with the last paycheck I ever received, a memorable one signed by the great American patriot Ross Perot as final payment for being media adviser to his 1992 campaign for president.

At this writing Lichi at age twenty-nine is still alive and healthy in the pension pasture at Two Bucks. Every day since she arrived, the sight of her has been a joy to my life. But each day has also been a struggle—not to make money, a futile endeavor for a small breeder—but just to hold my place in one of the most exciting, exhilarating, and mind-boggling adventures a man can undertake.

The year I started, the thoroughbred industry was just beginning to recover from a devastating financial crunch caused by the savings-and-loan debacle and accompanying real estate reevaluation in the late 1980s. In the year I just lived through, 2008, which may go down in history not only as the fall of George W. Bush but as the fall of everything, thoroughbred horse racing went through the most tumultuous year in its modern history.

There had been storms before, but never one that hit so fast on so many fronts. It was a cataclysm that could only have been produced by the perfect combination of external forces beyond anyone's control and years of internal failures that invited them. In many ways, what happened to horse racing was a microcosm of what happened to Wall Street and the world's economy as a result of consequences unforeseen and greed unforgivable.

As usual with anything involving horses, this story is conflicting and replete with intriguing villains and lovable heroes, both human and equine. Some are unforgettable, none more so than Monarchos's most successful son, Stones River, who did not make it to the Derby; his ill-fated stablemate Eight Belles, who did; and, of course, their cowboy trainer in the big white hat—J. Larry Jones.

Wherever and however this exciting ride through the thoroughbred world ends, I will never be able to characterize it as well as Yvonne Azeff, the amazing young woman who rode

Monarchos in the mornings for the trainer Johnny Ward and who played a key role in preparing him for the Derby.

A year later Yvonne suffered a severe head injury when her stable pony slipped coming off a Florida track. While she was hospitalized and in a deep coma, a picture of her atop a galloping Monarchos was placed near her bedside. When she finally regained consciousness, it was the first thing she saw when she opened her eyes. The first words out of her mouth were "Riding on a cloud."

PART ONE

RUMBLINGS

— 1 —

A LILY FOR THE DEPARTED

Something had definitely gone haywire. Breaking into tears at the realization that Greg Norman had just failed to win the British Open at age fifty-three to become the oldest golfer ever to win a Major Championship is hard evidence of pending emotional collapse. I had never cheered for Norman before in my life, even twenty years earlier when he was the best golfer in the world. He was always too cool and aloof for me. But those were tears running down my face and a real sob being choked back in my throat.

Fortunately, my six-year-old grandson and namesake, whose tears disappear as quickly as his cookies, was too engrossed in a sizable video planet war going on in his hands to even notice. He had arrived in my bedroom to announce, "Gramma sent me to tell you to come downstairs and start the grill."

At Two Bucks Farm, we always eat "the best" when the two grandsons are visiting. The "best" in my view—as I have been warned repeatedly over the last twenty-five years—is also the most unhealthy and hedonistic. Stuff like we were having that July Sunday: steaks; cheesy, scalloped potatoes; bread and butter; and multiberry pie with thousand-calorie crust. Only the salad would get dietary approval from the chef preparing it all. That would be the dominant female, Gramma, or to me Mary Anne, gourmet cook extraordinaire and amateur dietitian. Her idea of healthy eating leans toward brussels sprouts, tiny taste-less squashes, and stuff dredged up from the bottom of the China Sea, preferably soaked in health-protecting garlic.

Her infrequent concessions to dietary decadence are directly attributable to the grandsons' father, a South Carolinian who grew up as I did, eating whatever meat could be barbecued and whatever vegetable could be fried and fit on the plate with gravy, biscuits, and cornbread. And he was raising his sons that way, while still graciously slipping into their culinary education some of his mother-in-law's more elegant contributions such as spaghetti with clam sauce and calamari, although bypassing them himself.

Truth be told, all the men in the dominant female's life were addicted to the secret of succulent southern cooking most con-cisely defined in Tom Wolfe's novel *A Man in Full*. As Wolfe tells it, following a typical southern feast including pork-seasoned green beans, skillet corn, and berry pies, the plantation owner host invited the black cook from the kitchen to hear the acco-lades being passed on her meal. Asked specifically by one of the Yankee female visitors how she made so many different dishes so tasty, the cook was perplexed and slow to answer.

Finally, she said, "Just grease, honey."

This was not just any Sunday dinner at Two Bucks. It was a going-away meal for Sigita Budrikaite, our tiny Lithuanian farm manager for the last decade. Her contributions to the success of Two Bucks racehorses could only have been greater if she had owned and funded the place as well as she took care of the ani-mals. The boys love Sigita. And they are not alone. Our business model contains a standing contingency plan dusted off and updated every time she goes back to Europe that takes into account the possibility that she might decide to stay. It is called "Complete Dispersal of Breeding Stock."

Without her, we wouldn't be breeding thoroughbreds anymore. And that Sunday afternoon in July, there was an unspoken awareness that we might not be doing it much longer with her either. To me, the breeding industry appeared to be in free fall.

A few days earlier, the 2008 July yearling sale at Fasig-Tipton's Lexington paddocks—the first and only opportunity for Kentucky breeders to market their one-year-old horses—had been dismal from start to finish. Nearly half of the six hundred or so horses cataloged had gone unsold. And these were not average horses. They were among the most carefully culled, best-conformed, early maturing yearlings offered by some of the best thoroughbred breeders in the world.

For years, glowing sale reports and inflated but meaningless sale averages had masked the illness growing in the industry's underbelly: massive overproduction in the face of a shrinking market of end users and a racing industry in steep decline. In two short days, inevitability had become reality. And reality had landed especially hard at Two Bucks Farm, long a pygmy operation struggling to survive among giants, mainly on the strength of having bred Monarchos, the winner of the 2001 Kentucky Derby, whose siblings had generated more than $1.6 million in yearling revenue. In recent years, the July Fasig-Tipton sale, which featured a special section on the offspring of new sires, had become our most reliable source of income. Monarchos had been among the first crop of his sire, Maria's Mon. And more recently, the farm's mares had produced big-time racehorses from the first two crops of the young sire sensation Broken Vow, who stood at the same farm as Maria's Mon.

In a business where survival depends on the old axiom "take horse to sale—bring home money," we had sometimes brought home as much as $400,000 from the Fasig-Tipton July sale. But this year four Two Bucks horses had gone to sale and three had come home unsold, along with a measly $20,000 that would be obliterated by entry and sale costs. Among the returnees was one of the best yearling colts who ever drew a breath at Two Bucks. He was a son of Monarchos, more like his sire than any I had ever seen. He had no conformation flaws of consequence, no veterinary issues, no lack of size or charisma nor deficiency of pedigree. He also had no interest from buyers and was withdrawn from the sale without going through the ring to avoid a public devaluation.

As I was preparing to load him into a van for his return, an even more stunning blow was delivered. With no warning, I felt a sharp pain in the back, in the vicinity of my right kidney. The thought of having been stabbed ran through my mind. But there is no backstabbing at Kentucky horse sales, just front-stabbing, usually by slick, smiling charlatans armed only with deception and a sharp mastery of a flawed system that promotes fleecing of the unaware.

Within minutes, the blood in my face had been washed out by a gush of cold sweat that dripped from my neck and forehead. Food poisoning, I surmised from my sitting position under the shade tree. An hour earlier, I had carelessly and courageously consumed a sale-quality cheeseburger, complete with a pithy slice of tomato now suspected of being a salmonella carrier.

"You don't look so good," said a friendly consignor, who had chaperoned one of my unsold yearlings from his sale barn to my van.

"Well, what do you expect for a guy who's just been robbed—and poisoned—by Fasig-Tipton?" I responded.

"I hear you," he said.

But I could barely hear him. And things got worse by the minute. Eventually Sigita arrived to help me drive home and unload the yearlings, and two hours later I was in the emergency room of the closest hospital, begging anyone within the sound of a weak voice for any painkiller within their reach.

Kentucky is a cauldron of nearly blind patriotism. Veterans in pickup trucks compete to see how many SUPPORT THE TROOPS color ribbons can be fitted onto the surface of a single tailgate. In the local barbershop that summer, men would actually cry out in anguish at a cable news suggestion that Barack Obama had a chance to be elected president. Yet no one here even raises an eyebrow about guys named Mohammed or Abdul.

That is because Woodford County is the heart of the racehorse business, the state's number one economic engine, and no one has been more important to this endeavor in the last twenty years than a guy named Mohammed ("Sheikh Mo" to us), but he is better known worldwide as Sheikh Mohammed bin Rashid Al Maktoum, the ruler of Dubai. Of all our rich absentee owners, he and his brother Sheikh Hamdan are clearly the biggest spenders.

They are also the best liked and most respected, mainly because of the way they meticulously maintain and expand their vast land holdings: sprawling Gainesborough Farm near Versailles, imposing Darley at Jonabell, high on a hill behind Lexington's Blue Grass Airport, and Hamdan's multiple Shadwell Farms, which seem to be everywhere. Not only do the sheikhs overpay their employees and contribute liberally to local charities; they never try to squeeze dollars out of their horses or the people they do business with—a rarity among their peers, had they any.

Now similarly highly regarded by at least one Woodford countian is Dr. Mohammad Abdul Motalib of Bangladesh, an emergency room physician at Bluegrass Hospital. This is largely

due to the first words I heard him utter in his British accent—
"Two Di-laudids"—presumably to keep my moaning from alarm-
ing the Mexican families who gather in his emergency room for
their only contact with the U.S. health care system. So many
new Mexican citizens are born at Bluegrass Hospitals that they
had to hire a multilingual nurse who knew how to say "push" in
Spanish.

In no time it seemed—thanks to the "two Di-laudids," a
highly addictive narcotic similar to morphine—Dr. Motalib was
back at my side explaining that a CAT scan had detected four
stones in my right kidney, including one four millimeters in size
stalled at the entrance to my ureter.

Obviously convinced the stone could find its own way out,
Dr. Motalib promptly evicted me from the ER and away from its
Dilaudid supply with instructions to "drink a lot of water and
walk it off." And I found myself in the hands of M.A., who had
just returned from a trip to South Carolina to pick up the grandsons, ages six and seven.

"See, too many dairy products. I told you," she said. "How
much milk do you drink every day? A quart at least."

Someone answering her own question is not nearly as irritating when you are trying your best to die.

One of my life's blessings is a quarter-century-long marriage
to a highly educated biochemist, whose main regret is not having gone on to become a Cornell-trained medical doctor special-
izing in research. The lack of an MD after her name, however,
has not stopped M.A. from diagnosing and prescribing treatment for any malady she comes across in dogs, horses, plants,
and people, including herself.

A few years back, despite a plethora of doctors on her case,
she was the only one to figure out that she had contracted a
mutated strain of *Clostridium difficile*, a bacterium common to
the digestive tract of horses, that was suddenly killing humans

all over the Northeast, including Maine, from where she had just returned. It apparently was still a mystery to ER doctors in Kentucky, even though medical breakthroughs do arrive here faster than new movies. This *C-dif* bug, which flourishes where broad-spectrum antibiotics have wiped out its natural enemies, can fatally shut down the digestive process of man or beast. Among older Americans who contract it, the mortality rate is 25 percent.

Fortunately for M.A., one of the ER physicians, a female she insists, prescribed a drug called metronidazole that kills *Clostridium*, which—fortunately for me—meant that M.A. was still around to take over my treatment from Dr. Motalib. She immediately seized all the necessary credentials, including my brand-new, never-before-used Medicare card, as well as the prescriptions for nausea and pain tucked in my shirt by my Bangladeshi savior. She had them filled and returned them with a caveat.

"The water is more important than the medicine," she said. "You have to drink at least three gallons a day."

"That's a lot of water," I said.

"Horses drink ten gallons. You can do it. By the way, that tree needs water, too. Did you water the trees today?"

She had had water on the brain for some time. We were driving down the long front lane at Two Bucks, which is lined with fourteen-year-old Green Mountain maples, twenty-five or so, some still suffering from the drought of 2007. One was clearly punier than the others. Before going to South Carolina, M.A.—after an Internet search—had diagnosed the tree's illness as an attack of bore beetles, which she suspected was threatening all the others.

Watering all the Green Mountain maples on Two Bucks lane is an all-day affair, requiring the repeated emptying and refilling of a 210-gallon tank in the back of a pickup truck. Had I been forced to water them all that day, she could have planted me somewhere in the line.

Luckily, no bore-beetle assault on the trees had occurred. My own eyeball scrutiny of the dying tree had revealed it to be the nearly girthed victim of a thirsty midget woodpecker called a yellow-bellied sapsucker. Having quenched his thirst on the way south earlier in the spring, the little jerk had left only the one maple in dire need of the drought-survival watering tactics suggested by M.A.'s Web research.

"I'll take care of it," I said, and did, a physical act made possible only by the obviously still active two Dilaudids.

The next forty-eight hours are a blurred recollection from the fetal position and near-comatose state that became my refuge, and from which I was roused periodically to deal with the daily crises consistent with horse farm management—things like kittens being born inside hollow barn walls, dead skunks being delivered in truckloads of bedding, or a groundhog being cornered in the bathroom by the Jack Russell terrier. There was the usual "it just broke" machinery report, this one on our ancient diesel-powered, zero-radius mowing machine.

This is one of M.A.'s favorite pieces of equipment, which she rides up and down the perimeter grass strip along the road frontage, where from time to time she also insists on operating her own lightweight weed trimmer. Whatever her intentions, this behavior sends signals not only that she is extremely vigorous for a grandmother, but that her husband is a lazy lout too cheap to afford immigrant labor like everyone else.

A faulty piece of equipment so important to the farm's image had to be subjected to her emergency diagnosis, which ultimately required a trip chauffeured by M.A. herself to the Lexington mowing machine dealer for the replacement part. Fortunately the cramped interior of her Jaguar transport mandates the fetal position, pained or not.

The following day's crisis was less urgent but longer-lasting: a predictable farmworker frenzy when a small bulldozer belonging to a barn remodeling crew got stuck in parking gear, closing off the lone bottleneck on the farm road and limiting movement to pedestrian traffic.

Luckily the impediment did not restrict exodus from the house to the main road. Because later that afternoon, with the bulldozer still in park, the employees still afoot, and M.A. off in her Jaguar with the grandsons, I shamelessly drove myself down Two Bucks lane, past the dying Green Mountain maple for which I had renewed sympathy, and directly to the Bluegrass Hospital ER, where I intended to request immediate euthanasia.

Though I would have settled for "two Di-laudids," the man from Bangladesh was nowhere in sight. But a new set of radiographs confirmed that I was blocked as tight as the farm road, machinery full of gas, and none of the motors working. The ER doctor gave me two new prescriptions and an appointment with another physician for the following Monday—a three-day interval I had little hope of surviving.

Back home, M.A. again confiscated all my prescription drugs, perusing them like a narc intent on arrest. "It's the pain pills that are shutting down your digestive process," she said, authoritatively. "I wouldn't take any more of those. And this broad-spectrum antibiotic, you don't need that either. That's bad. But you have to take this one."

She was holding up one of the vials like it was a silver bullet. "Flagyl," she said, remembering the brand name for metronidazole.

"Flagyl saved my life. Probably what saved Little Bold Belle, too. You could have what we had," the "we" being my wife and my horse.

Little Bold Belle is one of our best mares, the dam of Unbridled Belle, a multiple graded stakes winner of over $1.5 million, and more recently the dam of Monarchos's most promising son, Stones River, already a stakes winner at three. The spring after

M.A. contracted *Clostridium difficile*, Little Bold Belle nearly died from an equine version, *Clostridium perfingens*. She was in one of the world's most expensive equine hospitals for thirteen days, lost more than two hundred pounds, and was sent home to die, which she stubbornly refused to do. Her hospital bill was over $20,000, more than Mary Anne's. For that amount of cash, both woman and horse could have spent a week at the Drake Hotel in Chicago and gone shopping on Michigan Avenue.

M.A. shook the metronidazole vial before my eyes one more time.

"You better take these."

Whether I did without fail and at the proper intervals is beyond my recollection. The next two days were only an agonizing haze—during which I flopped around in search of a comfortable position. In spite of all the medical attention received and scientific expertise offered, no one had delivered what I really needed. A plumber.

A lot of people who regularly take care of horses no longer can smell them, although horses have a distinct odor readily apparent to most humans. But many horsemen retain a keen sense of smell otherwise.

Sigita, who has been around horses all of her life, can smell a rotovirus infection in a foal long before any clinical signs become apparent. But I rarely smell anything less pungent than gasoline. Over the years my sense of smell has deteriorated even more than my eyesight and hearing. Not only do the smells of horses and their spore escape me; the scents of cabbages boiling, meat smoking, biscuits baking, and—sadly enough—perfumed-drenched women are all beyond my discernment.

But there is something about the *C-dif* bacteria or its pharmaceutical enemy, metronidazole—no one seems to know which—that heightens a human's sense of smell to an incredible degree. At some point during the delirium days, my long-missing sense of smell returned, enhanced exponentially. There was nothing, it seemed, that I could not smell. Not only could I smell horses again; I could detect differences in them. I could smell vegetables that I never knew had scents, flowers and perfumes from ridiculously far away, deodorizer fumes in elevators, and the body odors of people who passed me in the drugstore. I felt like a dog. They could have used me to sniff luggage at the airport or track escaped criminals through the woods.

The most disturbing aspect of it all was that I could smell myself. Neither hours in the Jacuzzi nor long showers with M.A.'s fragrant bath oils could keep me from smelling myself. Could this be the mysterious pheromone that somehow attracts us to the opposite sex? If it was, how could any woman have ever been attracted to mine? Can a person smell his own pheromones? Who knows? Whatever was going on had honed my sense of smell to the same level of acuity that lets skin detect heat, or makes hair follicles move to static electricity. For the first time, I understood how horses can differentiate one human from another by smell, or pick up on a rider's fear or confidence, which I always believed they did. Something—drug or disease— was setting new parameters by which my brain processed and reacted to whatever was being picked up by my keener senses.

What other possible explanation for crying over Greg Norman and a golf tournament? And what about the delusions that awaited me when I answered the summons to start the grill? When I showed up downstairs, it was from the perspective of an out-of-body experience.

I watched myself start the grill for Sunday dinner, free of pain for the first time since Tuesday, no longer fetal-bent but ramrod straight. And I saw my farm manager, Sigita, out of her farm manager uniform of jeans and sneakers, in makeup and dress-up Sunday clothes. And wasn't that a hint of perfume in her hair wafting across the room?

She was presenting something to M.A. It was a huge lily, deep red and white, which for some reason looked familiar.

"I grew it in my yard," I heard Sigita say.

M.A. took it immediately to the kitchen sink, cut and arranged it into a large vase of water. Soon a sickening sweet aroma engulfed first the kitchen, then the entire house, and finally even the patio where I was grilling. It was a smell out of my past, only magnified a thousandfold by whatever had hold of my senses.

Then I realized what it was. A stargazer lily, one of the most fragrant flowers on earth and with which I had a history. When I was a child in Tennessee, members of my family had spent many hours in and around a funeral home owned by my grand-father's best friend, the local sheriff, whose political clout was rooted in his undertaking business.

As the sheriff's sidekick and principal deputy, my grand-father led the funeral processions on his police motorcycle and was the unofficial mortuary security man in his off-hours. My mother was a regular volunteer political worker and virtually camped during election seasons in campaign headquarters two floors above a basement "embalming" chamber. I was often left to wander among the viewing rooms, where the departed were laid out and where two odors became imprinted in my sensibil-ities forever.

One was that of embalming powder, which burned my nose, and the other was the overwhelming, sickening sweet smell of stargazer lilies. They were omnipresent in funeral homes all across the South, a permanent disguise for the smell of death and embalming powder. The lilies could be found at the ends of the caskets, serving as backdrops for the wreaths and other flo-ral arrangement that moved in and out with the corpse.

These remembrances rode the aroma of Sigita's stargazer lily into my brain. Embalming powder, funeral processions, long-gone relatives, and viewing room conversations from sixty years ago. Again I felt tears streaming down my own face.

All my formal education being in the arts, not the sciences, I can only surmise a physiological connection between human emotions and senses. The day Monarchos won the Kentucky Derby, my ability to hear vanished for ten minutes after he crossed the finish line. And that July Sunday on the patio, my hearing became as acute as my sense of smell.

From far across the large music room in my old Kentucky home, I heard M.A. tell Sigita that she was taking our grandsons on a fishing trip the following Friday. What the hell was that about? I had heard the story many times of her catching a thirty-five-pound muskie when she was a girl. But that didn't make her Izaak Walton. What did she know about fishing? I, on the other hand, had been a fishing guide as a young man. I had caught more fish in my life than M.A. had eaten, and that's saying something. Besides, grandfathers are supposed to take grandsons fishing, not grandmothers.

And then it dawned on me. The return of smell and hearing, the sharpness of vision, the absence of pain in my gut, the emotions riling right under my skin. Maybe I wasn't really downstairs starting the grill. Not in the flesh anyway. Obviously I had died, maybe at the precise moment Greg Norman blew the British Open, and no one knew it yet. Or then again maybe I had died days before while watering the tree, and everybody was over it already. Nobody was crying, that's for sure.

Yes, indeed, this could be my own wake. That would certainly explain the funeral flower Sigita had brought from her backyard to the new widow at Two Bucks. A lily for the departed.

2

THE LAST STEROID DERBY

The question had always been which would come first—bankruptcy or death. From the moment of temporary insanity when someone decides to try to make his living raising racehorses, the lurch forward toward both is inexorable. At Two Bucks the gap between the two narrowed with each year's profit-and-loss statement. And in my mind at least, on that Sunday afternoon in July 2008 they had joined in a stretch-run duel to the wire.

If indeed death had won in a photo finish, the family diagnostician surely would attribute the outcome to a life of culinary debauchery. She regarded me as a modern-day Dorian Gray whose picture aged with each sinful, grease-drenched breakfast at the Keeneland Track Kitchen.

It had to be all those dairy products. A four-millimeter calcium deposit is actually rather a small price to pay for—as the mad poet of my generation Bob Dylan observed—having "sucked the milk from a thousand cows." But even a Phi Beta Kappa biochemist from Northwestern can be guilty of oversimplification. My demise—if indeed it had occurred—was considerably more complicated.

Some people who recover from close encounters with the grim reaper report that at some point events from the past flash through their minds. Now I know that for someone who spent twenty-eight years in a dying business—newspapers—this can take the form of an obituary, appropriately botched and error-filled.

The *New York Times* of my delirium reduced an extraordinarily diversified and adventure-filled sixty-five years to a seven-year relationship with the Kentucky Derby, beginning with the 2001 version Derby won by my homebred Monarchos and ending with the corporate-sponsored 2008 version, aggravatingly "presented by Yum Brands." A televised act of self-destruction, the obit of my dreams declared, and undoubtedly a contributing factor to my own death.

Now I understood. This was all about atonement—not only for a life of unhealthy eating but for carrying with me from one troubled profession to another the nasty habit of telling everything I know. On the Sunday before the 2008 Kentucky Derby, the real-world *New York Times* had announced under my byline that the upcoming edition of the world's greatest horse race would probably be the last ever run on steroids. It was an ugly truth no one wanted to hear.

The best part of a morning on the rail at the Keeneland race course in Lexington that spring was the regular appearance of Curlin, the 2007 Horse of the Year. The big chestnut stallion had recently vanquished international competitors in Dubai to become the undisputed champion of the world. Fully mature at age four, he was an intimidating presence, a gleaming red, chiseled example of what a precise regimen of feed, proper exercise, and pharmaceuticals can do to an already beautifully conformed natural athlete.

When he cut loose from his pony to gallop, it appeared he might at any moment sprout wings and take off along with the neighboring jets at Blue Grass Airport, leaving grounded and awestruck the herd of current Triple Crown nominees preparing on the Keeneland track for the 2008 Derby.

The sight of this fire-breathing Pegasus not only scattered the equine paparazzi but inevitably evoked commentary from the railbirds, among them two of the most loquacious and opinionated: John T. Ward, the trainer of Monarchos, and me. A couple of genetically engineered disturbers of the peace, we were imbued by our extraordinary good fortune with expertise on all matters involving the Kentucky Derby, which we seldom kept to ourselves.

Much of what we said was merely conventional wisdom, like how shameful it was that Churchill Downs had tacked "Yum Brands" onto the name of a world-famous race owned by the Commonwealth of Kentucky. But every now and then, Ward would come up with stuff nobody else had said.

"You know," he said that morning, after watching some muscle-bound Derby hopefuls go by, "this could be the last Kentucky Derby on steroids."

Only the most naive newcomers to the Sport of Kings would have considered the comment shocking. Certainly not the kings themselves, since steroids long have been a common and legal training technique in thoroughbred racing. There are old-timers who insist that even the magnificent physical stature of the great Secretariat was not all genetic and contend that his early problem settling mares may have been a by-product of steroids.

Steroids were a regular regimen for halter and running quarter horses in the 1970s. And their arrival under the Twin Spires was first noticed by trainers there when the prominent quarter horse trainers entered the thoroughbred world in the 1980s and changed it forever. Nowhere has steroidal impact been more obvious than on the sleek, powerful two- and three-year-olds that get pointed toward the Triple Crown from their yearling sale days. If home-run king Barry Bonds had as many shots of Winstrol as the average traveler on the Derby trail, his head would be the size of Yankee Stadium.

Winstrol, or "Winny," an injectable version of stanozolol, is what Roger Clemens's trainer claims he shot into the Rocket's tush in 1998. It is also the most popular anabolic steroid in the world of equine athletes. Most trainers are loath to reveal what they give their horses in the way of feed or other nourishment, but veterinarians agree that in many stables a monthly shot of Winstrol is pretty much a routine part of preparing thorough-breds for sales or training top-of-the-line racehorses. Some give it every two weeks. A trainer friend of mine, whose horse happened to be temporarily housed in the barn of a leading trainer at Churchill Downs, once had to fend off a veterinarian he witnessed down the barn aisle injecting every horse with its regular dose of Equipoise, another testosterone-based steroid. Sorry, the vet said, admitting that just a few stalls away he had already administered a dose to the stable pony by mistake.

Having observed the steroidal effects on so many quarter and paint halter horses in the 1980s and having followed Curlin's career path, I had little doubt that Curlin had been on Winstrol or something similar for at least half his life. So I used him in my *Times* report as the most prominent example of the commonplace.

It is questionable whether Winstrol can make a man or a horse run faster. But using it cost the sprinter Ben Johnson his gold medal in the 100 meters at the 1988 Olympics. And there is no doubt it increases appetite, muscle mass, strength, red blood cell production, and aggressive behavior—all of which enhance most athletic competition.

Yet in most racing jurisdictions, there was nothing illegal about a horse getting it. And as human athletes claim, stanozolol is a valuable therapeutic medication that speeds recovery from injury, enhances the positive effects of training, and builds endurance for man and beast alike. Trainers who insist they never heard of it or allowed it to be administered to animals in their care are not likely to be listed among those atop the trainer standings.

Concern about steroids had pretty much been limited to trainers who didn't use them and dedicated breeders who realized that drugs were distorting not only the appearance of young horses at weanling (less than one year old) and yearling sales but also the performance of juveniles in the two-year-old sales and the important early stakes races that determine Triple Crown candidates and future sires, which portended detrimental long-term effects on the future of the sport itself.

It doesn't take a genius to know that keeping the best-known horses in competition until they fully mature at five and six years old will create a fan following and enhance the sport's popularity. But their owners are always in a hurry to retire them from racing, citing risk of injury and subsequent financial loss.

The truth, as insiders know, is that the longer horses are on a steroid regimen, the more likely they are to be permanently damaged. Long-term regimens not only deplete hormones and retard liver function but also strip muscles of the fat between the sinews, increasing the chance of tendons and ligaments stripping away from the bones during exercise.

Fear of the impact of steroids on the long-term health of these animals, especially the fertility of mares and stallions, is also a partial but unspoken justification for a couple of otherwise seemingly inscrutable traditions in the racehorse industry. Champions of both genders usually are sold at the apex of their track success and routinely vetted by buyers for insurance purposes. Yet fertility assessments are almost never included in the routine because a lot of these horses would not pass, and that would deprive sellers, agents, and insurance carriers of vast sums of revenue. Instead the horses are insured against long-term infertility.

Steroids like Winstrol and Equipoise invariably have negative short-term hormonal impact such as shrunken testicles and reduced semen production in males and small ovaries and limited estrus cycles in females. Most horses can recover in a few months. But some never do and fail to approach in the breeding shed their success on the racetrack.

Shrewd breeders always wait a month or two before booking their mares to first-year stallions off the racetrack because it takes six to eight weeks for steroids to clear so the real horse can begin to show up. In the first thirty days after cessation of a steroid regimen, that gorgeous sale Adonis or Triple Crown hero can shrivel up like a raisin in the sun, his hair falling out in clumps and his eyes resembling those of a hungover sailor back from shore leave.

Stallion farms often blame racetrack injuries or come up with fictitious reasons why the new addition to their stud roster cannot be shown to the public until weeks after his arrival. Even when his natural self emerges, there is no assurance his speed and competitive spirit were not chemically induced, and are not likely to be passed on.

Yet in the months before the 2008 Derby, there had been a fortunate merging of latent industry concern and public issues. Congressional scrutiny of steroid abuse by human athletes coincided with the racing industry's fear that Congress, under constant pressure from casino and other gambling interests, might reconsider the exemption pari-mutuel wagering enjoys from federal laws prohibiting gambling on the Internet. The threat was increasing at precisely the time when tracks were looking to these Web-based, advanced deposit platforms that offer multi-track wagering, companies such as Youbet.com and TVG.com, as the revenue streams of the future. Soon, congressional committees regulating Internet gambling would be on television asking industry lobbyists how bettors can be sure the outcome of races is not being influenced by steroid abuse.

Three years before, the Horse Racing Board in California, where the steroid controversy was born and where horse breeders have more influence than they do in Kentucky and New York, had officially concluded that steroids are in fact "performance enhancing," and the state adopted tougher drug policies. Specifically, California sought to stop the practice of giving horses "milkshakes"— sodium bicarbonate solutions—to reduce fatigue and demanded longer withdrawal times for therapeutic medications such as Winstrol and other drugs that can enhance performance.

Emboldened by California, buyers, owners, and breeders in Kentucky and Florida—where most big-time racehorses are raised and sold—had finally taken up the cause to rid the sport of steroids and made their case before regulators and state legislative bodies. Steroids had long been illegal in Iowa, which has little thoroughbred racing, and late in 2007 the Pennsylvania and Delaware racing commissions had signaled that the drugs would be illegal for the first time in 2008.

Even more foretelling, the industry's two leading sale companies, Keeneland and Fasig-Tipton, long loath to do anything that might deter the potential consignor of a blazingly fast two-year-old or a high-dollar champion filly fresh off the racetrack, were formulating potential antisteroid policies for their conditions of sale.

There was also a building industry awareness and concern over a drug called clenbuterol, a bronchodilator used to clear up lung infections common to racehorses. It has steroidal effects and when given at certain intervals prior to racing is regarded as performance enhancing.

All but five of the horses expected in the 2008 Derby field had been purchased at public auction, the majority at six-figure prices. And at least seven, including the likely favorite Big Brown, began their journey to Churchill Downs by roaring down the track in the two-year-old training sales, where steroids and clenbuterol were most common.

Many future Derby hopefuls then training at Keeneland, in early quest of the graded stakes money that would launch them toward the Triple Crown battle in 2009, already sported the unnatural size, muscle, and maturity consistent with steroid regimens. But their shrivel period might come sooner than anyone expected.

In the minds of the two Keeneland railbirds, steroid regulation appeared a near certainty in Kentucky, California, and New York, the three most important racing jurisdictions. Considering that trainers believe at least 95 percent of the horses in California, where medical rules are the most stringent and enforcement the most vigorous, train and race on clenbuterol, that drug might well be on its way out, too.

This suggested a dramatic and seismic shift in how the magnificent animals whose images exhilarate Triple Crown fans will get to the competition in the future. In the face of new state and federal regulation, the 2008 Derby might not be the last "presented by Yum Brands," but it would surely be the last to be run on steroids. The journalist still in me couldn't resist putting the conjecture in a newspaper, not just any newspaper but the *New York Times*, which circulated it on its worldwide news service. The initial reaction to the *Times* piece, published the Sunday before the Derby, was tepid. A few naive fans of Curlin and his trainer, Steve Asmussen, accused me of not knowing what I was talking about. But there was no denial by anyone connected with the horse. The three original—and by then minority—owners were all notorious lawyers being held in a Kentucky jail as potential "flight risks" while awaiting trial for swindling clients in a diet-pill damage lawsuit case. The majority owner, the wine magnate Jess Jackson, a dedicated industry reformer and a proven disturber of the peace himself, was silent on the subject, as was Asmussen.

But the idea of Kentucky Derby horses on steroids was new to most people. And it landed on an already volatile public landscape that would become volcanic.

Any time a female takes on males in a competitive athletic endeavor, she is an automatic underdog. Even in the equine world, where speed and not size or strength is the issue, boys get the nod because the genes of males have always been more highly regarded than those of females, which of course is bunk.

To understand the root of this particular gender prejudice, nothing is more enlightening than the makeup of thoroughbred racing's most important organization, the Jockey Club. Of its one hundred members in 2008, ten were female. More important, of the nine "stewards" who really run things, only one was a woman, a disproportion similar to male-female influence on the writing of the Bible—and with similarly misleading results.

The most likely female Derby contender in 2008 was a big, strapping gray filly named Eight Belles, owned by Rick Porter, a Delaware auto dealer whose hard-knocking colt Hard Spun had finished second in the 2007 Derby. Although Porter was red-hot with Derby fever, handicappers were cool to the filly. Despite a couple of impressive stakes conquests against her own gender at Oaklawn in Arkansas, Eight Belles was not considered a serious challenger to the colts.

Just below females on racing's prejudice scale are cowboys, undoubtedly one of the most romanticized and unfairly portrayed figures in American lore. Cowboys were the heroes of my generation, racing across the silver screen vanquishing villains and rescuing damsels in distress.

They never threw the first punch, fired the first shot, sang a sour note, or sought unfair advantage in any situation. Perhaps more than anything else, that vision—real or mythical—reflects the most admirable and widely held self-image of America as a country. But today the term *cowboy* has lost some of its luster, most often heard in public discourse as an adjectival description of the reckless shoot-first, think-later foreign policy of George W. Bush, the forty-third president of the United States.

Bush owns a ranch in Texas, where he raises brush, and he was often photographed in boots and jeans and hands on his hips as if ready to draw double six-guns. But as a cowboy, the commander in chief was all mouth and no horse. Anyone who knows real cowboys knows Bush is no cowboy.

Thoroughbred racing, however, is now rife with "cowboys," most of them migrants from the vastly different world of quarter horses. They might as well be wearing an "O" brand for outsider. When D. Wayne Lukas first moved in at Churchill Downs in the 1980s with his cowboy hat, flower boxes, and stalls deeply bedded with golden straw, he was derided as "the best gardener in horse racing." And then he quickly became the sport's most popular and successful trainer, dominating the Triple Crown races like no one else in modern times.

A decade later, Bob Baffert, an Arizonan perpetually in jeans and cowboy boots, made a similar impact, winning consecutive Kentucky Derbys in 1997 and 1998, and losing to a Lukas-trained horse by a nostril in 1996. In the new millennium, the most consistently successful thoroughbred trainers have been Todd Pletcher, a former Lukas assistant, and Steve Asmussen, both sons of quarter horse trainers. Each had to elbow his way to the top along the only path open to cowboys—through the winner's circle. Both Asmussen and Pletcher benefited from the achievements of Lukas and Baffert, but they also learned from their mistakes. Unlike their forerunners, Pletcher and Asmussen left behind the cowboy attire of their youth—and for good reason. Something about blue jeans and high-heeled boots sticks in the craw of the thoroughbred establishment, whose culture and style are decidedly uncowboy.

Denim jeans are common among all trainers for morning work hours, but never in the saddling paddocks in the afternoons, certainly not at stuffy old Keeneland, swell Saratoga, or the big Triple Crown races. Even at casual but upper-crust Del Mar in California, where cowboys are held in higher esteem, beach bum attire is more in vogue than hats and boots. Whenever television cameras come on anywhere, thoroughbred racing prefers its star trainers to look more like bankers or CEOs.

This may be a grudge held for decades against an Arizona-born, leather-faced cowboy named Rex Ellsworth, who came to Kentucky in 1933, loaded up a bunch of cheap mares and fillies onto an open flatbed truck with wooden slatted sides, and hauled them back to California. By the time he got there, the horses had eaten the canvas off the top, but he came back later, tried to buy the famous stallion Nasrullah, yet went home with a cheaper stud named Khaled.

In 1955 Ellsworth returned to Kentucky, this time with an unorthodox trainer named Meshach Tenney and one of the fastest racehorses that ever lived, Swaps, the son of Khaled. Swaps won the 1955 Kentucky Derby and was named Horse of the Year in 1956, as Ellsworth's stable became the third in history to win $1 million. But Ellsworth's cowboy ways—he once punched Swaps in the head with his fist in front of witnesses—never sat well with the thoroughbred gentry, and Ellsworth was eventually accused of animal cruelty later in his life when his horse herd was found neglected and undernourished.

Ellsworth left a stain other cowboys have always had to ride around to be accepted. The traditional broad-brimmed western hats are particular objects of disdain. A Texan and a former quarter horse trainer friend of mine—and perhaps the only wearer of cowboy hats that will ever be elected to the board of the exclusive Keeneland Association—he always paid the price in derisive comments aimed at his back. Just his appearance at a yearling sale once incited a very un-Keeneland-like remark by one of his fellow board members: "That guy needs two of those hats," the fellow said. "One to shit in and one to cover it up with."

The Texan's hat was more of a narrow-brimmed Lyndon Johnson model, considerably less obtrusive than the white monsters that have become the trademark of the latest successful cowboy interloper, J. Larry Jones, the trainer of Eight Belles.

A native of western Kentucky, Larry Jones grew up on a farm that raised cattle and soybeans, his decidedly bowed legs all the evidence necessary to know he has ridden horses for most of his fifty-three years. For half that time, he has been a thoroughbred horse trainer, laboring mostly at Ellis Park, a hardscrabble track built around a cornfield near the Ohio River not far from where he grew up.

Once described by one of the airbags on the TVG horse-racing cable channel as having been "born with a wooden spoon in his mouth," Jones has struggled to overcome inferior horses and poor prospects throughout his training career. But both improved significantly when a filly in his barn named Island Sand won the $1 million Delaware Handicap in 2005.

Jones first began to attract public attention during the 2007 Triple Crown season as the trainer of the iron horse Hard Spun, as much for his cowboy style and unique training methods as for his horse's gritty performance in the three classics. Although he weighs 180 pounds, Jones personally gallops many of his top horses in the mornings, not only the sturdy Hard Spun but also Eight Belles and her tiny barn rival Proud Spell, who was entered in the Kentucky Oaks, the prestigious filly race that is run the day before the Derby at Churchill Downs. It may be no coincidence that the horses Jones rides personally are often the ones who achieve stardom. The skill of a horse's gallop rider in the morning is often the reason it wins in the afternoon.

"I just love to ride," Jones says. "That's probably when I quit training . . . when I can't ride anymore."

By design Jones also regularly employs heavier riders, some weighing almost as much as he does. This causes smirks and raises eyebrows among the traditionalists, who believe the heavier load puts unnecessary stress on the horse's bones, and therefore try to employ the lightest exercise riders possible. When I sent Jones a small two-year-old filly in 2007, I was warned, "You better hope he doesn't get on her himself every morning."

The gallop riders for other trainers usually employ short stirrups and crouch atop their mounts in the manner of race jockeys, butts raised in the air. But Jones and his larger gallop riders straddle their horses, feet planted in stirrups dropped to the level of the horse's belly or longer. Not only is it more comfortable; the riders are more stable and therefore less likely to be maintaining their balance with a tight rein on the horses' mouths. With less of a hold, the Jones horses gallop considerably faster and longer than the others.

The trainer himself cuts a peculiar figure on the tracks in the morning. He favors a pair of white western chaps with orange trim and a vest to match, topped off with a white crash helmet that could have belonged to Evel Knievel. His horses sport white bridles (a fad started by Lukas), and his stable saddles have burnt-orange seats. Even his stable pony, a mammoth paint named Pal, is a standout—about 1,400 pounds—and tricolored yellow, black, and white. With Jones in the lead, his fleeting posse lapping everyone else's horses, there is a circus atmosphere about him that can be off-putting were he not so genuine and affable.

Well aware of his own eccentricity, Jones was once passed on the racetrack in the morning by a hapless exercise rider aboard a runaway horse. Exiting the track, the cowboy encountered the horse's trainer. "You should tell that boy what everybody else knows: that if he passes me, he's going too fast."

When applied to Jones, the term *cowboy* fits in the finest and most romantic sense, true to the clichés by which he is described by lifelong acquaintances. A "book you can judge by the cover," they say; "a man whose word you can take to the bank." He is, in the words of my old boss Ross Perot, a true original who hates clichés, "somebody you can leave your wallet with, or your wife."

Contrary to first impressions, there is no showboat to him. And unlike most trainers who began working as someone's assistant, Jones is nobody's protégé. So his horsemanship was honed by whatever he's learned raising and riding them. Galloping his horses harder and longer is a training tool proven effective by his own experience.

Carrying the extra weight every day, he believes, strengthens his horses' bones rather than weakens them. And with fifty to sixty pounds less on their backs in the afternoon, the ground they have been covering every morning seems to fly by under their feet. Jones doesn't win every race, but his horses are seldom far off the wire. Almost never are they struggling home, veering from fatigue.

Jones is the epitome of a hands-on horseman. The first time we met he was bedding Hard Spun's stall at Keeneland. A barn helper I know was present once when a van carrying Jones's horses arrived at Keeneland at 2:30 a.m. Surprisingly, the driver who got out was Jones.

He personally unloaded each horse himself, pointing out that it was his responsibility, not that of his grooms. While most of his peers ship their horses from track to track with big van companies or fly them on planes across the country, Jones most often hauls his stable stars to stakes races in his own truck and trailer, catching up with phone calls during the trip.

This is a guy who mixes his own feed and whose veterinarian bills are routinely a small fraction of those in the larger barns of top trainers with which he is competitive. And he and wife Cindy, his top assistant and the first gallop rider he ever hired, seem to know whenever a hair turns on any horse in their barn.

"I can usually tell when a horse has a problem and what it is," she says, "but Larry can always figure out why. That's why he is our leader."

Once you have had a horse in Jones's barn, you want all your horses there, which is why it was such a great irony when the 2008 Kentucky Derby took him from obscurity to infamy in a matter of hours.

By race time, most knowledgeable insiders had figured out that the Derby field included eighteen slow horses and two fast ones—Big Brown and Eight Belles, neither of whom were considered likely to last the mile and a quarter. Big Brown had the outside post, number 20, which was considered a handicap. And Eight Belles had drawn post position number 5, from which she was likely to break quickly and burn herself out in the front of the pack. Besides, she was a filly by a sire not known for producing stayers. The experts were wrong as usual. Both fast horses had perfect trips and plenty left at the end, Big

Brown slipping up the outside untouched to run most of the race in midpack, and Eight Belles settling in easily behind the slow leaders in a clear stalking position.

Both started to run at the quarter pole in the middle of the final turn, Big Brown making a big move on the outside that took him past the field, including Eight Belles, who was cruising in the second rank of horses on the rail. The only one with anything left in her tank, she fired, too, and took off after him. The two easily ran off from the pack, but Big Brown had gotten the winning jump and was five lengths ahead when they hit the wire.

Eight Belles had her ears pricked when she crossed the finish. Her stride was long and lovely, not a sign of distress showing anywhere. Young Gabriel Saez, who the day before had won the Kentucky Oaks on the other Jones filly, Proud Spell, had kept his Derby mount clear of traffic and running free the entire way. The trouble began when he tried to pull her up, well after rounding the clubhouse turn. First one ankle gave way, throwing all her weight on the other, which cracked as well. She went down in slow motion like a big train running off the rails. Unable to stand again, she had to be euthanized on the spot.

The image of the big black filly lying in a heap beneath the famous Twin Spires struck a raw public nerve, a link between her shattered front legs and drug and whip abuse in horse racing having been instantaneous. Some people blamed Jones for running a filly against the colts in the first place, even though she was the physical superior of most and had easily defeated all but Big Brown. Not surprisingly, the uninformed zealots of People for the Ethical Treatment of Animals (PETA) were in the forefront of the lynch mob.

Their spokeswoman wanted criminal charges brought against Jones, whom they suspected had run the filly on drugs, and Gabriel Saez, the jockey they perceived guilty of excessive whipping near the finish line.

The Joneses were devastated. The trainer did not see the breakdown and didn't know what had happened until he saw his jockey riding back on a horse with the television commentator and ex-jockey Donna Barton Brothers. By the time Jones made it to the backstretch where Eight Belles had collapsed, the filly had already been euthanized, a decision he did not question.

"Nothing has ever hurt me more," a visibly distraught Jones told reporters the following day. "This is the greatest tragedy of my life."

Unlike many big-name trainers who are curt when they win and downright hostile or unavailable when they lose, Jones is the same in good times and bad. He is friendly and accommodating and—true to the spirit of the mythical image of the cowboy—ready to stand up and take whatever is coming to him, good or bad. Armed only with plainspoken candor, he faced the media onslaught virtually alone.

He defended the decision to run Eight Belles against the boys, pointing out that she was actually bigger and stronger than most of the colts, and he said that his twenty-year-old jockey had not whipped excessively, that in fact Saez had given her the perfect ride. To refute the drug abuse charges, he ordered a necropsy he knew would prove she had nothing illegal in her system.

Only a few friendly voices from inside the industry, including mine, were raised in support of the trainer's explanations. All of us pointed out how often self-destructive thoroughbreds break their ankles kicking stall walls and running across the pasture even without anyone on their backs waving whips.

The average Derby watcher could not possibly know that horses like Eight Belles in the care of people like the Joneses are among the most pampered and protected creatures on earth. They get more attention than children and more prompt medical care than the average patient in a hospital emergency room.

Animal rights activists would have none of it. Jones and Eight Belles's owner, Rick Porter, were deluged with hate mail, much of it so vicious that Jones quit reading racing news on the Internet and stopped answering his phone.

The firestorm raged on without him. Normally horse racing gets only the publicity in the mainstream media that it can afford to purchase. But having unfolded on network television on the one day the whole world was watching, the story of Eight Belles had all the elements necessary for a modern media melodrama: a female victimized by a cruel and villainous industry and ultimately ridden to her death by greedy, callous, and glory-seeking male tormentors.

Even knowledgeable, committed horse lovers sympathetic to the sport and familiar with the fragile nature of the beast inadvertently threw gasoline on the fire. My friend Jane Smiley, the Pulitzer Prize–winning novelist and expert horsewoman who thinks nothing about jumping horses over four-foot barriers for them to land on one spindly leg, wrote a typically eloquent and heart-wrenching tribute in the *New York Times* to the courageous female who ran herself to death in the interest of proving gender equality. In the *Washington Post*, the columnist Sally Jenkins conjured up images of Christians being fed to the lions in a Roman circus when she wrote that Eight Belles had died for the entertainment of wealthy and overdressed Derby spectators.

As has become the norm in the twenty-four-hour cable news cycle, the more ugly and more absurd the allegations, the hotter the fire burned. Bloggers suggested—on no evidence—that Eight Belles had been seen limping at Keeneland in the weeks before the race. And on the backside of Churchill Downs, a rumor spread that Cindy Jones had so opposed the running of Eight Belles in the Derby that she now planned to divorce her husband as a result of the tragedy. It is true that Cindy Jones took the loss so hard she considered leaving the racetrack life. And there was no doubt the strain tested their twenty-year marriage.

"It was really tough for both of us," Jones told the *Keeneland Magazine*, "especially Cindy. She got really upset that I kept doing interviews after the Derby and she took the insults toward me more personally than I did."

But as people who know her would suspect, Cindy Jones ended up putting the horses first. The couple had just won the Kentucky Oaks and finished second in the Kentucky Derby, an extraordinary achievement. But there was neither time nor room for elation in their lives—or for further disruption.

Before the Derby, most of their stable had been moved to Delaware Park, where they had relocated following Hard Spun's Triple Crown season of 2007. Their most important client, Porter, had acquired his own barn at nearby Fair Hill, a Pennsylvania training center where he had nearly forty horses in training. With the arrival of the two-year-year-olds in May, the Joneses' string would grow to over a hundred horses, more than double their normal numbers.

For all those years in a perennially hard business, Larry and Cindy Jones had been best friends, a relationship they credit for seeing them through the Eight Belles crisis. Horses had been the center of their lives and would continue to be. But despite the strong bond between them and the support of their owners and friends, the pressure of more horses, more staff, and sudden, unrelenting notoriety covered the Jones stable with a pall of depression.

A few days after the Derby, its leader came face-to-face with the sort of reckoning that often accompanies the trauma of death and its crushing aftermath. He and Cindy had finally escaped Kentucky, where they had been in the eye of the storm, and had followed their horses to Delaware, where they would be stabled for the summer.

As recounted to his close friends, including a reporter for the *Blood-Horse*, a leading industry magazine, they were spending the night in a Days Inn motel near Delaware Park. Cindy was already asleep, but Jones was still up reading the Bible, he said, searching for answers that might provide solace from the public shellacking he had taken from people who blamed him for the death of Eight Belles.

"We had tons of mail we opened we probably shouldn't have," Jones said. "People telling us how bad we were, how cruel we were for racing horses, and what we had done to this horse. Those letters really hurt. And I had also listened to the radio the Monday after and heard people on radio saying they knew for a fact we injected her ankles on Wednesday. These people just don't understand. No vet even entered her stall that week. We could prove that they were lying. That hurt me personally."

What Jones said then took place while he was reading the Bible could happen only to someone of unusual faith under the most difficult of circumstances and ultimately be acknowledged only by someone of rare courage and confidence.

In the midst of a violent thunderstorm, a clap of thunder shook the thin walls of the room. It was like nothing he had ever heard before, so loud he thought his wife had been aroused. "So, you're awake," he said, sensing a presence in the room. But it was not Cindy.

"He was there," Jones said, meaning his creator. "It all became clear to me after he said, 'She wasn't your horse, Larry. She was my horse. You can trust that she didn't suffer and she didn't die in vain.'

"That set old Larry back where he came from. My life changed after that. I knew everything happens for a reason and he has a plan. It won't ever be revealed, but it gave me the comfort knowing that this was out of my control. If I didn't have my faith, I wouldn't have gotten through it."

To those who might question the nature of that experience, Jones has a ready response: "I can tell people that horses talk to me. I tell them I understand what they say and they tell me I must be some kind of horse whisperer. They say, 'You're gifted. That's great.' But I tell them God talked to me that night, they say, 'You're a nut.' But it happened."

One of my best friends for forty years, an extremely bright woman with a high-level education, once told me in the same vivid detail and with equal conviction of a similar encounter with the Lord in her kitchen. I believed her, too.

PART TWO

RATIONAL BAD BEHAVIOR

3

THE DINNIES

For three generations the name Arthur B. Hancock has been synonymous with the breeding of superior thoroughbred racehorses. Early in the past century, the first A. B. Hancock, an industry pioneer, moved his horses west from Virginia, established Claiborne Farm, and is now considered by many the man most responsible for rooting the endeavor in Kentucky. Later, his son Arthur "Bull" Hancock Jr. became the establishment leader and a prime force in moving from Europe to the Bluegrass the bloodstock that became the epicenter of a $300 billion global industry. And in June 2008, the third-generation A.B. turned renegade reformer and urged the federal government to step in to prevent the construct of his ancestors from crumbling down on his head.

When the U.S. House of Representatives called horse racing on the carpet following the televised breakdown of the filly Eight Belles at the 2008 Kentucky Derby, the lone breeder on the witness list was Hancock, the owner of Stone Farm and the senior member of Kentucky's most celebrated horse-raising family. Looking and sounding more like a history professor than a hard-boot horseman, Hancock spilled the beans about what was wrong with the racehorse industry: it was rife with drug abuse and void of leadership.

"We are a rudderless ship," he said. "And the way we are going, we will all end up on the rocks."

Even more remarkable, Hancock contended that the only way to avoid disaster would be for the federal government to rewrite the Interstate Horse Racing Act of 1978, the lone federal statute regulating the sport and one that the industry had spent millions trying to keep unchanged, specifically to mandate uniform drug and safety regulations and revise a failing business model.

No industry other than perhaps big oil is more traditionally Republican and more opposed to government regulation than the thoroughbred hierarchy, within which Hancock is enormously respected but also viewed, as one conflicted admirer put it, as being "wired a little differently than the other Hancocks." Still, his testimony before Congress was an act uncharacteristic of Bull Hancock's eldest son, a man so conservative one of his oldest friends refers to him as "political Nazi." It stunned even his fellow reformers and was considered heresy by most of his peers.

In a telephone conversation ten days earlier, Hancock had told me what he planned to do and why. He and I are not close friends in the sense that we travel in the same circles or visit in each other's home. But we both have strong ties to my hometown of Nashville, where his grandfather was a prominent lawyer. And we have been cohorts on issues that affect our common passion for the breeding of horses—especially the long-term effect of drugs on sales and performance.

Earlier that spring Arthur had traveled to our alma mater, Vanderbilt University, in Nashville to attend graduation ceremonies for his son Arthur B. Hancock IV, who he hoped would follow him as master of Stone Farm and continue the tradition of the Hancock family.

"I would like very much for young Arthur to succeed in this business as I have," Hancock told me. "But I don't want to leave him the business the way it is now. I'm not even sure there will be a business for him if something is not done. We've got to get rid of the drugs, and we have to have some leadership."

Six years earlier, in what I recall to be our first telephone conversation, Hancock had been just as passionate on the same two issues. He had recently resigned as a member of the board of the Keeneland Association after it purchased Turfway Park, a race course in northern Kentucky in partnership with a company involved in casino gaming, which Hancock believes is incompatible with the pari-mutuel gambling that supports horse racing. He had gone public with his reason for resigning: the three Keeneland trustees made the decision, and the board was informed only as an afterthought.

"I didn't even get a chance to vote 'no,' so it looked like I was for it," he said.

About the same time, he had declined to run for reelection to the board of the Kentucky Thoroughbred Owners and Breeders Association (KTOB). Largely due to my friendship with John Ward, the trainer of Monarchos, who was about to take office as the KTOB president, I had been invited to stand for election to Hancock's spot. I wanted to know why he was not seeking reelection.

"That seat must be the one set aside for troublemakers," Hancock said, which I took the way he meant it—as a compliment. "First of all, that bunch almost never does anything. And when they do, everything is already decided before the meetings and the board is just a rubber stamp."

That somebody as prominent as Arthur Hancock, whose farm had produced three Kentucky Derby winners, had finally aired his familiar litany of complaints in Washington was heartily welcomed by those of us who had long shared his perceptions and admired his courage. These were not simply the newly formed opinions of a single renegade, but those of a largely underground reform movement that had been building for years among breeders, trainers, and even a few veterinarians. Hancock had expressed some of the same sentiments in the *New York Times* racing blog "The Rail" shortly after the Derby. So had a few others with much less standing in the game, including me.

But the salient point in the argument—that only the federal government could force uniform racing and drug rules on the thirty-eight different racing jurisdictions—had never been made in a forum as public as the *New York Times*. For more than a quarter of a century, the industry had focused its lobbying and expended most of its resources to cover up its ugly secrets and keep sacred its exemption from interstate gambling bans.

As a young man, I had watched the Tennessee walking horse industry in my home state behave the same way, presenting a respectable face to the government and the public while hiding a rotten underbelly of abusive training practices known as *soring*, which keep animals in constant pain and leave them permanently crippled.

In my first job as an editor at the *Tennessean*, Nashville's newspaper, I managed an undercover investigation of the practice by another young journalist, Wendell Rawls, a schoolmate of Arthur Hancock's at Vanderbilt who would go on to become a brilliant Pulitzer Prize–winning reporter for the *New York Times*. His resulting series of stories attracted the attention of both animal rights activists and a Senate committee headed by Senator Joseph Tydings of Maryland. In a circus-like atmosphere typical of congressional hearings, we hauled a sore and crippled walking horse to Washington for a press conference on the lawn of the Capitol. Rawls and I, both in our early twenties, delivered testimony to the Tydings committee that resulted in passage of the Horse Protection Act, which is the scourge of the walking horse industry to this day. Nearly forty years later, Rawls's old roommate was bringing down the same kind of pressure on his own business.

"In my opinion, only a federal racing commission or commissioner can save us from ourselves," Hancock told the committee, knowing full well that the only stick in a commissioner's hand would be the threat that any state refusing to comply with uniform rules of racing would lose its ability to conduct parimutuel betting via transmission of interstate signals. And later, Representative Ed Whitfield, Republican of Kentucky, and a longtime acquaintance of Hancock's, specifically warned that the committee might well recommend an amendment to the law if racing failed to clean up its act.

To an industry with a history of being best motivated by the sight and smell of its own blood, Hancock's plea and the Kentucky congressman's response were unambiguous. A wound had been opened in public. While it may have been the most significant and stunning moment in the hearing, a vast array of so-called industry movers and shakers—none of whom had been invited to testify—had to endure an equally embarrassing assertion. Hancock had rattled off a list of the top-ten industry organizations, which along with the thirty-eight separate state racing commissions, he said, are all "fiefdoms" with "Nero-like C.E.O.s," each one envisioning "himself as the savior of racing and most of them don't even own a horse . . . No one is in charge."

That no one is in charge no doubt came as a huge surprise to those who believed they were—the very "kings" for which the sport is named—an aging, shrinking group of industry elite known derisively behind their back as "the Dinnies."

By now it is clear that in America anybody can grow up to be president. But however great your faith in the American dream, you cannot grow up to be a "Dinny," the name by which Ogden Mills Phipps, the long-reigning chairman of the Jockey Club, is known throughout the industry and a moniker that has rubbed off on his extended family of intimates. It is now a generic synonym for what is viewed as the sport's ruling establishment.

Dinnies do not come with bootstraps by which they can pull themselves up. Either you have to be born a Dinny as was he, the grandson of Henry Phipps, founder of the Bessemer Trust and Andrew Carnegie's partner in U.S. Steel; or you can become one by marriage, as did William Stamps Farish, the grandson of the founder of Humble Oil, who married into the Du Pont family. Together Phipps and Farish have served as chairman and cochairman respectively of the Jockey Club for the last twenty-six years, during which time their influence on the sport has been pervasive.

The Jockey Club, indisputably the most important and powerful organization in horse racing, is the keeper of the studbook with control over registration, naming, pedigrees, and racing statistics vital to all competition and sales. As organizations go, it has no peers within racing—and few outside—in fund-raising prowess or political clout. Its membership consists mainly of the wealthiest, most powerful, and most well intentioned of the sport's enthusiasts and some of the industry's most respected horsemen, veterinarians, executives, and experts.

However, not everyone who puts on a tuxedo for the Jockey Club's most visible display of power, the Saratoga dinner bash preceding its annual and much ballyhooed Round Table, is a Dinny. For many members, bootstraps were critical for their attaining the stature necessary for an invitation to join. If the truth were known, Phipps and Farish may turn out to be the only full-fledged Dinnies, although fellow members such as G. Watts Humphrey, whose grandfather was secretary of the

treasury in the Eisenhower administration, and Stuart Syming-
ton Janney Jr., whose mother was a Phipps, may qualify as well.

From the rung on the ladder that determines my perspective,
it is not always easy to tell a real Dinny from a surrogate
wannabe Dinny, of whom there are legions. When viewed from
below, the shape of those on a ladder above exhibit pretty much
the same characteristics.

A partially blocked view of the top is one of the drawbacks of
being a "pygmy" in the horse business—a precisely accurate
assessment of my status by the late John R. Gaines, the founder
of the Breeders' Cup, who could see things better from higher
up. Although Gaines was rich, powerful, and brilliant, he was
never a member of the Jockey Club, a group he regarded as "self-
appointed guardians of the turf" and who regarded him as a
boorish interloper. But as the moving force behind the industry's only major steps forward in the last fifty years—the formation of the Breeders' Cup and the founding of the National
Thoroughbred Racing Association (NTRA)—Gaines was constantly testing the reins by which the Dinnies held the horse
industry.

Gaines's bestowal of my "pygmy" status had come in the
mid-1990s, during the planning stages of the NTRA, when he
still envisioned it as the office of a commissioner of racing that
could govern the sport in the fashion of professional football,
baseball, and basketball. As part of his planning, Gaines had
summoned me to the library of his Lexington home more than
once to pick my brain about how a commissioner would function, what he should be paid, and what skills were demanded by
the job.

A perfect commissioner, I told him, would be a tough organ-
izer with superb diplomatic skills such as my friend Hamilton
Jordan, the former chief of staff for President Jimmy Carter,

with whom I had worked in Ross Perot's 1992 presidential campaign. Jordan was a consultant on Gaines's project and somewhere along the way suggested that my background in newspapers and knowledge of public policy might be helpful to their cause. Gaines dismissed it out of hand, terming me "a mere pygmy" and of no value in dealing with "industry poobahs." He had that right.

Early in our relationship, it was clear that Gaines and I had one thing in common: neither of us would last long in any organization we couldn't run. And having risen to Dinny status in the hierarchy of the newspaper business in my previous life, I no longer had the patience to work well with others and was suspect of any group that would have me as a member. Gaines, however, was still intent on leading an industry that did not want to be led and that had rejected his attempts time and again.

Successful leaders in any endeavor are usually consensus builders, but Gaines explained to me that building consensus in the thoroughbred business had proved impossible. "These men are not like the owners of football and baseball who elect a commissioner and let him fix the problems," he said. "And no one can build a consensus because the builder himself automatically becomes an impediment to the building. Resentment of the builder becomes the stumbling block. The only way to move them is to throw out an idea so compelling they want to seize it and take the credit themselves."

That was my first lesson in Thoroughbred Horse Organizations 101, taught by someone who had learned it the hard way. When Gaines entered the thoroughbred world in 1962, it was still operating much as it had for the last fifty years. Heir to a Gaines Dog Food and Florida land fortune, he had already learned enough in his grandfather's standardbred business to know that the real money was in stallion syndication. This industry segment was then safely tucked away in the hands of a few shrewd Kentucky farm owners, breeding legends such as Bull Hancock at Claiborne Farm, John Galbreath of Darby Dan, and Leslie Combs of Spendthrift.

Their common business plan was to acquire the best race-horses in the world and carve up the ownership into forty shares that they then sold mainly to people who boarded mares on their farms, the idea and basis for foal value being exclusivity. Combs, the P. T. Barnum of the horse business, had revitalized the practice after World War II by selling twenty shares of a horse named Beau Pere for $5,000 each.

Pretty soon the business model had increased the number of shares to sixty because an innovative outsider named John Gaines was proving you could raise more money that way and outbid competitors for each stallion prospect. Twenty years later, after his Gainesway Farm had established itself as a premier stallion maker and Gaines had carved out a respected place in Lexington as a civic leader and philanthropist, he came up with the idea of the Breeders' Cup, a day of racing near the end of the calendar offering lucrative purses funded by nomination fees from stallion and foal owners. Initially, it looked like this idea was so compelling it could not fail. But it would have failed had Gaines not agreed to step back from his own creation and let it be run by "the guardians of the turf."

Diplomacy not being Gaines's strong suit, he had left a trail of ruffled feathers along his route to success. His aversion to pretense and intolerance of fools had marked him a natural adversary of the thoroughbred hierarchy, which at the time was a smooth mixture of the rural Kentucky guile of people like Combs and the eastern elitism of the Phippses and the Whitneys. A graduate of Notre Dame, Gaines conceded them nothing in wealth or education. But he was blunt, confrontational, and quick-witted, exactly the kind of born leader who could take over a meeting and intimidate a committee. Had he been bred in the purple and admitted to the Jockey Club on his father's sponsorship, he would have made a great Dinny.

Instead he was their worst nightmare. In the end Arthur's brother Seth Hancock, who had succeeded their father at Claiborne Farm, whose stallions were critical to the success of the Breeders' Cup venture, refused to participate as long as John Gaines was involved. Claiborne Farm was where Ogden Phipps and his son Ogden Mills Phipps, who had been admitted to the Jockey Club at age twenty-four, boarded one of the best broodmare bands in existence. Without Claiborne Farm's participation, there could be no Breeders' Cup, so Gaines had to go.

Over the next twenty-five years, the Breeders' Cup was run in the finest tradition of trade organizations—a large representative board that basically rubber-stamps the decisions of a small executive committee. It was led first by Will Farish and Watts Humphrey, then by D. G. Van Clief of Virginia and the longtime Keeneland czar James E. (Ted) Bassett, all Jockey Club insiders.

Despite widely diverse and conflicting interests, the "fiefdoms" within the horse-racing world perpetuate themselves just as do the average corporate board of directors. Sitting officers virtually "fix" elections to the board by controlling the nomination process, easily done by an appointed committee certain to carry out the wishes of those already in office.

These nominations are heavily weighted toward easily flattered newcomers or obvious followers who will fall in line—and away from people like John Gaines. The nominators sometimes pick troublemakers by design (as in my case once) or accidentally (when Gaines-like bully tendencies have gone undetected). But their numbers are invariably too thin to make a difference.

Fittingly, considering that Kentucky has been the center of the racehorse industry for years, the state remains a sterling example of all that is wrong with it. Since the days of Daniel Boone in a place where horses drive its only economic engines— agriculture and tourism—the Bluegrass horse crowd has been traditionally ignored by much of the political establishment and often demonized by the rest. So getting anything done is near impossible.

Most of the influential horsemen such as Farish, whose Lane's End stallion station is the most important of U.S.-owned breeding farms, and Robert Clay, the master of prestigious Three Chimneys Farm, are prominent Republicans.

Farish, a close friend of former president George H. W. Bush and a former ambassador to Great Britain, is a publicly low-key but highly skilled and forceful behind-the-scenes politician. He, Clay, and many others in the Jockey Club are intimately familiar with the Washington power levers that have kept the 1978 horse-racing act free from tampering by gambling opponents. As a group, they have been important to the prodigious fundraising ability of Kentucky's senior senator Mitch McConnell, whose efforts in Washington on behalf of the thoroughbred and walking horse industries are viewed as a "protection racket" by both rival gambling interests and gambling opponents. Yet McConnell and his backers have been helpless in the Republican-controlled state senate in the Kentucky capital of Frankfort, where the influence of evangelicals and other antigambling forces has repeatedly thwarted key legislative goals of the horse industry.

Democrats have done no better, even when their party controlled both executive and legislative branches. The lack of unity, constant bickering, and institutional enmity between Churchill Downs and the political establishment in Frankfort have doomed most legislative initiatives before they ever get off the ground. The first real effort at consensus building statewide, an organization known as the Kentucky Equine Education

Project (KEEP), has been hamstrung by the identity of the consensus builder, former Kentucky governor Brereton C. Jones, the
owner of Airdrie Stud. Although Jones was among those who had
pushed John R. Gaines out of the Breeders' Cup management
two decades earlier, the two joined forces—at least temporarily—
to form KEEP and wrestled temporarily for control until Gaines
died in 2005. But Jones is a Gaines-like figure himself and about
as popular among Frankfort legislators as Gaines was among the
Jockey Club stewards. And so far KEEP's main goals of significant
tax relief and new casino revenue for racing have been as elusive
in Frankfort as change has been to the Dinnies.

Gaines would rock the rudderless boat of horse racing as
long as he was alive. Despite steadily failing health, which
moved him from cane to walker and finally to wheelchair, he
finally—and almost single-handedly—forced into existence the
NTRA, which he wanted to pattern after the powerful NASCAR
organization, which has built automobile racing into the most
watched sport in America. The idea, originally proposed in the
mid-1990s by the Lexington advertising man Fred Pope, was to
give owners a bigger say in racing politics by essentially creating
two classes of racing in which revenue from fan interest in the
majors helped subsidize the bottom. By early 1997, after a hundred owners had signed on, Phipps summoned the leaders
among them to a private meeting in Palm Beach. Neither he nor
Farish, then the chairman of Churchill Downs, supported the
fledgling organization, then called the National Thoroughbred
Association, which they saw as a competitor to the Thoroughbred Owners and Breeders Association (TOBA), which they
already controlled.

Basically the Dinnies hijacked the project by joining it,
involving the Jockey Club, Keeneland, and the Breeders' Cup—
the three wealthiest organizations in racing. They turned what
was an owners' initiative into what Ray Paulick, the former

editor in chief of the *Blood-Horse* magazine, later termed a *fuster-cluck* of industry organizations, "which by their very nature could never paddle in the same direction."

Ultimately the NTA became the NTRA, an expensive marketing and lobby operation that when starved for revenue was merged with the Breeders' Cup—a deal sweetened with an undisclosed amount of cash from the breeders' stallion and foal nomination fees. Predictably, instead of a commissioner's office that might rival the supremacy of the Jockey Club, the NTRA became an organization of questionable effectiveness. After five years of near bloody insurrection by irate breeders, the merger was reversed. Now the two operate under separate boards but both under control of the same people.

When Gary Biszantz, the founder of Cobra Golf and a horse-racing enthusiast for most of his life, was added to the boards of the Breeders' Cup and TOBA in their corporate board-style "elections," he took it as a compliment to the leadership and acumen he had exhibited in business. If Biszantz was a racehorse, he would run up front and be hard to catch. After starring in basketball and golf in college, he followed his father into the auto business, establishing a major Ford dealership of his own and then founding Cobra, which he built into the second-largest maker of oversize golf clubs in the country before selling it to American Brands to become a full-time horseman.

At his first board meeting Biszantz was seated next to John Magnier, the owner of Coolmore and a billionaire ranked the tenth-richest man in Ireland, whose rivalry with Sheikh Mohammed for global dominance of the thoroughbred world had been its main economic engine for years. Magnier was attending his first meeting as well. Both men sat stunned as D. G. Van Clief, the Breeders' Cup chief executive, breezed through the meeting collecting "aye" voice approvals on his agenda list in rubber-stamp fashion and then adjourned the meeting.

Biszantz said Magnier couldn't believe his eyes. He got up and said, "I'm going home. I flew all the way from Ireland for this?"

No shrinking violet, Biszantz asked Van Clief who had set the agenda and when. Van Clief said it had been done in a private session an hour earlier with Will Farish, Watts Humphrey, and Robert Clay, all perennial stalwarts of thoroughbred organization boards. None of the three had been present for the actual board voting, according to Biszantz.

"Where are they now?" Biszantz wanted to know.

"Oh, they're playing golf," Van Clief replied. "They had an early tee time."

In 1999, after years of service in the trenches on committee after committee and ponying up contributions to virtually every industry initiative, Biszantz was admitted to the Jockey Club and ascended up the ladder to be vice president of TOBA. And when in 2002 he got a call from "the committee" offering to make him the chairman of the TOBA trustees, he was even more flattered. This was Dinny-status-level stuff. Then the caller said, "But I have to tell you, Gary, we're a little worried about you."

What worried them was his John Gaines–like tendency to grab the bit in his teeth and run with it, which he did, serving four straight terms and pushing so hard for uniform drug rules and the championship tour idea that he almost got them both accomplished—almost.

It was during his term that TOBA revived the old Gaines-Pope "major league" of racing idea, which ultimately became a corpse in the arms of a Biszantz-appointed task force that ran headlong into opposition from the Dinnies. The uniform drug rules remain a divisive, explosive, and still unsettled issue today. Four years after his tenure atop TOBA ended, Biszantz was still pushing, this time as part of the small group of reformers trying to maneuver the federal government into forcing thoroughbred racing into serious, well-funded self-regulation.

The story of the Breeders' Cup and the NTRA is a parable for the racing industry, which flopped around like a chicken with its head cut off following the breakdown of the filly Eight Belles before mustering statements of regret and awareness. Flopping around is really all a headless chicken or organization can do.

The first response of the NTRA was to plot an expensive new advertising campaign to counter the wave of criticism. What the business needed, it was said, was a first-rate "public relations" official to answer media questions instead of "these people who took it upon themselves to speak for the industry," presumably meaning Hancock, myself, and a handful of others who did not duck the media onslaught after the Derby disaster. Three Chimneys Farm, the breeder of the fallen horse, justified its silence in the face of press inquiries by saying that the farm had decided it was "not the proper time to be making a public statement."

To industry insiders, there was no question why the bridge of the rudderless ship was empty in the storm. It was no place to be for puppets on a string, at least not until it became clear whether Larry Jones had raced a drugged or previously injured horse. Everybody had to agree on what to say.

"It is all about control for Phipps and . . . Farish," Paulick wrote in his blog, "The Paulick Report." "Whether it's Jockey Club president Alan Marzelli bullying NTRA executives on when to hold meetings and who to invite, or surrogates for Phipps and Farish populating industry boards and leadership positions, they want to make sure nothing moves forward without their stamp of approval."

The impotence of many industry organizations can be explained by their lack of money or relevance. The Jockeys Guild (the jockey union), for example, is perennially broke, and the veterinarian groups seldom open their pockets or raise their voices on issues not involving horse safety or their own income stream. The only organizations that can even lay a claim to leadership are those Paulick listed as within "the sphere of control" of Phipps and Farish. They are the Breeders' Cup; the NTRA; TOBA, which controls the American Graded Stakes Committee and the *Blood-Horse*; and the New York Racing Association.

Seldom does one of these four institutions make a spontaneous move without prior consultation with a Dinny. Rather, they plod along in lockstep with the Jockey Club in accordance with whatever is outlined in its annual Round Table, a sort of state-of-the-industry presentation that Paulick contends is no round table at all but a "throat-clearing exercise for industry poobahs." He says Phipps "goes over every speech with a fine-tooth comb, cutting out things he doesn't like and adding points he wants to have made."

"It's a precisely orchestrated show that leaves nary a stanza for improvisation," the former *Blood-Horse* editor wrote. "And there is no question about who the conductor is . . . waving the baton."

Robert McNair, the owner of the Houston Texans pro football team, came to the thoroughbred business in the early 1990s about the same time I did. He came from Texas as one of the fifty richest Americans, the founder and owner of Cogen Technologies, an energy company that Enron would buy from him in 1999 for $1.5 billion—mostly cash, according to *Forbes* magazine.

I dropped in with a "golden" parachute from Tribune Tower in Chicago, a newspaper editor fired, the industry publications accurately noted, for being a pain in the ass to the corporate bean counters who had taken over the company.

McNair and I have yet to meet, but among our first investments was a $60,000, 20 percent share in a horse named Kozak, half brother to the champion Fly So Free. A miserable failure as a racehorse, Kozak turned out to be worthless. But with McNair as a partner I had at least been a loser in good company.

That's where our parallel paths diverged back to where they belonged. But we both recovered nicely, McNair with the purchase of 2,000 gorgeous acres near Arthur Hancock in Bourbon County that he developed and named Stonerside after a nearby creek. And I landed on a considerably smaller but nonetheless lovely 132 acres in Woodford County that Mary Anne and I named after two white-tail bucks that lived there. McNair started his breeding program by purchasing the entire thirty-six-broodmare band of the fabled Elmendorf Farm, and mine was built on three daughters of the stallion Dixieland Band, among them Regal Band (the dam of Monarchos), whom I purchased for $14,000.

As breeders, we both had extraordinary early success. In 1998 McNair bred the hard-knocking colt Congaree, who beat Monarchos in the Wood Memorial, the last prep race before the 2001 Kentucky Derby. But at Churchill Downs, Congaree ran out of steam in the last furlong, and Monarchos breezed by him to win easily. Congaree went on to win five Grade 1 stakes races before he was done, and McNair later bought a share in Monarchos, which raised both horse and owner in my esteem. I was among the first in line to breed a mare to Congaree.

Earlier McNair had teamed up with Arthur Hancock to breed the 2000 Kentucky Derby winner Fusaichi Pegasus, who sold as a yearling for $4 million in 1998, the year Monarchos and Congaree were born. McNair's half share of that bonanza exceeded my total sales revenue for the next few years and validated further the already established disparity in our business acumen, which of course had long been apparent to the "leaders" of our industry.

The year after Monarchos won the Kentucky Derby, John Ward, one of the few reform-minded insiders, whose main client, John Oxley, is a Jockey Club member and formerly one of its nine stewards, was slated to become president of the Kentucky Thoroughbred Owners and Breeders Association, an organization originally formed as an alternative to the established, nationwide Horse Benevolent and Protective Association. Out of the blue came the call from the organization's executive director asking me to run for Arthur Hancock's recently vacated seat.

"I wouldn't get ten votes," I told him. "You might as well forget it."

"Oh, you'll get elected," he told me. "I can guarantee that. Johnny Ward wants you on the board."

And miraculously I did. But it was a humbling experience and my second lesson in Thoroughbred Horse Organizations 101. Largely due to my friendship with Ward, I got choice assignments and was able to influence committee recommendations, most of which never saw the light of day. Embarrassingly, the KTOB often ended up taking the opposite public position on issues from the one my committee had recommended. Before my service, the KTOB was widely regarded as an impotent organization that was actually a hindrance to progress in the Kentucky General Assembly, where most of its efforts were aimed. And nothing Ward or I did changed that one iota.

When Ward's term ended in 2005, so did mine. And due as much to my personality as my net worth, my relationship with all the Dinny-controlled organizations since has been limited to writing them checks to register my foals, qualify my racehorses, and purchase inferior-quality seats for my racehorse clients at the Breeders' Cup.

Meanwhile McNair's natural charm and established business prowess got him a seat among the Dinnies, in the high-rent section reserved for people of wealth and power. He was quickly elected to the board of TOBA, the nationwide and more prestigious version of the KTOB, and recruited to appear in an industry television commercial. An overachiever all his life, McNair naturally believed they wanted him to lead, which would have been a good idea.

In 2003, when Gary Biszantz was running loose as TOBA chairman, McNair was chosen to oversee a project with the working title of the Thoroughbred Championship Tour, which was the brainchild of some like-minded but equally naive and well-intentioned board members who believed that McNair's standing and experience in the National Football League made him a natural for the job.

McNair, the Canadian businessman Eugene Melnyk, NetJets founder Rich Santulli, and Sheikh Mohammed each kicked in $100,000 to jump-start the project.

The idea was to raise the sport's profile and expand its fan base by creating a "major league" of racing that would pit the best horses of their class in a series of televised weekend events like pro-sports playoffs leading up to the Breeders' Cup. Similar to what Gaines and Fred Pope had tried to do in 1997, it would require a $25 million investment, the support of the well-staffed Breeders' Cup, and the political power of the Jockey Club to elicit cooperation from racetracks that for the most part shared the Dinnies' dim view of change.

The project languished for two years before finally expiring under the weight of opposition by G. Watts Humphrey and Will Farish, who controlled the executive committee of the Breeders' Cup. "They did all the work, raised all the money, and did everything right," said a TOBA insider. "But it was like when you were in college and turned in a project expecting to get an A and it comes back a D. They turned it over to Watts, who was liaison with the Breeders' Cup, and it died right there."

The failure of the Thoroughbred Championship Tour was blamed largely on track intransigence involving scheduling conflicts and the new organization's insistence that it control media and wagering rights. But McNair is said to have taken the defeat as a personal rejection, not just of his advice and expertise on the project, but of his willingness to become a leader in an industry in which he had invested well over $100 million. It was at that moment, according to a close associate, that McNair decided he had no future in the thoroughbred business and began making plans to leave it, which he would eventually do.

At the time, the management of the combined Breeders' Cup and NTRA operations rested safely in the hands of the old guard loyal to the Dinnies. The Thoroughbred Championship Tour debacle had coincided with an unpopular board decision to raise stallion nomination fees and a rising tide of protest from breeders who believed the NTRA was squandering the Breeders' Cup's $40 million treasury built from their nomination fees. Moved once again only by the signs of internal bleeding, the Dinnies allowed the existing management to be pushed into retirement. Staff salaries were cut, the executive staff was trimmed, and the merger with the NTRA was reversed.

When the dust had settled, the bylaws of the Breeders' Cup were rewritten, setting up a familiar system of control. Now a large board of forty or more is elected democratically on the basis of votes awarded to nominators according to the amount of money they have paid in during the last year, which gives breeders more voice. But then in a classic example of backroom politics, the board elects a smaller group of thirteen trustees, who then elect the officers.

Not surprisingly, Will Farish's son Bill, a member of the Jockey Club and a new generation of the old guard, emerged as the president of the Breeders' Cup. He has since been reelected to a second term.

Despite the longevity of Dinnies in high places, their perennial occupation of the first-class seats, and their ability to fill the key jobs and stack the committees, Arthur Hancock was right on the money when he said nobody is in control of horse racing. In truth it has been out of control for at least two decades, during which the thoroughbred market and the very nature of the beast on whose back it rides have been subverted by new forces well beyond their reach and perhaps even their recognition.

Right under their noses, in the auction pavilions they rule and the historic racetracks around which they socialize, the tough, durable classic representatives of the breed—those of the famous names that adorn their statuary such as Man o' War, Citation, Seabiscuit, and Bold Ruler—were replaced by an entirely different animal: the sale horse.

4

THE SALE HORSE

Due to her tragic death under the Twin Spires of Churchill Downs in May 2008, the filly Eight Belles will likely go down as a celebrated but miscast example of all that was wrong with thoroughbred horse racing. But that dubious honor actually belongs to the Green Monkey.

No, that is not something I ate on a bad sale day. It was something the thoroughbred industry swallowed.

The Green Monkey was a big, gorgeous red horse, mature for his age, with a wide white stripe accenting intelligent eyes. His quality and speed suggested Triple Crown. The marketing minded among us even viewed his unusual name as a possible rival for fan appeal with that of Funny Cide or Smarty Jones.

Named after a Barbados golf course once called "the most expensive in history," the Green Monkey became the most expensive racehorse in history in 2006. At the sale of two-year-olds in training held at Calder Race Course near Miami in February of that year, the Irish Coolmore shelled out $16 million for the Monkey, surpassing the $13.1 million paid for Seattle Dancer in 1985.

The golf course turned out to be terrific; the horse turned out to be, well, an embarrassment. Unable to seriously contest any of his three races, he ultimately retired to stud in Florida for a paltry $5,000 breeding fee.

Eight Belles and the Green Monkey have more than a little in common. Both were bred for speed and sales appeal. Their sires both stand at the same stallion farm, Taylor Made, which incidentally is the largest consignor of thoroughbreds to auction in North America and one of the industry's most efficient marketing machines.

As a sale horse, Eight Belles was a bargain at $375,000. According to standard industry economic models, selling for three times the $125,000 stud fee of her sire, Unbridled's Song, she was profitable but not excessively so. Certainly she was not the kind of "home run" horse for which Unbridled's Song is famous, having sired twenty-one offspring that have brought $1 million or more at auction.

When she was sold as a yearling, the top-selling filly in her sale went for $3.2 million, and the top colt for $11.2 million, a few months after the Monkey set the record. Such million-dollar horse-for-money swaps have been the norm in the thoroughbred business for a quarter of a century, driven mostly by a twenty-five-year rivalry between the ruling family of Dubai, one of the United Arab Emirates, and the Coolmore conglomerate of Ireland.

But none was more dubious and illustrative of such madness than the saga of the Green Monkey, who will go down in history as the prototype of the modern thoroughbred "sale horse"—a commodity that became for the racing industry what the subprime mortgage derivative was for Wall Street—a kind of overvalued product that sucked the money out of the market until it was gasping for survival.

Perhaps more significant, the "sale" animal shifted the thrust of Kentucky's successful racehorse breeding industry away from the classically bred yearling that had been the envy of the world and had dominated racing globally for more than a half century. In its place was left an early maturing muscle horse that can set records for speed and return megaprofits for covering an eighth of a mile as fast as a quarter horse. But on the track the "sale" horse has been largely a disappointment and in the breeding shed a long-term disaster.

In 1971, the last horse to win the English Triple Crown went to stud at Bull Hancock's Claiborne Farm. Nijinsky II was the epitome of the classic racehorse, a son of Northern Dancer who had spent his entire racing career on the grass tracks of Europe at classic distances of a mile and a quarter or longer. Not only had he won all five of his starts as a two-year-old at shorter distances, to complete the English Triple Crown and become European Horse of the Year in 1970, he'd had to win the Doncaster St. Leger Stakes at a mile and three quarters.

Such a combination of pedigree, precocity, and stamina was just what the American market wanted for its Triple Crown candidates. So over the next decade Nijinsky II's get were among the brightest stars that came out at night at the prestigious Keeneland July sale and Saratoga August, an older summer sale held at the upstate New York spa by Keeneland's competitor Fasig-Tipton.

The offspring of Nijinsky II averaged $800,000 in 1982, $1.3 million in 1983, and the mania reached its apex at Keeneland in 1985 when his son Seattle Dancer sold for $13.1 million, becoming the most expensive yearling in history.

It was a classic case of supply and demand. Farms like Claiborne still clung to the old business model of breeding their stallions to sixty or seventy mares each year, and half the resulting foal crop or more belonged to wealthy clients who bred to race, not to sell. Fillies were usually half the crop and more likely to be retained by their breeders. And some of the colts that showed up in the sales were clearly inferior animals with conformation flaws of one kind or another, usually offset knees and errant ankles.

By the time Seattle Dancer pranced into the sale ring, the heated competition for the best Kentucky colts—between the Maktoum family of Dubai and the Coolmore conglomerate—had been under way for years. The profiteers from that sale included perhaps the most powerful American in the business in those days, Warner L. Jones, the chairman of Churchill Downs, and the man who would replace him in that role, Will Farish, both members of the Jockey Club elite.

Virtually all the expensive, royally bred summer sale animals like Seattle Dancer ended up in the hands of the Dinnies or their global counterparts to run in the most important classic races at the most fashionable tracks under the most famous colors. In short, Nijinsky II was the kind of racehorse sire around which the thoroughbred industry elite built its business and based its travel plans.

The classic horse is still the dream of Jockey Club members, Arab sheikhs, oil barons, and instant billionaires from the get-rich-quick worlds of digital technology and exotic financial instruments. A special animal carrying the right combination of blood, class, athleticism—and luck—is what is needed to win the Kentucky Derby, the Breeders' Cup Classic, the Epsom Derby in London, the Prix de l'Arc de Triomphe at Longchamps, and the $5 million purses in Dubai.

Winners' circles, however, are restricted to the owners of the fastest horses, not those with the most impressive net worth or the highest society credentials. Nor could the exhilaration of bidding wars and Seattle Dancer–size bonanza profits remain the private preserve of the landed gentry and their blue-blooded stock that has been passed down through generations.

Pinstriped speculators from Wall Street were only a fraction of the new gamblers attracted by the seven-figure numbers on the neon at Keeneland and Saratoga. They were joined by bold men in big white Stetsons and women in boots and tight blue jeans, ambitious lads in plaid caps from the fields of Ireland, and tweed-clad risk takers from the betting shops of Great Britain, natural-born gamblers all, in search of a piece of the action. Some of them even knew a little something about horses.

On September 13, 1974, about the time Nijinsky II's first foal crop was heading to the track, an upstart trainer won his first stakes race at a small thoroughbred track in California, saddling a horse he owned named Harbor Hauler, and taking home a $6,312 purse. Change had broken through the gate. And right under the very noses from which it was being looked down upon, it would alter both the kind of horses being bred, raised, and sold in the Bluegrass of Kentucky and the very nature of the market for which they were intended.

It would take Darnell Wayne Lukas fourteen years to win his first Kentucky Derby, which he did with a precocious giant filly named Winning Colors. His Derby champion lost the Breeders' Cup by a "lip" later that year to a mare named Personal Ensign, owned by the Phipps family, in a race regarded as one of the greatest horse races ever, largely due to the way Personal Ensign came from the back of the pack in the slop to nip the Derby champion at the wire and retire undefeated. But it may also have been a seminal event in the sport's history.

Personal Ensign was the epitome of what the best in the sport had always been, a homebred owned by the most prominent family and from one of the finest broodmare bands ever assembled. She was raised on the three thousand acres of Claiborne Farm, sired by a Claiborne stallion, and saddled by a native Kentuckian named Shug McGaughey, who has spent most of his career as the private trainer for the Phipps family.

Winning Colors was something else again, a sale horse bred by tiny Echo Valley Farm, which would have fit inside one of Claiborne's forty-acre paddocks. Though she was descended from a historically respected family, her grandmother had been a free throw-in as a foal on the side of a $45,000 mare. Her sire was a French export named Caro, who came to America carrying the herpes virus and was best known as a sire of broodmares. Due mainly to the racing success of a relative, Chris Evert, also bred by Echo Valley and named after the tennis star of the time, Winning Colors was cataloged in the 1986 July Keeneland sale, where Lukas found her.

A Wisconsin native who grew up on a farm and earned a master's degree in education, Lukas had left his basketball coaching profession to train quarter horses in 1968. Over the next ten years he trained twenty-three world champions. Since that first thoroughbred stakes victory in 1974, he had become one of the most colorful and best-known trainers in the thoroughbred world with more than two hundred horses in his public stable.

At the sales Lukas was himself quite an attraction. Though he still wore cowboy hats and jeans while training in the mornings, he would stroll the sale grounds hatless, handsome, and silver-haired, in colorful shirts open at the collar, pleated trousers, and shiny dress shoes. Other buyers tracked him at a distance just to see which horses he was inspecting, sparking unsubstantiated rumors that consignors actually paid Lukas just to look at their offerings.

His major client in those days was Eugene Klein, a Californian who wanted to win the Derby as badly as his trainer, and over the years Lukas had purchased many expensive colts for the endeavor. Winning Colors was exactly the kind of horse

Lukas liked, massive and muscular like the quarter horses he had grown up around. She looked like a colt. And not just any colt—a big, tough colt. Though listed as roan in the catalog, she was a shiny gray with a wide stripe on her face, flashy like the man perusing her. So when the hammer fell at Keeneland just one year after Seattle Dancer's sales record, Lukas bought Winning Colors for Klein for $575,000.

The filly started only twice as a two-year-old, unusual for any horse Lukas was aiming at the Derby. But she won both races handily, and when the first Saturday in May 1988 came around, she was his only Derby entry, also an oddity for the man who usually had several horses in the gate. By now, Lukas was 0 for 13 in the world's greatest race. In Derby history only two fillies—Regret in 1915 and Genuine Risk in 1980—had ever beat the boys, and hardly anyone believed Lukas's filly could become the third.

Among her competitors that year were two Claiborne-raised horses: Forty Niner, owned by the farm, and Seeking the Gold, owned by the Phipps family. Forty Niner's trainer was Woody Stephens, the face of the racetrack establishment who was born in Midway, Kentucky, the very center of the breeding industry. Stephens had a huge stable, too, and an ego to match. He made no bones about the load of resentment he bore for Lukas. The filly didn't belong in the Kentucky Derby, Stephens told the press, and had no chance of winning.

Stephens didn't know what he was talking about. Winning Colors had the quick start typical of quarter horses and cowboy training techniques. She took the lead early and gamely held off the late run of Forty Niner to beat him by a neck. Seeking the Gold finished back in the pack. The new guard had given the old an embarrassing licking.

While Personal Ensign's exciting victory in the Breeders' Cup before a television audience later that year represented a measure of revenge, it was hardly a setback for the upstarts. In retrospect, it was a metaphor for how the thoroughbred traditionalists would respond to the challenge by the new.

Like so many other responses to change by the Dinnies in the years to come, Personal Ensign's victory was merely a holding action that allowed them to remain in place.

Six more times in the next ten years, the blanket of Kentucky Derby roses would be laid across the necks of horses led by "cowboy" trainers: three by Lukas, two by the California invader Bob Baffert, and one by an ex–rodeo bull rider named Carl Nafzger. None had ever rung a big bell at the sale. And more often than not, they physically resembled Winning Colors more than Personal Ensign.

Still, the bred-in-the-purple pedigrees of horse and owner would remain the premier consideration in the minds of upper-echelon sellers and buyers. For more than thirty years, the blood of top stallions was concentrated in the mares living on the most storied Kentucky farms: Claiborne, Three Chimneys, Lane's End, Mill Ridge, and Overbrook. The farm owners, all Jockey Club members with their own base of wealthy clients, controlled the shares in these stallions and the breeding seasons available to outsiders.

Year after year the produce of these expensive matings continued to be the focus of the select sales, traded primarily among the Kentucky elite and the two foreign powerhouses, Coolmore and the Maktoums. Their proceeds drove up sale company revenue, averages, medians, and every other statistic by which the health of the thoroughbred breeding industry was measured.

In 1986, when Lukas bought Winning Colors, Keeneland sold 2,264 yearlings for $177.5 million. Well more than half the revenue—$104.4 million—was spent on the 256 sold in the select July session. By 2007, the numbers had risen to 3,558 for a record $399.7 million, with 324 horses accounting for nearly half the revenue—$182 million.

Happily ensconced in this tiny top sliver of the market, the establishment Dinnies had no reason to worry about losing control of their industry. They were entitled to their position, after all, having inherited it from their ancestors just like the great blood of their horses.

But lose it they would. The charismatic sale horse with size, speed, and muscle would come to dominate every segment of the market, including theirs, and change the nature of horse breeding for years to come.

In the late 1980s, most horses arrived at thoroughbred sales looking as if they'd just been led out of the pasture and had the mud brushed off. Their bellies bulged from the rich spring Kentucky grass, and their hair shone from its excess protein. Forced exercise had been limited to a few weeks of hand walking, so there was little tone to their muscle. Many were plain-headed, a little coarse, and still rank to lead.

The world of quarter horses, where my equine education had been gleaned, was different. I'd spent a decade learning to prepare weanlings and yearlings for shows to be judged on the same criteria as sale horses: temperament, conformation, muscling, and coat preparation.

Yearlings were lunged or trotted behind ponies for weeks, their necks and throatlatches reduced pencil-thin from glycerin sweats, the hair inside their ears shaved down to the skin. Their eyes were often accented with liner and their muzzles oiled. By sale or show time, they had learned to stand for hours tied to a wall and pose like statues during inspection. And one other thing: a lot of them had been on steroids since the day they were weaned off their mothers. In the halter and racehorse segments the drugs were as routine as hay, water, and oats to make them grow faster and stronger and appear older than their chronological age. They also made the horses more aggressive.

Equipoise, a brand name for the anabolic steroid boldenone, a form of testosterone that builds strength and appetite, made the females and geldings look and act like males. In the ring they would rear and strike.

Winstrol, meanwhile, made young males so difficult to control at show or sale time they were often given a second drug called Regu-Mate, an estrus suppressant in females that controls hormonal distractions. Otherwise, a line of 1,200-pound stallions waiting in a narrow corridor to enter a halter class might become a pecking-order dispute with the handlers caught in the middle. The drugs used to grow and condition the animals into sale or halter show standouts required that other drugs had to be administered to manage them.

None of my horses, quarter or thoroughbred, was ever raised on steroids. But the lengthy and painstaking sale preparation process of diet, grooming, and exercise had given my Two Bucks weanlings and yearlings an appearance so strikingly different that some traditionalists laughed at them—and at me. But they drew the attention of buyers.

The first weanling colt I ever offered at Keeneland, from my mare For Dixie, attracted a $100,000 bid on the first auctioneer's call in 1996 and was hammered down for $150,000. He was eventually named Misbah and raced by Sheikh Hamdan, one of the Maktoums. He was from the first crop by the 1992 champion two-year-old Gilded Time, a thick-chested sprinter so chiseled and muscular he could have been a quarter horse halter champion. Another Gilded Time weanling colt sold well in that sale and went on to win $655,000. The Gilded Time babies looked just like their sire, precisely what D. Wayne Lukas and the growing number of migrants from the quarter horse business were used to seeing.

About the time Two Bucks horses began showing up at Keeneland sales, so did a distinctive truck and trailer rig bearing Texas license plates to unload a dozen or so beautifully prepared thoroughbred babies for the yearling sales. The thoroughbred world had discovered Roger Daly, a master sale and show horse fitter from Aubrey, Texas, north of Fort Worth. Everybody in the quarter horse world knew that, given 120 days, Daly could turn an unruly lump of coal into a sale diamond.

The quarter horse prep techniques—treadmills, neck sweating, appetite enhancers, and pharmaceuticals—were already in vogue elsewhere in the industry among ambitious and upwardly mobile outsiders, many of them from the quarter horse world, who were beginning to set trends not only in the sale preparation of horses but in the breeding of them as well.

Good racehorses come in all shapes, sizes, and degrees of limb contortion. Neither Seattle Slew nor Mr. Prospector, two of the most important sire influences of the last thirty years, were much to look at. Among their least-desired genetic gifts to the breed was a high percentage of badly aligned front leg joints and in Mr. Prospector's case thin, fragile hoof walls. But these drawbacks were regularly trumped at the sales by the one quality that would replace class, blood, and endurance as the most important in the thoroughbred: speed. Soon their plain and often bad-legged offspring were being mated to a handsome descendant of Northern Dancer named Storm Cat, another source of precocious speed.

The stud fees commanded by Mr. Prospector and Seattle Slew remained in excess of $100,000 for most of their careers. At the height of Storm Cat's popularity, he was even more expensive—$400,000 and higher in some instances. His sons and daughters were not only fast but also uncommonly beautiful and charismatic, as was he. The offspring of all three were generally out of top mares and therefore confined to the tiny top sliver on the market, where the high dollars they commanded kept them beyond the reach of average buyers and sellers.

Their genes good and bad, however, were abundant and readily available in the expanding yearling market through their less prominent descendants. There, legions of trainers, bloodstock agents, and speculators in search of a fast horse and a fast buck combed the barns in the footprints of the well-established equine evaluators like Lukas and Baffert, who had won his second Kentucky Derby with Real Quiet, a fast but bargain-priced great-grandson of Mr. Prospector.

The new shooters dwarfed in number the elite traders at the top. Their purchases were holding up the bottom of the sales, soaking up the best individuals from an oversupply of inferior-pedigreed or physically flawed yearlings.

When resold again six months later, these choice "pin-hooks" provided consignors, sales companies, horse haulers, veterinarians, and bloodstock agents a second bite of the same apple, making up the revenue shortfall for the growing numbers of horses that had either been sold at a loss or not sold at all.

Virtually overnight the new industry segment, made up of "pinhookers" and based primarily in Florida, had become the shopping center of choice for wealthy buyers in a hurry to compete with the Dinnies on the Triple Crown trail.

For better or worse, a true Dinny always preferred to see his well-bred two-year-olds under saddle for the first time jogging down his own private farm tracks or leisurely cantering across the grass in late August or early September toward the end of the Saratoga race season after the riffraff had gone home.

In the unalterable and pervasive caste system of the thoroughbred world, the training sales—where the two-year-old horses were being sold—were considered the more proper venue of the cowboy trainers, lower-food-chain bloodstock agents, and speculators—and as the natural market for conformational rejects and modestly bred animals they could afford.

That changed in March 1995, when a horse bought for $200,000 the previous August at the Saratoga yearling sale sold for a record $1.4 million at the Barrett's select sale for two-year-olds near Los Angeles—a $1.2 million return in seven months for a flamboyant New York investment broker named Ernie Paragallo.

A son of the 1990 Kentucky Derby winner Unbridled and carrying the speed genes of his great-grandfather Mr. Prospector, the colt was a beautiful gray yearling with a loose-jointed walk whose bargain price at Saratoga was due to rumors that he had veterinary issues. Unbridled had yet to prove himself as a sire but had quickly gained the reputation for throwing foals with offset knees.

However questionable the colt's front wheels, his marvelously long, ground-eating stride enabled him to set a record for covering an eighth of a mile in 10.2 seconds while making it look easy. This record-setting "breeze" fueled the auction frenzy at Barrett's, but Paragallo would later have to return the $1.4 million to the buyer, Hiroshi Fujita, after postsale radiographs disclosed a small chip in the horse's right front ankle. The highly publicized turn back was a blessing for Paragallo, considered a rascal by some, and an embarrassment to the late "Mr. Fujita," who was beloved by many. The colt went on to become a brilliant but unsound racehorse and a smash hit as a sire of speed-burning sale toppers. In a twist of Shakespearean-level irony, he turned out to be Unbridled's Song, the sire of Eight Belles.

Though he was bothered by bad feet that probably prevented his winning the Kentucky Derby in 1996, Unbridled's

Song's combination of grace, beauty, speed, and big profit would become the new business model for thoroughbred sale success. And he became the epitome of the sale horse sire.

In his first decade at stud, twenty-one of his offspring sold for $1 million or more at public auction. One of his sons, Songandaprayer, ran the first half-mile fraction of the 2001 Derby three seconds faster than ever, a pace largely responsible for Monarchos being able to run by the exhausted favorites to win the second-fastest Kentucky Derby in history. Upon their retirement, Songandaprayer instantly became a bigger attraction at stud than the Derby winner.

The price Unbridled's Song commanded at the Barrett's sale from a representative of a new wave of foreign buyers paved a path for the industry out of its late 1980s doldrums and changed forever the establishment's evaluation of the training sales as a market.

After belittling the sales for years as a place for rejects, Keeneland held its first "under tack" show and sale in 1993. The number of horses and the sale revenue were relatively small— 108 sold the first year for $6.8 million—and would remain so. But now the best pedigreed and most expensive pinhooks find their way to Keeneland's April two-year-old in training auction.

Unbridled's Song's ultimate success at the track and in the breeding shed was even more pivotal, signaling both an expansion of the Kentucky stallion business and a shift in the direction away from classic horses to sires of speed, a trend for the next fifteen years. In time, the quest for speed would be responsible for the rise of veterinarian influence on training methods and for the drug-induced enhancement of appearance at sales and performance at the track. It would also be a critical factor in the steady increase in the percentage of unprofitable horses.

Coupled with ill-conceived changes in sales policies that

produced unintended consequences, the speed horse first merged the middle and the bottom of the yearling market, then divided it again between sale successes and sale failures.

If ever a single animal could qualify as both, it was the Green Monkey.

There were 679 horses consigned to the Fasig-Tipton sale of July 2005, none better looking than the horse wearing hip number 522, Forestry's son out of Magical Masquerade. Had he the blue-blood pedigree of a true stallion prospect, he would have been a certain target of the Arabs and the Irish.

Dr. Dermot O'Byrne, the horse buyer for Coolmore, was on the grounds on a familiar mission: to make sure no good stallion prospect, especially one sired by a Coolmore stallion, got sold for too little money. As is often the case, he signed that year for the high-selling horse, a son of Giant's Causeway for $650,000. He passed on the Forestry colt, ostensibly because his dam's lineage did not measure up. But he was clearly a creature with speed in his blood. His sire had done his best running at a mile or less, his best win coming in the King's Bishop, a seven-and-a-half-furlong sprint at Saratoga. The pinhookers who buy at the yearling level to sell a year later were hooked.

When the dust had settled, Randy Hartley and Dean De Renzo, a respected pair of two-year-old conditioners from Florida, had bought the colt for $425,000—the most they had ever spent on a yearling and a monumental risk for someone in their business.

Seven months later they brought him to the premier under tack sale at Calder Race Course, where his appearance and performance drew so much attention that Hartley told a Florida newspaper he was wondering, "Have they got a board big enough to handle all the numbers?"

"Everyone was on him," Hartley said, including the two buyers whose presence revs up a seller's heartbeat: Coolmore's Demi O'Byrne and John Ferguson, who shops for Sheikh Mohammed. Obviously the long-running war between their principals had reached beyond yearlings and prize mares in Kentucky to the hard training tracks of Florida.

The attraction was how easily the Forestry colt had broken the ten-second barrier in his one-furlong breeze—an eighth of a mile sprint from a running start that had become the ridiculous measure of racehorse potential in the new speed market. He had stopped the timer in 9.8 seconds.

To appreciate the absurdity of this evaluator, it's worth noting that Secretariat ran the Kentucky Derby—ten furlongs or one and a quarter miles—in 1 minute, 59 2/5 seconds, which means he averaged slightly less than twelve seconds per furlong for the entire distance. Neither he nor Monarchos, the only other horse ever to break the two-minute mark in the Derby, apparently ever ran a timed furlong in less than eleven seconds in their lives.

Yet in the eleven years since Unbridled's Song's record-setting breeze at Barrett's—10.2 seconds—had rung the Japanese buyer's bell, the sub-ten-second furlong had become a training sale brass ring. Speed and top dollar now had a synonymous resonance with the consignors.

The faster a horse could run a furlong, the more a trainer or bloodstock agent could wring out of his buyer, the bigger the profit for the pinhooker, and the bigger the commission for the seller and the sale company—rational behavior across the board.

Not all two-year-old conditioners liked the new program. Horses do not naturally run a furlong with 120 pounds on their back in less than ten seconds. Some trainers refused to adopt the rigorous training regimens necessary to produce such results and paid the price in lost revenue.

Others quit sales training altogether rather than try to make a horse run that fast at such a young age. To get that kind of performance not only demands a special animal but also requires constant pressure, steroids, and other performance-enhancing drugs and painkillers, and even excessive whipping. Some trainers have acknowledged publicly that they try to entice such results by offering bonuses to riders who make a horse work in less than ten seconds.

Some horses survive the regimen and go on to become early and successful racehorses—the 2008 Kentucky Derby winner Big Brown, for example, and Monarchos. But they are in the distinct minority. Studies show that most horses passing through a two-year-old training sale don't make it to the races for eleven months, a statistic that negates the very reason for speed being a measure of value.

None of this seemed to matter when the battle was joined between the Irish and Arab representatives on February 28, 2006, at the Calder Race Course over the Forestry colt. The scene, as best described by Nicholas Clee, writing for the *Observer Sports Monthly*, was the stuff of which movies are made.

"Before long, his price had risen above $3m, leaving only two bidders: Demi O'Byrne, representing the Coolmore bloodstock empire of John Magnier, and John Ferguson, representing the Darley operation of Sheikh Mohammed bin Rashid Al Maktoum. O'Byrne and Ferguson, seemingly entrusted with limitless budgets, slugged it out past the $5.2m record price for a two-year-old, past the $9.7m Sheikh Mohammed had paid for a yearling in autumn 2005 and past the 20-year-old thoroughbred auction record of $13.1m.

"Spectators gasped as each mark was passed, swivelling in their seats to watch the protagonists. Ferguson signalled his bids with curt nods; O'Byrne, arms folded, responded to each raise instantly. At $14m, Ferguson raised to $15m. O'Byrne countered with $15.2m. Ferguson went to $15.5m.

"For the first time, O'Byrne hesitated slightly. Then he raised to $16m. It was too much for Ferguson. The gavel descended. There was an eruption of applause; the horse, startled, wheeled round and kicked tanbark over spectators in the nearby seats."

O'Byrne said of the horse: "He'd better be good." And Coolmore quickly named the most expensive horse they ever bought the Green Monkey, after the most expensive golf course they ever built.

The $16 million "sale" of the Green Monkey now evokes smiles and smirks from knowledgeable insiders, who frequently cite it as an example of the long-standing practice of inflated sale prices that misrepresents the state of the industry's economic health but more accurately portrays the state of its integrity.

Defending the extravagance that drove them to victory in what may be remembered as "the Monkey War," the Coolmore men said the speed displayed by their prize Monkey in the training sale breeze-up is what convinced them of his eventual worth as a stallion.

Biomechanics experts are often hired to make a slow-motion gait analysis as part of a buyer's "due diligence," and those who later watched the Monkey train at Todd Pletcher's barn were convinced that his extraordinary speed at short distances came from what is known as the *rotary gallop*, more common to quarter horse racing, in which the footfall pattern moves around the horse in a circle—left hind, right hind, right front, left front.

Most thoroughbreds employ the rotary gallop when leaving the starting gate but quickly switch to the more normal transverse gallop, which has a diagonal-based footfall pattern, left hind, right front, right hind, left front. The rotary gallop is what propels dogs and cheetahs. And it is the gait the fastest equine on earth—the quarter horse—employs to run gate to wire for a quarter mile (440 yards), where sub-ten-second furlongs are routine.

But quarter horses are not called that for nothing. The rotary gallop is also energy inefficient and cannot be sustained at longer distances. It is dependent on those powerful shoulders and short, bulging lower hindquarter muscles—the stifle and the gaskin—muscles that cowboy trainers found so appealing in the new "sale horse"—muscles that quickly lose their elasticity. My old Jack Russell terrier, Two Bucks Al, had thick muscles like that and after about fifty yards had to rest one hind leg while hopping on the other.

Fittingly, the Monkey will stand stud at the Florida farm of the pinhookers who made him famous, Hartley and De Renzo, who hope to augment his puny $5,000 opening season fee by making him a tourist attraction. To no one's surprise, Coolmore is said to have retained an interest in his stallion performance and will support him with mares from its vast and formidable collection. At that price he will only have to settle 3,200 mares in his lifetime to recover his purchase price. Assuming a superb average equine conception rate of one hundred pregnancies a year, he might accomplish that if he is still living and breeding at age thirty-five.

"He was just unlucky as a racehorse," John Magnier told the *Guardian*. "He got injured and he never really came around from it, but this is giving him a second chance. He's from a young family that is going to improve, and he has everything going for him in the breeding shed. Now it is up to the breeders to make him a champion."

The Coolmore boss knew where to drop the Monkey's future, in the lap of the hapless breeders at the bottom of the headless industry, who for the past decade seemed intent on breeding themselves out of business in quest of the "home run" horse: the mindless bunch of amazingly happy resilient gamblers who flock to the sale company table set by Coolmore, the Dinnies, and the Arabs, in quest of a Hartley–De Renzo–like feast, only to leave most frequently with crumbs.

These are my people. If the Green Monkey has a human counterpart, I am it. We are it.

5

SHENANIGANS

Until a man gets old enough to worry about death, the two top items on his agenda are sex and money, the order depending on the time of his life—and maybe even the time of day. Unbridled excess in either is a recipe for addiction and disaster. Jails, divorce courts, and homeless shelters are rife with supporting evidence.

Horse sales—one of the more addictive aspects of the horse business—are all about money. At a top-level thoroughbred yearling auction, $100 million might fly by on the tote board in a single day. It is spectacular gambling to the nth degree, fascinating even if you are merely a spectator.

In the world of politics, which is similarly intoxicating, an acquaintance of mine with a phenomenal record of success and a glowing future used to throw parties to celebrate his triumphs. In a moment of euphoria, he succumbed to an offer of crack cocaine. Eight years later, a ravished fifty-year-old hopeless addict, he had lost his health, his family, his wealth, and his future.

There are moments like that at horse sales (probably some involving cocaine, too, though I have never seen it). Mine came in 1995 at the sight of a Canadian megamillionaire named

Frank Stronach literally running into a Lexington sale pavilion to bid on For Dixie's first foal, a nine-month-old colt that had cost about $15,000 to raise. Ultimately hammered down for ten times that amount to an even more excited bidder, the colt represented my first big profit for Two Bucks. I was hooked.

Sales have been pretty much downhill for me since, but like thousands of others I go to watch them if not to participate. Horse sales are circuses with lovely horses for elephants, mint juleps for peanuts, where clowns abound, beautiful women are frequently on parade or being flaunted, and fortunes fly through the air like confetti.

The man who gave me the best advice on how to survive in the horse business (take horse to sale, bring home money) was no longer around in the summer of 2008 to see me flagrantly unable to follow it. At age eighty-six, upon his retirement, Robert Courtney Sr. had had enough.

"It's a great game and I've had a great run," Courtney told the *Blood-Horse.* "I've been very fortunate but the game has outgrown me."

As usual, his timing was impeccable. Courtney had sold his farm and could watch from an easy chair in his new house downtown as his beloved horse business collapsed again, along with the rest of the economy. He had seen that the market for the kind of horse Courtney had made a living raising for sixty-seven years had virtually disappeared, its worth on an auction block about the same as a subprime mortgage in downtown Detroit.

Courtney's reputation for selling $1 million worth of yearlings, including the multiple Grade 1 stakes winner Fit to Fight, out of a mare he bought for $11,000 had made him the role model for my horse business endeavor, which ironically began at the bottom of another real estate–induced downturn nearly twenty years before as the savings-and-loan scandals rocked the U.S. economy.

The stories of Courtney's accomplishment and that of Donald

Sucher, who bred the Derby winner Winning Colors off his small farm, constituted the kind of seductive lore dripping off the lips of new associates encountered in the exploration of a second vocation.

Though he had raised and sold some very good horses, Courtney's peers to a man introduced him to me and eventually sent him off to retirement with identical words of praise—testaments not necessarily to his horsemanship or business acumen but to his unerring ethical conduct and courage to chart his own course since the day he bought his first mare in 1941.

Why those particular qualities? I asked one of his old and my new friends. "Because they are so rare in this business," he said. "As a group, we are as herdbound as our animals and not nearly as honest."

The consensus estimation of Courtney's legendary integrity and steady course over the years came as a sharp and reassuring contrast to the more intriguing tales of high risk, chicanery, deal making, and high reward that draw gamblers and speculators to the sale grounds but terrify and drive away others.

When I first started frequenting thoroughbred sales in the late 1980s, the most popular yarn of sale scheming concerned the record-setting sale of Seattle Dancer, the $13.1 million yearling still being a plum recollection about the high-rolling heydays and lunatic prices of the recent past.

Warner L. Jones, the colorful and powerful chairman of Churchill Downs and a principal owner of the colt, had just died of cancer, spurring offhand recountings of his exploits at the height of the boom days in the late 1970s and early 1980s when he was often the leading consignor in the July sales.

The $13.1 million record sale, ballyhooed for years as the signature success in racehorse breeding, was according to scuttlebutt much like that of the Green Monkey two decades later—not all it appeared to be.

One version of the rumor had Warner Jones preselling the horse for half that amount to D. Wayne Lukas and his partners, who then ran up the price on the eventual official buyer, a British bloodstock agent bidding for the British bookmaker Robert Sangster and his partners at Coolmore. A second version had the Coolmore players in on the deal and splitting the overage without Sangster's knowledge.

So widespread were the stories that reporters began pursuing them, ultimately provoking denials all around except from one of Lukas's partners, a Texas banker and horseman named Mel Hatley, who is reported to have told a reporter on tape, "We [Lukas and company] all got together and bought that horse before the sale."

Glenye Cain, a reporter for the *Daily Racing Form* and the author of the book *Homerun Horse*, took the tale of the tape to Jones's partner Will Farish, a future U.S. ambassador to the United Kingdom and now a trustee of Keeneland, where his Lane's End Farm is often its second leading sale consignor. According to Cain, Farish said he didn't believe that Hatley was actually part of Lukas's group of buyers and therefore would not have intimate knowledge, and that even if he was, Hatley's advancing age might explain his confusion on the matter.

Gossip or gospel, both the record-setting $13.1 million Seattle Dancer sale and the $16 million record breaker twenty years later remain more suspect than legitimate in the minds of some industry insiders. Yet before the public and sale newcomers, these legal but possibly underhanded bonanza paydays are hoist like victory trophies, to be admired and emulated.

There is a reason the word *shenanigan* looks Irish and is most commonly traced back to the Gaelic word *sionnachuighm* as the source, meaning "I play tricks." Though it may have roots in German, English, and Spanish as well, it's the lads of my own mother's bloodlines whose names pop up in any discussion of the improprieties that plague modern thoroughbred sales.

While hardly alone as purveyors of intrigue and skullduggery, the Irishmen must at least be credited for viewing it as more gamesmanship than outright venality. They play it the way they do soccer and politics—with brutal tenacity often explained by their native poets and philosophers as a kind of genetically engineered revenge of the oppressed, a nonviolent taking up of the guns against English Protestants.

In truth, the economic war of the thoroughbred sales grounds is not all that far afield from the Emerald Isle's epic struggles to get up off the carpet. When John Magnier, the master of Coolmore, began charming horses in his youth as a stallion handler in his native land, Americans rich from the industrial revolution were pillaging the best bloodstock of his country and the rest of Europe.

He watched the Kentucky breeding industry flourish on the blood of horses his country could not afford to keep, and then send their descendants, like Sir Ivor, back across the Atlantic to win the English Derby and the Arc de Triomphe. Until he could afford to outbid the Americans for champions like Nijinsky II and Seattle Slew, his only hope was to outsmart them, which he did frequently with a war chest filled partially with the money of others, often Englishmen like Robert Sangster and later Michael Tabor, both rich from their betting shops.

By the mid-1990s, however, Magnier had won the battle against Americans for horseflesh and become the leading worldwide trader of stallion semen for revenue. And his only true competitor left in world sales rings was Sheikh Mohammed, then the bold and ambitious son who would succeed his father as ruler of Dubai. A penchant for never letting another's bid be the last for a horse that struck his fancy set the sheikh up as a perfect rival for a master of shenanigans.

A common industry theory is that in the Green Monkey war both sides got caught up in what has become an egotistical struggle between two powerful and ambitious men: Magnier and Sheikh Mohammed. "This was two obstinate people who don't like each other very much bidding against each other," Tony Morris, the *Racing Post*'s breeding expert, wrote in his explanation of the sale.

With the industry in an uprising over such practices and both camps so naturally closed-mouthed about their operations, it is impossible to verify the precise circumstances. Six different insiders have given me six different versions, all with different figures but with the same conclusion: not what it appeared to be.

That is the only plausible explanation for what the *Racing Post*'s bloodstock editor, Rachel Pagones, called the Irish "leap into la' la' land" on a horse they had already passed on because it lacked the pedigree page to make a great stallion. Both Demi O'Byrne and his employer, John Magnier, have ignored for years fast horses whose pedigrees did not pass muster.

The problem with this theory is that it is only partially believable. There is no question that Sheikh Mohammed knows what he likes and will not let someone else's willingness to pay prevent his getting it. Maybe, but not likely, he loved defeating Coolmore enough to bet nearly $16 million on a horse that once ran a sub-ten-second furlong but had little if any chance on paper of siring a classic winner.

Clearly, Magnier has proven himself too clever and competent as a businessman to bet that kind of money in a blood rush. Over the years he has consistently outfoxed the competition at every turn and almost single-handedly brought Europe back to the top of a worldwide industry.

As a profitable provider of racehorse stallion semen to the world, Coolmore has no equal. And Sheikh Mohammed has frequently been the loser in Magnier's various business show-downs. No one who knows Magnier and his taste in horses believes him foolish enough to value the Green Monkey at $16 million—$6 million maybe.

Who knows? But from the bottom to the top, the perception is that Sheikh Mohammed finally got his fill of being had at the very auctions his money had been holding up for the last twenty years. Without him, there would have been no one to bid against the Irish as they moved to corner the market on great bloodstock.

One British turf writer, James Underwood, contends, "Something happened nobody will talk about" that set off Sheikh Mohammed's revenge to take the Irish up the summit and push them off. Industry sources offer up two possibilities.

It might well have occurred in the fall of 2005, fewer than sixty days after the Green Monkey sold as a yearling, when the rivals hooked up on a true stallion prospect in the select portion of Keeneland's huge September yearling auction. By this time Keeneland had folded its elegant July night sessions into the first two days of September, again restricted to the best of the best in bloodstock and the wealthiest and boldest of buyers.

Among the best horses bred anywhere are those raised by Martin Wygod, a wealthy Californian who went to high school in New York with the Hall of Fame trainer Bobby Frankel and at age fifteen cooled out hot horses for Woody Stephens. Having the high-selling horse at the largest and most prestigious yearling sale in the world is quite an accomplishment for a breeder, so when Wygod put in his reserve bid on a lovely son of Storm Cat out of his great race mare Tranquility Lake, he told a Keeneland official he wanted it high enough to make his colt the sale topper.

There was every reason to believe he could be. The colt was a beautiful son of America's favorite sire, whose stud fee that year had risen to $500,000. His mother, a daughter of Rahy, had won two Grade 1 races and $1.6 million. Her first foal, a full brother named After Market, was a promising two-year-old.

Last but not least in importance, another Storm Cat–Rahy cross had produced the Coolmore stallion Giant's Causeway, the Horse of the Year in Europe, and at $300,000 headed toward becoming the second most expensive stallion in the world. Keeneland told Wygod a reserve somewhere in the neighborhood of $8 million or $9 million ought to do it.

The Arabs had no reason to believe the colt had any connection to Coolmore, and there is no evidence that it did. Martin and Pam Wygod were long-respected breeders and had consigned him through the Mill Ridge Farm consignment of Jockey Club member Alice Chandler, whose father was a founder of Keeneland and whose sales operation had an unquestioned reputation for integrity.

According to the sheikh's associate John Ferguson, "This was a horse Sheikh Mohammed felt was the best Storm Cat he had seen. From the moment Sheikh Mohammed laid eyes on this horse he thought it very important that he race in the Godolphin name. We were very keen to get him."

So when After Market's brother came into the sales pavilion, the only serious bidders were the two old rivals on opposite sides of the back ring, Sheikh Mohammed, in his familiar white T-shirt, doing his own bidding, with Magnier himself signaling Coolmore's response. This was auction theater at its hot-and-heavy best, its most famous and powerful actors going at it face-to-face with a familiar script. When Sheikh Mohammed got the bid at $8.6 million, there was a pause in the action as the Coolmore committee conversed around Magnier in inaudible tones.

To give his bidders time, the auctioneer John Holmberg said, "First one to $10 million wins."

Finally, the Irish came out of the huddle with a bid of

$9 million, a $400,000 raise, at least $300,000 more than expected or necessary—a tactic normally used to intimidate competition. But after all these years, the Irish surely knew that Sheikh Mohammed would not be intimated by $300,000. He fired back instantly, and the two sides rocked back and forth until the Irish failed to respond to the call for $9.8 million. Sheikh Mohammed had his horse, which had been more often the case than not through the years, and it was a horse pretty much like the one the Irish already had.

A few days later at a gathering of prominent breeders at a Kentucky dove shoot, someone who claimed to know the Wygods quoted one of them as having told a mutual acquaintance that the colt had been quietly sold to the Irish before the auction for $6 million, which meant the Irish were bidding on a colt they already owned. A man who knew the Wygods said he doubted they would do that, to which another man retorted, "Anybody would do that. It wouldn't surprise me at all."

Whether this particular "something" happened or not, it would never be acknowledged outside the Wygods' tax returns, and there would have been no way for Keeneland or Mill Ridge to know if it did. But what is said in a dove field almost never stays in the dove field. Like the doves, it flies from one field to another, building perception—if not reality. The Arabs are notorious dove hunters.

Another "something" more assuredly happened the same year when the Dubai ruler unexpectedly departed from the undeclared "boycott" of Coolmore stallions to purchase a red-hot two-year-old sprinter named Henny Hughes, sired by the Irish-owned stallion Hennessy. At the time the horse was racing spectacularly out of the barn of Coolmore's favorite U.S. trainer, the Frenchman Patrick Biancone.

Just the mere idea of a purchase by the Arabs of a horse out of Biancone's barn startled knowledgeable insiders, who knew it could not have been done without Coolmore involvement that would drive up the price.

The Irish buyer O'Byrne had passed up that particular Hennessy colt the year before at the Fasig-Tipton July sale, where the horse was sold to a pinhooker for $180,000, and bought another Hennessy colt instead for $650,000. So had Sheikh Mohammed's man John Ferguson, who in that sale preferred to pay $950,000 for a colt sired by a stallion owned by Sheikh Hamdan, his boss's brother.

When either O'Byrne or Ferguson buys a yearling sired by a young stallion that is owned by his boss, the sale is immediately suspect as an obvious effort to help the stallion get off to a good start—another reason sale averages and medians are worthless as barometers of industry health.

Now, after Henny Hughes had won his first three races for the pinhookers, both the big guns that had ignored him came back. Ultimately the gleaming red colt made a lovely birthday present for Sheikh Mohammed's son, who had his own Zabeel racing stable—but at what price?

Not only had Henny Hughes been made considerably more expensive by the Irishmen; they reportedly rubbed it in verbally that fall when the Zabeel team's new runner was beaten in two important juvenile stakes races in New York by a son of the Irish-owned stallion Giant's Causeway. When someone reported Sheikh Mohammed's anger to Magnier at a Kentucky party, the Coolmore boss reportedly replied it was not his concern that "Sheikh Mohammed can't take a joke."

The Irish always could. But in the eyes of many, Magnier and Maktoum have become leading men in a theater of the absurd, the irrational extravagance of their behavior more entertaining than harmful. Viewed as sort of victimless crimes at the top, their epic battles over the blue-blooded stock bred by the Dinny elite nonetheless set the tone and style for everything happening in the market below, the men themselves and their roles of hunter and prey reflections of its character.

At the middle and lower levels, migrant cowboys, gamblers, and pinhookers lured by the scent of big money were cherry-picking the less expensive produce of breeders such as Robert Courtney and his imitators in search of the horse fast enough to top a training sale and win a short two-year-old stakes race, even if not sturdy and long-winded enough to last the Triple Crown.

As in the short-term reward games played on Wall Street, there would be no ethnic restrictions or economic class distinctions among the victims of the quest.

My first exposure to these shenanigans came on the very first colt I offered at Keeneland: the Gilded Time colt out of For Dixie in 1995. Even as Frank Stronach, a rich newcomer, was racing to bid on the colt, I was weighing a surprising last-second offer to sell my baby before he entered the ring. The deal, conveyed to me by my closest new friends in the business, offered a presale price of $100,000 and a split of everything over that amount that the weanling could attract in the bidding. The offer was said to be from "the Irish"—an array of players so vast and vague the exact source is never clear. And the deal was proffered so late in the game at which I was so new that the bidding had started before I could make heads or tails of it.

"I'll just take my chances in the pavilion," I told them finally.

The colt ultimately went to a Florida pinhooker for $150,000, well sold though money may have been left on the table. But in August 2003, my decision not to go along with another attempted scam at the exclusive Saratoga sale in August cost me at least $100,000.

My entry in the sale, hip number 72, was a full sister to Monarchos and perhaps my best opportunity to add monetary gain to what thus far had been mainly emotional reward for my good luck. A dark bay beauty she was, regally bred, free of conformation flaws and boasting a perfect set of radiographs, which means that X-rays of her knees, hocks, and ankle joints showed she had no bone abnormalities.

A couple of presale appraisals by experts put her value at $350,000 to $500,000, precisely the kind of horse that big-money buyers list for possible acquisition due to her residual value as a broodmare. True to form, representatives of a well-known farm, with an unlimited line of credit with Fasig-Tipton, showed up on the first inspection day. Pleased with what they saw, they dispatched their veterinarian to read the radiographs and to evaluate the workings of her throat with an endoscope. Knowing those radiographs to be perfect and the throat more than adequate, I was already allocating the sale proceeds in my mind.

Saratoga sales are small, and horses arrive on the grounds three days beforehand. With fewer than two hundred passing through the ring over three night sessions, everyone seems to know when a horse has been vetted, and usually by whom. Vets and agents talk so much among themselves that consignors generally know before the horse enters the ring which buyers—if any—are "on the horse."

Soon another prospective buyer, this one a small-time bloodstock agent, inspected the filly, and without any veterinary involvement informed the consignor he wanted to prebuy the horse for $350,000, an offer rejected when relayed to me. He obviously believed the filly would bring more than that in the ring two days later in the first night session.

Having run a slight fever during her first few hours on the sale grounds, she was yet to be seen by many of the top buyers. Mysteriously, though she had been shown ninety times on the first full day, only the bloodstock agent ever came back for a second look. No one else had the filly "vetted"—highly unusual for such a pedigreed filly sibling of the second-fastest Kentucky Derby winner in history.

The explanation became clear when the bloodstock agent showed up the second time, informing the consignor that he—and not the first group of lookers—was the true representative of the farm that had the filly vetted. He and the others, he said, planned to buy a couple of fillies for the elderly farm owner, who had authorized them to spend up to $500,000 for each. They had in mind an even more voracious scam than was offered on the For Dixie colt. All the excess bid over the prebuy amount was to be kicked back to them when their buyer—the primary victim—paid the sale company.

But already I had been victimized and didn't know it. After my rejection of the initial $350,000 offer, word had quickly spread among other buyers and their veterinarians that hip number 72 had already been vetted by the famous farm and had failed to pass muster. This had a dual effect of providing the agent an excuse for not buying a filly included on his employer's list and having it validated by the market.

With only one "vetting," the veterinarian was easily identified and confronted concerning the report. Not true, he said, the filly had passed with flying colors and had been added to his client's short list. But it was too late. If the bloodstock agent was legitimate, the lone buyer was gone and my filly "dead in the water" just hours before sale time.

At the last minute, my consignor came up with another prospect, a regular customer who had bought Two Bucks yearlings before and agreed to bid up to $250,000 for my filly. There was no choice but to submit my reserve bid at $249,000 or keep the filly, which I could not afford to do. She sold for $1,000 over the reserve, the only live bid coming from the prearranged customer.

Had my consignor not been a consummate deal maker and

underground player himself, the sister of Monarchos might have gone unsold, as had happened to him at the same sale in 1999, the victim of a false rumor spread through the grounds that he might be a *wobbler*, a term used to describe a horse with an abnormality in his spinal column.

But the consignor of his sister four years later was so integral a part of the sale fabric that he could even relay to me the hip numbers of two other fillies whose consignors the bloodstock agent identified as having allegedly agreed to his deal. Both fillies ended up being listed as sold for $500,000 and signed for by the famous farm.

A few years earlier, this same kind of sale scheming had cost a Florida consignor the sale of the colt most appraisers had predicted to be the Saratoga sale topper at somewhere close to $1 million. After refusing a presale offer from a prospective buyer, the woman was warned that unless she agreed to a presale, she might not have a sale at all.

Sure enough, word spread through the grounds that the horse had failed to pass veterinary scrutiny. When he went through the ring, he brought only $160,000 in live bids and was not sold. The following spring, he brought $360,000 in a two-year-old training sale, less than the prebuy deal the consignor had been offered at Saratoga. The buyer? The same guy who made the presale offer. Later raced, the horse became a Kentucky Derby prospect in the barn of D. Wayne Lukas, winning two graded stakes and placing in three others.

These are neither isolated nor exaggerated incidents, but rather common occurrences at every sale in the last twenty years. While not illegal, they are hardly entertaining, victimless shenanigans. Moreover, sale scheming is only one wave of a plague of detrimental sale practices and trends that have left victims galore, including the quality of the horse, the health of the breeding industry, and the reputation and future of the sport itself.

6

SUBPRIME SALESMANSHIP

A woman whose spare time is spent studying the history of failed societies can be very helpful to a man in the horse business. Any commercial breeder with my history of success at sales is fortunate to have the shoulder of a learned arbiter of right from wrong on which to sob.

"Social scientists have a term for what is going on," M.A. declared one day when she caught me sobbing. Well, not sobbing like I did about Greg Norman not becoming the oldest guy to win the British Open, just whining that while Two Bucks horses were winning on the track, they were losing at the sale grounds.

"We haven't had a profitable sale horse in a year and a half," I said.

"Those people at the sales are sheep," she said. "The original Asch experiments proved people can even be persuaded to give the wrong answer to a question just because somebody else does."

"The original what experiments?" I asked.

"Never mind," she said. "They're about herd mentality. Studies show that wherever there is an absence of knowledge and conviction, it can be a problem. Equity markets are no place for herd mentality. Once somebody goes first, the others don't want to be left behind. They all go after the same thing."

I had to remember this was coming from the skilled diagnostician of a broad range of society's ills including dying maple trees, kidney stones, and lousy eating habits.

"That sounds like the horse sales."

"This guy says a few people can ruin an entire society by rational bad behavior that is good for them and bad for everybody else," she said, patting the spine of a dog-eared copy of a book she had cupped in her arm. M.A. is a believer in continuing education, and this was her bible of diagnosis, the work of a prize-winning California social scientist that I had seen her carrying around before.

"The few make a lot of profit, which seems rational, while everybody loses a little and does nothing about it," she explained. "So the few keep doing it until everybody fails, including them."

What's the name of that book? I wanted to know.

"*Collapse*," she said. "So don't say you weren't warned."

In the predawn haze the elegant old Keeneland Race Course is difficult to discern from the adjacent Blue Grass Airport. Track barns are lined up like airliners on parallel runways, the size and shape of the silhouette heads in lighted windows the only clue to distinction. On both sides of the highway, hulking beasts are constantly moving silently in the cool shadows, leaving white vapor trails in their wake.

Among their other commonalities is security with a capital *S*. Airport management frets constantly—and obsessively it seems—over the possibility of a terrorist attack. Why, only God and Allah know. And across the street, Keeneland appears equally concerned that someone will park in the wrong place.

Long before dawn on the days of racing and sales that fill the Keeneland calendar, fluorescent-jacketed road guards are posted at major intersections. Strung between them are thousands of yards of white rope blocking off the entrances to the huge parking lots, ostensibly to prevent early tailgaters from setting up in bus lots or blocking the path to the drive-through betting windows. Where there is no string, there are orange cones, green barrier gates, and DO NOT PARK signs, so many that more than one thoroughbred breeder has considered the possibility of cone, rope, and signage supply to Keeneland being a more profitable enterprise.

There is no shortage of security employees, either, some of whom are notoriously vigilant. One once interrupted a television interview in progress because the participants didn't have the proper credentials. Another once ordered a tour group off a pathway to the saddling paddock, proclaiming that their shoe heels might damage the rubber brick surface on which the horses clomp and kick regularly with nailed metal shoes.

Exactly what is it that needs protecting? A treasure, that's what, probably the single most important institution in thoroughbred racing.

Despite all its cones and ropes and fastidious security personnel, Keeneland is the most user-friendly racetrack in the world. Unlike many others, there are no chain-link barriers to the backside where the horses live and train. So anyone successful enough to find a parking place is free to roam through the barns and mingle with the dozens of riders, veterinarians, blacksmiths, owners, and bloodstock and jockey agents. And those who can utter with familiarity the names of the Keeneland CEO or any of its three powerful trustees can usually bluff their way to any spot they want to be.

Twice a year Keeneland puts on one of the premier race meets in the world, never having departed from its motto—

"Racing as it was meant to be"—which has been its goal from the day Hal Price Headley spurred the formation of the Keeneland Association in 1935 and bought the first 147.5 of its 907 acres. For sixteen days in April and seventeen in October, the $600,000-plus in daily purses attracts the best of horses, the most successful of trainers, and—of course—the best people.

When Keeneland is racing or selling—which it does six times a year—there is no place in America other than the trustees room at Belmont Park and the clubhouse at Saratoga Race Course that the Dinnies and their associates would rather be. And each of their New York haunts, state owned and cash starved, pales in style and quality against the pristine confines of elegant Keeneland. Fueled by the largest and most profitable equine sales company anywhere, it is undoubtedly the most lucrative private business in the world of horse racing.

Ray Paulick, the longtime *Blood-Horse* editor, estimates that over the last forty-six years Keeneland has collected at least $750 million in commissions on sale revenue of $13.5 billion. Because of its private nature and the history of secrecy surrounding its financial operations, there is no way to estimate Keeneland's wealth. Since it pays no dividends to its limited number of stockholders and operated for a short time in its history as a nonprofit cooperative, many people estimate its retained earnings over the years in the tens of millions to perhaps $250 million. The only way to track its expenditures is through charitable donations of $15 million since 1936, its sizable property expansion and improvements, contributions to industry projects, and the regular subsidizing of race purses, which alone could amount to as much as 40 percent of the estimated $10 million-plus in race purses given away twice a year.

By everyone's estimate the Keeneland sales operation is a cash cow that takes more money off the industry table and puts more back into the pot than anyone else. Both as an institution and as a venue in horse racing it has no equal. Yet its sales policies, which its competitors feel compelled to follow, are generally viewed by breeders, consignors, and buyers alike as predatory, damaging, and a departure from the association's original goal of preserving and supporting the critical breeding industry of Kentucky.

That assessment gets little argument from me. To the breeder or seller of horses, Keeneland erects the obstinate bureaucracy of an insurance company, engages in the profit-taking of a Fortune 500 corporation, and—most disappointingly—fosters shortsighted government-like policies that result in similar unforeseen, unintended, but often devastating consequences.

Along with the Jockey Club, its only peer in the industry, Keeneland and the sales companies that follow its lead must share responsibility for the rise of the sale horse, which soaked up buyers' money the same way the subprime mortgage instruments drew Wall Street capital.

They must also bear some responsibility for the largely unfettered spread of drug use that resulted in what trainers called a "chemical war" on the racetracks, and for the huge number of unwanted and unprofitable horses that have clogged the market in the past ten years. And like the federal government that they most resemble, Keeneland and the Jockey Club failed their leadership responsibilities by not recognizing and correcting the rational bad behavior to which they had become enablers.

Industry problems that get quick attention from the Dinnies and the organizations they control are those that the Dinnies encounter themselves—like a dog gnawing their ankle or barking outside their summer home at Saratoga.

In the mid-1990s, two "dogs" from the same litter were harassing Keeneland's prime revenue source and the Dinnies' most exciting social event: the Keeneland July sale. One was the nasty and time-consuming problem of postsale legal squabbles over yearlings that buyers wanted to return for one reason or another, usually some perceived unsoundness or physical flaw that had gone unnoted before the hammer fell.

The other was closely related: the presale X-rays of the horses's legs that buyers were ordering in an effort to avoid such postsale dissatisfaction. When word got around that a certain yearling had been X-rayed by a prominent buyer, herd mentality ensued. A popular horse could get X-rayed twenty times. This meant thirty-two shots of radium each time and a traffic jam at the consignor's barn that disrupted his day or night. There had to be a better way.

Keeneland, reportedly on the suggestion of Will Farish, chose an idea already in experiment in New Zealand of a repository containing a single set of X-rays for each horse entered into the sale. The $450 cost, it was determined, could easily be borne by owners of July sale yearlings, which seemed reasonable. In 1996, the first year of the repository, the 167 yearlings sold averaged just under $350,000 and fewer than 16 percent went unsold.

The repository idea was quickly extended to the much larger Keeneland September and November sales, where total entries would eventually soar past a combined ten thousand per year, and to the other major North American sales companies, creating not only a giant revenue stream for veterinarians but an even bigger problem for breeders that became known as "Goddam OCDs."

Virtually unknown and largely irrelevant to sales before the repository was created was the reality that at least 50 percent of all equine yearlings and an even higher percentage of weanlings are undergoing natural changes in their bone surfaces at precisely the point in their growth when they are being offered at auction.

These changes show up radiographically and present to veterinarians a problematic bone growth stage known as *osteochondritis* (OCDs), ultimately considered "issues" that have unnecessarily disqualified or seriously discounted literally thousands and thousands of sale yearlings and weanlings.

The pictures also picked up the previously unknown and irrelevant flakes and chips that fly off the joints of baby horses early in their life, more often among Kentucky thoroughbreds that tend to spend more time in barn stalls than horses born and raised in cowboy pastures or in the fields of Europe, Australia, and New Zealand.

Subsequent studies of 1,163 yearlings sold by Keeneland between 1993 and 1996, before the repository was instituted, showed that only 9 percent of the OCDs found on radiographs ever had any impact on the horse's ability to perform on the racetrack. In fact, 81 percent of the yearlings in the study went on to start a race at ages two and three. But no amount of scientific evidence or buyer education could reverse or even slow down the damage done by what became known as "the Keeneland suppository" for what it did to the bottom of the horse market. The results of the study, done by a New Zealand researcher in conjunction with Colorado State University, might have been best used if flashed in neon letters on the front of the sales ring.

As is often the case with great new ideas, the baby had already been thrown out with the bathwater. The presence of an OCD or chip off any leg joint would become virtually an automatic deterrent to sale in a market already in oversupply, with most buyers chasing the perfect sale horse that could be pinhooked for a profit. Almost immediately a second new Keeneland policy ensured that the baby could not be recovered.

In 2002, in the face of declining revenues and participation, Keeneland shockingly abandoned its historic July sale. The decision fit the classic rational behavior mode of the modern American corporation, one made solely in the economic interest of those making it, in this case the two segments of the industry that neither raise nor own nor race horses but merely collect commissions on the sale of them.

For years Keeneland and its lone true competitor, Fasig-Tipton, had been providing the same three midyear opportunities to sell yearlings, each aimed at a particular level of the market.

Keeneland's July sale and Fasig-Tipton's August sale at Saratoga were redundant small sales, each generally fewer than three hundred high-end pedigrees raised mainly by the Dinnies to ultimately be fought over by the Arabs and the Irish. Fasig-Tipton had held a similar-size July sale for animals whose pedigrees did not qualify them for Keeneland's elite gathering or its own extravaganza at the Saratoga Spa. These three sales attracted early-maturing animals and seldom soaked up more than 25 percent of the yearlings, leaving three times as many for the big Keeneland finale in September, which featured a select early two-day section for July-quality horses.

As foal crops grew, these back-to-back sales had become more of a chore for both sales companies and large consignors like Lane's End and Taylor Made. But the upcoming 2003 yearling crop had been decimated by the Mare Reproductive Loss Syndrome of 2001, a plague caused by tent caterpillars killing foals and fetuses, including many from top mares normally aimed at the two July elite sales and boarded at places like, well, Lane's End and Taylor Made.

Suspending the Keeneland July sale made economic sense in that revenue from those yearlings would migrate naturally to the first week of September, saving preparation and sale-holding costs for both Keeneland and the large consignors. This left the summer market entirely to its hungry competitor Fasig-Tipton, whose small July sale would eventually grow to nearly eight hundred horses. And the September sale, already the largest in the world, would soon outgrow even Keeneland's vast physical layout.

The first combined Keeneland September sale in 2003 cataloged 4,294 yearlings, despite 2,500 foals and fetuses from that crop having been lost to MRLS. That year 1,360 yearlings, nearly 30 percent of the catalog, went unsold, many of them pulled out of the sale or bypassed as a result of "issues" raised in the repository. Despite the construction of six new barns, the numbers of yearlings cataloged in September continued to grow in each of the following years, forcing a corresponding reduction in the amount of time 75 percent of these horses were available on the grounds for inspection.

Horses sold in the relatively tiny Saratoga August auction and what ultimately became a four-day "select" portion of the Keeneland September sale are routinely available for inspection for at least three days before the hammer falls. At Keeneland, their catalog positions are determined by a computer program that takes into account factors ranging from the racing success of the dam's family to the initial letter in her name.

But the factor weighted most heavily by the computer is size of the stud fee involved in the mating. Horses with stud fees of $100,000 or more, most often being offered by the top six or seven most important consignors, usually take up the first 700 to 800 catalog positions in the first two days. Those with fees between $40,000 and $100,000 fill the next two days.

These first four days routinely produce half the total commission revenue of the sale company and the consignors. Getting a spot early in these four days encourages breeders toward the more expensive stallions and tends to drive up both stud fees and sale commissions—consequences not necessarily unintended.

Once the first 1,200 or so revenue producers pass under the hammer at Keeneland, the speed of the auction increases dramatically in perfect lockstep with the decline of food service and the size of the stud fee.

At Fasig-Tipton, yearling placement takes the size of stud fees into account as well but is more subjective in that it includes individual physical inspection and whatever trend wind is blowing through the historically dwindling but increasingly influential middle- and lower-level buyers in search of the big sale horse.

Each year after the advent of the repository and the combined September sale, Keeneland and Fasig-Tipton cataloged and sold more yearlings than the year before and reported increases in both gross revenue and average until 2007, when the long-ignored cracks at the middle and bottom of the business began to show at the top.

The monster Keeneland September sale reached its peak in 2006, selling 3,556 yearlings for $399.7 million. Invariably the multimillion-dollar sale toppers and the random "home runs" hit by lucky pinhookers made headlines and fueled more interest by more people in breeding more sale yearlings, at a time when the number of people producing homebreds to race continued to decline.

Underneath the hoopla, a perfect storm was brewing. Between 1994 and 2005, the size of the North American foal crop grew 10 percent, from 35,351 to 38,500, and has since remained relatively stable at around 37,000—about a third of which are born in Kentucky. But pinhook sale successes and the influx of speculators drove the percentage of foals that were being offered at public auction up 27 percent during this same period.

Each year more of the horses counted as sold and included in the record revenue numbers were unprofitable. And the number of horses cataloged but unsold was increasing. In 2007, 10,160 yearlings were listed as having changed hands at public auctions, while another 3,800 went home unsold. But even these numbers do not reflect the persistent decline in horses sold profitably or the horses involved in sales listed fraudulently as sold.

Most of these unsold and unprofitable animals had been disqualified by "repository issues" either before or during the sale because mere acknowledgment of any blemish—significant or not—usually excluded them from core buyers whose taste in horses and penchant for risk were rising with the stud fees. The contrast between the "home run" horses of 1993 and 2006 tells the tale.

Among the group of influential buyers most responsible for changes in the yearling market were the Florida pinhooker Jerry Bailey and his partner Ken Ellenberg, representatives of the growing class of high-risk takers whose living now depended on having the fastest, best-looking horses in the training sales the following spring.

The sharp-eyed Bailey's credentials as a horse-market-savvy trendsetter were established in 1993, when he bought the cheapest horse at the elite Keeneland July sale. Bailey paid $40,000 for an undersized but well-made grandson of Mr. Prospector whose radiograph "issues"—had he any—were unknown because the repository had yet to be invented.

Although the colt, eventually named Thunder Gulch, twice failed to meet his reserve bids in subsequent "breeze-up" sales, he was ultimately sold to the Irish for a reported $500,000 and ended up winning the 1996 Kentucky Derby for the utmost trendsetters: trainer D. Wayne Lukas and owner Michael Tabor, John Magnier's new Coolmore associate.

Ten years later, as a group Jerry Bailey and friends had moved decidedly upscale. Whether at Keeneland, Saratoga in August, or Fasig-Tipton in July, they were shopping for a bigger, better pedigreed, more imposing animal with "issue"-free radiographs and flaw-free conformation—a far more expensive horse that when sold later to the Irish or the Arabs would make them rich and famous. It was no accident that 2006, Keeneland's biggest year, was also the year of the Green Monkey's record sale.

Stallion owners, breeders, and consignors were not slow to identify what "the market" wanted. The formula was simple: breed as many high-quality mares as possible to the half dozen or so heavily hyped "stallions of the month" known for speed genes. Quickly, their overfed, often steroid-boosted offspring flooded the sales, often as many as fifty or sixty by the same sire in the same sale at the same time.

There they would be culled by conformation flaw and radiograph down to a precious few that ultimately would drive up revenue, sale averages, and—of course—commissions for every sale segment through whose hands they passed. Whether anybody realized it or not, they were building what some skeptical breeders viewed as a chemical herd.

In July 2006, at the height of the "sale horse" bubble, I brought a son of Monarchos eventually named Stones River to the Fasig-Tipton yearling sale. The experts who had graded Monarchos when he passed through the Saratoga yearling sale in 1996 had faulted him for being "a little small" for a colt born in February, for being "light behind," which meant his rear end was not as wide and powerful as was desirable by then, and for a right knee that appeared "a little flat," a condition short of being "back at the knee"—an obviously inverted joint that might not stand up under the stress of training.

Reflecting the physical traits that can be passed along in genes, Stones River was similarly evaluated a decade later at the Fasig-Tipton July sale. Although a month younger when sold than was his sire, Stones River benefited from the fact that his dam was a full hand taller than the dam of Monarchos, so he was big for his age and appeared even leaner and rangier.

These sale "issues" easily could have been avoided through the employment of sale preparation techniques widely used then and now by many successful yearling conditioners and consignors. The concerns over lack of size and muscle mass would never have arisen had the colt been raised on steroids.

A monthly injection of Winstrol stimulates appetite, speeds bone growth, converts fat to muscle at an accelerated rate, and multiplies the effect of regular exercise on treadmills and other equivalents of weight lifting by humans. The slightly convex surface or "over at the knee" appearance of knees can be disguised by the proper administration of an antibiotic called tetracycline, which temporarily relaxes tendons so they actually appear normal. A more permanent correction to a flat or back-at-the-knee appearance can often be achieved by repeated injections of iodine into the growth plate behind the knee.

Monarchos, who had a great natural walk, was for some reason walking a little stiffly at Saratoga in 1996. His consignor, Brookdale Farm, was a stickler for ethical conduct, so he was still walking stiffly when he went into the sale ring and failed to bring his reserve. Had he been in any number of neighboring consignments, Monarchos would have been given a dose of the muscle relaxant Robaxin, which was common at the time, or if the stiffness was pain-related a daily dose of an anti-inflammatory corticosteroid. They were available and in use all over the sale grounds.

One effect of a steroid regimen is loss of elasticity in the muscles, which often inhibits the loose, slinky walk yearling buyers have come to equate with fast horses. Another is that excess testosterone can make colts overly aggressive and difficult to handle. Not only can't they walk for inspection; they often refuse to, jumping around and making themselves impossible to evaluate. The answer to this problem was more drugs.

By the time Stones River went to sale in 2006, ambitious consignors of big, good-looking but bad-moving yearlings were actually showing them on a daily horse-size combination dose of the tranquilizer Valium and the muscle relaxant Dantrium. One veterinarian called to treat a horse with a bad reaction to the combo said she barely escaped being injured when the horse just "suddenly collapsed" during her examination.

Stones River never got to the sale ring in 2006, due to a lack of interest on the part of buyers. His only serious looker was my friend Cot Campbell, the owner of Dogwood Stable, who'd had previous luck buying Two Bucks yearlings from that sale who turned out to be stakes winners. Among them was the filly Cotton Blossom, bought by Campbell the previous year for $210,000. She went on to earn Dogwood nearly $1 million on the track and later sold as a broodmare prospect for $1.9 million.

Yet Campbell walked away from Stones River when a veterinarian found a "small shadow" on the radiograph of his right front ankle that "might" involve his suspensory ligament though he could not be sure. Campbell's veterinarian was the only one who visited the repository to look at the radiographs, for which I had paid $500 a set on each of the four Two Bucks yearlings in the sale.

At Fasig-Tipton that July so many big, well-muscled, loose-walking yearling colts were on the grounds awaiting Campbell's inspection there was no point in his taking a chance on Stones River. But the real chance he was taking was that the next colt he saw might not be the perfect specimen that he appeared. The combination of speed genes, abnormal size and maturity, and conformation perfection had become the essence of the new sale horse with the complete cooperation of all concerned—

except Mother Nature, who still tended to deliver them frequently in the same old crooked packages.

A characteristic of horses passing through elite summer yearling auctions in the 1980s and '90s was the preponderance of small animals with crooked front legs. Having owned and raised four different breeds of horses, I have no doubt that thoroughbred babies are much more likely to be born with a higher incidence of offset knees, contracted tendons, and irregular ankle formations. The lesser the quality of the sale and the deeper into the catalog, the worse these horses looked. But later in the fall sales, they were at least big enough to suit buyers.

Now, crooked horses are much harder to find, not because selective mating miraculously improved the breed overnight, but as a result of the progress and popularity of corrective limb surgery and other forms of growth plate manipulation that can affect conformation—procedures that for most of the last twenty years went undisclosed because of auction company reluctance to mandate it in their conditions of sale.

Unfortunately, some of the most popular and trendy sires of speed also passed along a high percentage of crooked limbs. Some of the most successful and sought-after blood today comes from Mr. Prospector's descendant Unbridled's Song, the engine that drove Taylor Made to prominence in the stallion business, and A.P. Indy, the son of Seattle Slew who made Will Farish's Lane's End Farm perhaps the leading stallion station in the world.

Soon, surgical procedures to correct angular deformities became a growth industry for equine orthopedic surgeons, with some of the biggest consignors offering the most expensively bred yearlings as their biggest customers. Both of Kentucky's elite veterinary clinics, Rood & Riddle and Hagyard Equine, do a booming business in "PEs"—periosteal stripping of the concave surface of the limb to stimulate blood flow to the growth

John Ward, the trainer of the
2001 Kentucky Derby winner
Monarchos and a leading
advocate for reform of
horse racing's drug rules.
(Anne M. Eberhardt)

The Hall of Fame trainer
D. Wayne Lukas. His success
at selecting and training
horses became the model for
generations of buyers and
trainers. *(Anne M. Eberhardt)*

The trainer Larry Jones atop Eight Belles, the horse
that changed his life and perhaps his industry.
(Anne M. Eberhardt)

Rick Dutrow, the outspoken trainer of Big Brown, celebrates his horse's victory in the 2008 Kentucky Derby. *(Anne M. Eberhardt)*

Michael Iavarone, the leader of IEAH, Big Brown's controversial Wall Street–based owners. *(Anne M. Eberhardt)*

Two weeks after his Derby win, Big Brown coasts to victory in the Preakness. But, like so many others with Triple Crown dreams, he would falter in the Belmont Stakes. *(Anne M. Eberhardt)*

Kentucky breeder Arthur B. Hancock III sees his industry on the path to self-destruction. *(Anne M. Eberhardt)*

Ogden Mills "Dinny" Phipps, chairman of the Jockey Club, the most powerful organization in American horse racing. *(Horsephotos.com)*

Will Farish *(right)* and his son, Bill Farish, the owners of Lane's End Farm, America's most important breeding farm, outside their sale barn at Keeneland. *(Anne M. Eberhardt)*

Sheikh Mohammed bin Rashid Al Maktoum (*left*), the ruler of Dubai, and John Magnier, the head of the Irish conglomerate Coolmore, regularly competed to buy the best horses. *(Anne M. Eberhardt)*

The Green Monkey, the horse their rivalry turned into the most expensive racehorse ever. *(Horsephotos.com)*

Fasig-Tipton's Kentucky sales ring became another acquisition in the ever-expanding Arab presence in the world thoroughbred industry.
(Anne M. Eberhardt)

The late Dr. Alexander Harthill,
the veterinarian who once was
the most powerful man
in American horse racing.
(Anne M. Eberhardt)

Stones River, a gray colt bred at Two Bucks Farm, with jockey Gabriel Saez on the track with Cindy Jones, following a stakes win at Delaware Park. *(Michael J. DiMenna)*

The author and his wife, Mary Anne, in the paddock before the Pennsylvania Derby. *(Michael J. DiMenna)*

The computer guru Satish Sanan (*front, center*) and the wine mogul Jess Jackson (*directly behind Sanan*), whose reform efforts earned them recognition as the "Righteous Brothers." *(Horsephotos.com)*

Sanan and Jackson's prize acquisition, Curlin, was a two-time Horse of the Year and became the richest racehorse ever. *(Anne M. Eberhardt)*

The 2008 foal crop at Two Bucks Farm. *(Photograph by Sandy Shiner-Swanson)*

The Two Bucks mare Little Bold Belle and her Strong Hope colt. *(Photograph by Sandy Shiner-Swanson)*

plate—and "screws and wires," a mechanical bridge that retards growth of the convex limb surface.

The efficacy of these procedures is widely debated. Some trainers like John Ward believe them merely disguises for permanently weakened bones and refuse to buy any horse known or believed to have undergone the surgeries. Others believe that if successful—a 50 percent rate at best—the joints are actually strengthened because a straightened bone bears the load more equally.

Early in his thoroughbred training career, Bob Baffert bought—reportedly unknowingly—a "screws and wires" product ultimately named Real Quiet that won the Kentucky Derby and missed winning the Triple Crown by a whisker. A failure as a Kentucky sire, Real Quiet moved to Pennsylvania. And in 2008 one of his offspring, Midnight Lute, won his second Breeders' Cup and went to stud in Kentucky for a $20,000 first-year fee.

Whether these procedures work or not, they definitely give an erroneous impression of possible genetic implications. The crookedness in a lot of mares and stallions is often repeated in their offspring. Yet surprisingly, the offspring of a crooked to crooked mating sometimes comes out with perfectly conformed legs. Go figure.

Most research studies support experts who believe the majority of angular deformities correct themselves in time. Skilled corrective shoeing can also be helpful. But natural growth and patient blacksmithing do not happen fast enough for yearlings on jet growth regimens headed for big-money sales and picky but often naive buyers in search of the fast buck.

The inability of important consignors to get their high-priced yearlings big enough and correct enough for buyers at the summer sales is the most often heard explanation for the demise of Keeneland July and the decline of Saratoga August, which led to the monstrous growth of the September auction.

However rational and shrewd the business decision by sale companies and consignors at the time, it was—like the creation of the X-ray repository—rife with unforeseen and disastrous consequences for most of the small commercial breeders. Over the last twenty years, the gambler's dream of selling a "home run" yearling such as the $9.7 million colt that Sheikh Mohammed bought from the Wygods in 2005, or the $16 million Green Monkey, created a wealth of "new" breeders. Bloodstock agents who used to visit my farm to cherry-pick my foal crop so they could mark them up for their clients are now my competitors.

Becky Thomas, a marvelously successful pinhooking pioneer from Florida, went into the breeding partnership business. She now breeds more mares than I do, supplies her clients with "homebreds," and takes more yearlings to sale than Two Bucks. The broodmare band of my friend Tracy Farmer, for years an avid buyer and successful "owner" who campaigned Albert the Great and Commentator, is three times the size of mine.

John Oxley, who bought Monarchos at a two-year-old sale in 2000, now markets far more of his offspring and competes at a much higher level. At the 2006 Saratoga sale, while I was bringing home unsold a half sister to Monarchos by the promising freshman sire and Belmont Stakes winner Empire Maker, Oxley sold a bigger, older, and flashier filly by his stallion Sky Mesa for $1.1 million to Sheikh Mohammed.

When I met Gary Knapp, the breeder of Big Brown, he was a finance and statistics expert fresh from an Alabama media and pension fund deal bonanza. Interested in polo horses, he owned no mares and no farm. But he jumped into breeding at the highest levels of the game and in 2006 topped the Keeneland September sale with a $9.2 million son of Danzig bought by—who else?—Sheikh Mohammed. But for every hit like that, there are thousands of misses. The odds on breeding a horse that gets caught up in an Irish-Arab bidding war are about the same as breeding a Kentucky Derby winner—1 in 35,000—if that. Knapp has now experienced both.

Framed in the never-ending dream of lottery-level rewards, the exclusion of imperfect youngsters by the repository, and the increasing oversupply of them at auction eventually created another more destructive perfect storm: the ultimate buyer's market. It pushed 75 percent of all yearling revenue into the last quarter of the year, creating cash flow problems for virtually everybody not trading "perfect" regally bred animals with the Dinnies, the Arabs, and the Irish conglomerate—and of course bloodstock agents, large consignors, and the sales companies collecting commissions on them.

When the Keeneland Association was closer to its roots as a breeder's cooperative, its huge cash reserves were used to grant advances to breeders on anticipated sales to help the farms meet payroll and pay stud fees that come due in September and October, before most yearlings are marketed. The modern Keeneland, however, wants the entry fees sixty days before sales, and distributions often do not reach breeders until sixty days after. But that's only a footnote to the real consequences of failed sales policies.

The headline news from the first day of the first Keeneland September extravaganza of the new millennium was that Sheikh Mohammed had bought a $5.5 million Storm Cat colt. The sales were interrupted on their second day by the 9/11 terrorist attacks in New York and Washington, after which Sheikh Mohammed and his brothers went home, but their representatives stayed behind to spend more than $20 million. That year twenty-seven yearlings sold for $1 million or more apiece, nearly all in the first four days, the sale topper being a $6.5 million purchase by the Irish of another Storm Cat colt.

Despite all the ego exercised and money expended in quest of the sale-topping horses—nearly $100 million spent on thirty sale toppers at Keeneland alone between 1990 and 2006—only two have won the Kentucky Derby or a Triple Crown race.

A.P. Indy, who sold for $2.9 million in 1990, won the 1992 Belmont Stakes, and Fusaichi Pegasus, who brought $4 million in 1998, won the 2000 Kentucky Derby. Both were Keeneland July sale graduates. Seattle Dancer, the $13.1 million phenomenon from 1985, though a serviceable sire of thirty-seven stakes winners, earned only $152,000 on the racetrack.

Of the thirty-five most expensive colts from the 2004 foal crop purchased at public auction, only one—the $1.5 million Cowtown Cat—made it to the 2007 Kentucky Derby, which meant that the other $88.5 million would be hard to recover. A 20–1 morning line entry, Cowtown Cat finished last.

Not all the high-price yearlings were busts. Rags to Riches, who sold for $1.9 million at Keeneland in September 2005, beat Curlin in 2007 to become the second filly ever to win the Belmont Stakes and also won the Eclipse Award as champion three-year-old filly. Any Given Saturday, a $1.1 million purchase the same year, formidably contested the Triple Crown as well. But the overwhelming majority have names no one but their purchasers recognize.

Jalil, the $9.7 million Storm Cat son who was at the center of the Arab-Irish bidding war in 2005, won a minor race in Dubai before coming to America to finish third in a $50,000 stakes at Suffolk Downs. Another Storm Cat sale topper, Mr. Sekiguchi, who sold for $8 million, won two of four races and just $85,000 in purses.

The big-bucks pursuit of speed has not fared much better. The Green Monkey, the world's fastest and most expensive two-year-old in training sale horse, never won a race. Only one sale topper in the six-year history of Keeneland's April two-year-old in training sale, Strong Contender, and one other horse in the top twenty, a filly named Point Ashley, ever won a stakes race.

Meanwhile, sharp-eyed buyers sifting the lower and middle segments of the market and throwback breeders fielding home-breds have dominated the famous stakes races and the Eclipse Awards.

Funny Cide, the gelding who captured the hearts of racing fans by winning the first two legs of the Triple Crown in 2004, was a $22,000 purchase. Real Quiet, another horse who barely missed the Triple Crown, was picked off by Bob Baffert for $17,000. By the identical amount Arthur Hancock bought back Sunday Silence, who also lost the crown on the final leg.

Seattle Slew, one of the three last Triple Crown champions in the 1970s, had also sold for $17,000. The other two, Secretariat and Affirmed, were both homebreds, as was Smarty Jones, who won two legs of the crown, and Birdstone, the horse who kept him from winning the Belmont.

Curlin, a son of the Lane's End stallion Smart Strike, was expected to bring over $250,000 when he went through the Keeneland September sale in 2005. But the radiograph report showed he'd had an OCD removed from a sesamoid. Along with his rather common head, the ugly ankle caused a dramatic discount. The trainer Kenny McPeek picked him up for a meager $57,000.

Once on the track, Curlin was so impressive that two industry newcomers, Jess Jackson of Kendall-Jackson wine fame, and Satish Sanan, paid a reported $3.5 million for an 80 percent interest—an amount already tripled by his earnings. Azeri, the three-time Eclipse Award–winning mare and 2003 Horse of the Year, was bought back as a yearling in 1999 by her breeder-owner Allen Paulson for $110,000. She went on to win three Eclipse Awards, seventeen of twenty-four races, and more than $4 million.

But the true worth of even the greatest modern horses such as Curlin and Azeri as breeding animals is clouded by what the Hall of Fame trainer Jack Van Berg described to Congress as the "chemical war" raging on the racetrack. Some experts, including veterinarians who oppose the use of anabolic steroids in racehorses, do not believe they are responsible for superior performances. None dispute, however, that a steroid regimen makes athletes—human or equine—stronger, more aggressive, more likely to shrug off minor pain in the middle of the race, and more likely to recover from injury faster than normal.

If all these medication by-products do not make for a better race record and a more valuable racehorse, why are they so widely relied upon? A study by the University of Pennsylvania Toxicology and Research Laboratory released in 2004 showed that 61.7 percent of 988 horses from thoroughbred and standardbred racetracks tested positive for at least one anabolic steroid. Nearly 18 percent had two or more in their system.

In 2008, long after the steroid issue had inflamed the public and the California Horse Racing Board had established a ninety-day grace period after which anabolic steroids would be considered illegal, 418 tests were administered on horses that raced at Hollywood Park and Del Mar, whose prestigious meet was nearing an end. Of the thirty-eight positives detected, twenty-eight were in the barn of the Del Mar meeting's leading trainer, John Sadler, and ten others from the second-ranking trainer, Mike Mitchell. Sadler had twenty-five wins, including five major stakes, and Mitchell had thirteen victories, including a Grade 1 stakes.

As board president of the California Thoroughbred Trainers in 2008, Sadler was privy to the storm over widespread drug abuse raging in the state since 2005, when Laura de Seroux, the trainer of Azeri, became the first California trainer to be cited for using them.

Two graded stakes horses in de Seroux's barn tested positive for the drug trenbolone, a derivative of nandrolone, which is considered the most potent muscle builder in existence. At the time, de Seroux was considered among the most vocal opponents of drug abuse in horse racing, an irony not lost on her. "People think I'm being hypocritical because I've criticized the use of drugs," she said. "But I don't think I'm being hypocritical in using them because everyone else is, too. I don't do anything illegal with my horses. My horses run clean. I'm all for oats, hay, and water."

In her explanation lay the root of the problem. To de Seroux and many of her peers, steroids are "clean" and as common as oats, hay, and water, and they are most frequently employed in the interest of a level playing field.

Of Azeri, by far her most successful horse, de Seroux said, "She didn't let anyone down, and she did it in great style. She's simply the fastest filly in the world now. You can't catch her early, and you can't catch her late."

There is no doubt that Azeri was a magnificent natural athlete and a superior racehorse who might have achieved stardom with one of the many trainers whose oats, hay, and water regimen does not include steroids. But would she have lasted long enough to set all those records?

Although born in 1998, the same year as Monarchos and Point Given, who survived the rigors of the track only until late in their second year of racing, Azeri raced for de Seroux and won her third Eclipse Award as the nation's leading older mare when she was five years old. Although she injured a tendon late in the season and was "retired," her owner, Michael Paulson, brought her back the next year, during which she won two magnificent stakes races for D. Wayne Lukas while competing against males and defeating the best younger mares in the world long after most fillies in her class had joined the broodmare band.

Barry Bonds, the most celebrated steroid user among human athletes, bloomed as a muscular strongman late in his career as well. Even if she was on steroids most of the time, Azeri's record is freakish. If not, it was a miracle, and the $14 million Michael Paulson expected for her first offspring not as absurd as it appeared.

During interrogations preceding testimony as a witness at the congressional hearings, Curlin's history of performing on steroids was confirmed by his majority owner Jess Jackson, who promptly and publicly ordered the trainer Steve Asmussen to stop administering them. The owners of Big Brown, the Triple Crown sensation of 2008, had no choice but to order an end to his steroid regimen, too, after his trainer, Richard Dutrow, confessed it in a stream of boasting about how much better his horse was than all the rest.

Neither Curlin nor Big Brown appeared as dominant on the racetrack after their owners ordered the steroids stopped. But both will go to the breeding shed, where in their first two years they will attract at least three hundred of the best mares in the world to their court, based on what appears to have been their superior racing records.

If their performance was chemically enhanced, the breeders are being cheated just as their opponents were on the racetrack. Arthur Hancock said as much when he testified before Congress on the long-term effect of drugs on horse breeding. "Horses are running on drug-induced abilities as opposed to natural abilities," he said. "When you breed those, you're going to be breeding more unsoundness."

Yet Robert Clay, the master of Three Chimneys, which bought the breeding rights to Big Brown before his steroid history became public, suggests that having trained and raced on steroids will not have an effect on the Derby winner's career as a stallion. If he means Big Brown's genes are not affected by months on steroids, he may well be right. But would Big Brown have won two legs of the Triple Crown and been attractive to Clay as a stallion had he not had an "edge" on the track?

Until both Curlin and Big Brown prove themselves in the breeding shed as effective sires, their racetrack accomplishments will bear—like the hitting records of Bonds—a virtual asterisk. A wise breeder would want their foals—and the offspring of Azeri for that matter—to arrive along with a racetrack life's supply of whatever it is the parent was running on. Otherwise, buyer beware. The two champions are at this point poster boys for the steroid era in racing.

When exactly the use of steroids in racehorses actually began is anyone's guess. But some senior members of the veterinarian community have acknowledged giving steroids to horses infrequently as early as the 1950s, when humans first began using them.

Jack Robbins, an eighty-eight-year-old retired California veterinarian, told the *Blood-Horse* magazine that he administered testosterone on a limited basis to stakes horses in those days and that indeed it did improve both appearance and performance. But for the most part, then as now, the drugs were intended therapeutically, mainly to increase appetite and speed healing.

Still, the history of racing competition suggests there are always participants in search of an edge. Contemporaries familiar with the training methods of Seabiscuit's enigmatic trainer Tom Smith say he used a "buzzer" or battery pack to hone his horse's rocket break from the gate, which he believed necessary to defeat War Admiral in their famous match race in 1938.

Denigrators of the late Frank Whiteley, the surly magician who trained Damascus and Ruffian, sincerely believe that his magic came from sniffs of cocaine and say they know people who claim they saw Whiteley coming out of the stalls brushing the white dust off his hands.

A few breeders whose mares did not settle early to Secretariat during his first year at stud now attribute the failure to impotency they believe was the result of the steroids that had produced his incredible equine physique. (Secretariat's heart was reportedly 50 percent larger than that of the average thoroughbred.) Steroids shrink the testicles and reduce sperm count and motility, which is one of the reasons fertility insurance is written on stallions coming off the racetrack without tests. Many would not pass, thereby queering the breeding rights deal and costing money to all concerned, including the insurers.

When horses like Big Brown and Curlin come along, their trainers are automatically suspected of taking an edge, too.

Steven Asmussen, who maintains a racing stable of two hundred or more horses, won more races in a single year—555 in 2004—than any trainer in history. He is consistently among the top earners and a routine competitor for the Eclipse Award as the leading trainer. He has also been cited twenty-two times for drug rule violations.

Rick Dutrow is a confessed drug abuser once ruled off the tracks in New York for five years for using marijuana himself. An incredibly candid and likable individual, he makes no bones about having been suspended every year since 2000 for some kind of racing rule violation or another.

In the early part of the decade, about the time he rose to the top echelon of trainers, on the advice of a veterinarian Dutrow began giving steroids routinely to his entire string of horses. During the week prior to Big Brown winning the 2008 Derby, one of his stakes horses tested positive for clenbuterol. Later suspended, then cleared by a hearing officer whose decision was appealed by Kentucky racing authorities, Dutrow once more said exactly how he felt: "As long as it [a penalty suspension] happens after the Breeders' Cup, I don't care. I was planning to take a vacation anyway."

Dutrow's cavalier attitude affirms the widespread belief that a high percentage of racehorses perform on some synthetic form of testosterone, especially geldings who race longer and have through surgery lost their natural means of production. Without testosterone supplement, horses are not likely to replace muscle as quickly as they break it down. So the banning of the anabolic substances are likely to have more long-range financial impact in the claiming ranks—the lower end of the racing food chain—than at the championship levels.

Yet over the last few years, it has been the suspensions of big-name trainers for illegal drug use that has made headlines and roused the curiosity of the public and the anxiety levels of professional gamblers, many of whom bet millions of dollars a year on racing outcomes.

So far in the first decade of the new millennium, any list of leading trainers has included the same five names: Steve Asmussen, Rick Dutrow, Todd Pletcher, Bobby Frankel, and Dale Romans. And at least once during that time, each of the five has served a suspension for a drug positive, and in each case for the same medication: mepivacaine.

Mepivacaine is not a steroid but a nerve-blocking painkiller. Contrary to what might be the initial interpretation of people not involved in racing, mepivacaine is not normally used to mask pain so a horse can run down the racetrack. Because of its quick and thorough action, mepivacaine is simply the drug of choice vets use to numb tissue for suturing or for diagnostic testing.

A horse that bangs its eye on the gate and gets sutured might still show traces of the drug when it wins a race later in the week. Even if a painkiller was needed to help some lower-class claiming animal get through the race, vets would most likely use something else. At their level, they are probably not "nerving" their valuable horses to keep them in training. Each has so many horses under his care that keeping one off the track until it heals affects neither the vet nor the horse's owner financially.

Still, the suspension of leading trainers for illegal use of a painkiller is a serious problem. Like steroids, painkillers are a symbol of the drug culture in racing that is ruining the game. This came home to me in June 2008, upon encountering the wreckage of the drug culture in my own racing stable.

I was at Delaware Park, looking in on a well-bred Two Bucks filly by a highly regarded sire. My partners and I had placed her with a well-known trainer who kept a barn at the Fair Hill training center in Maryland and had a reputation as an uncommunicative curmudgeon, which turned out to be an understatement.

The filly had left for Maryland eight months earlier dappled out in full flesh without a mark on her, a compact but beautifully conformed and sweet-moving two-year-old that I hoped would become the cornerstone of a second-generation broodmare band made up of the daughters of the mares with which we began Two Bucks. The day after her arrival the trainer called to report that she had injured her knee during the trip and was lame. Whatever else there was to know about her in the next few months he kept to himself. Whenever I ran him down on his cell phone, he was always somewhere other than where she was.

Although the filly had performed gamely in her first two races, getting a fourth in her first race and second next time out, what now stood in the stall before me that June morning can be most charitably called a wreck. She was thin, her hair coat haggard, and her feet erratically shod, not one matching another in shape and size. One front foot was heavy with a hoof-shaping compound called Equilox, applied in an apparently unsuccessful effort to keep her left forefront from banging her rear right hind.

Most noticeable was the lack of long muscles along her back

and across her croup, a clear sign that she had displaced her sacrum joint connecting the spine to the hips. Sacrum displacement is a common malady of racehorses and one that goes regularly undiagnosed by the well-intentioned people licensed to train them and the veterinarians paid to care for them. Most veterinarians cannot adjust a sacrum, a simple procedure for a good equine chiropractor. They can only recommend a rest, which would usually take the horse out of the trainer's barn for a long period, or treat with drugs the other joints and muscles that become sore as the horse adjusts its gait to reduce the pain. That the injection of sore joints is one of the most expensive and overused procedures in a racetrack vet's bag is probably just a coincidence.

The obvious degeneration of long muscle on the filly's back and the overdevelopment of the shorter stifle and gaskin muscles in her hindquarters also cleared up a mystery that had prompted my trip to Delaware in the first place: an outrageous $1,585 bill for her May veterinary maintenance, including $300 to inject her overused stifle joints. She was obviously being kept on an extensive drug regimen to treat symptoms of problems that could be cured only by a combination of rest and chiropractic adjustment.

The young assistant trainer in whose hands my most valuable, blue-blooded animal had been placed was amiable, well intentioned, and proud of his work. But he obviously had no idea what had gone wrong with her. While he was away overseeing the training of other horses on the track, I had been observing her closely in her stall. In addition to her dislocated sacrum, she had a dropped sternum and was clipping her right hind ankle with her left forefoot in an effort to maneuver away from the pain. The assistant trainer's offer to take the horse out of her stall to parade around for the owner was even more disappointing.

"That's not necessary," I said. "I've seen enough."

Even as I was wondering how fast I could get agreement from my co-owners to move her elsewhere, I received a call from Arthur Hancock, who was recounting through my cell phone an experience of his own to illustrate his contention that veterinarians have way too much influence on the training of racehorses. Having informed his trainer's veterinarian that he wanted drugs administered to his horse only to treat illness, the veterinarian responded, "But Arthur, you want to win, don't you?"

In the case of the Two Bucks filly, she was not being given drugs that enhanced her performance on the track. Rather, her joints and organs were being flooded with medications, some of them steroidal in nature, in an effort to keep her sound and in training. By injecting her hock and ankle joints, the vets were treating the symptoms of her problem but not their cause.

Rather than inform an owner that his lovely, expensive, well-bred horse is being sent home a failure, trainers often depend on veterinarians to keep them on the track. An owner friend of mine recalled a time when he got his race mare home in good order, but she would not get in foal. Finally she was sent to a clinic for evaluation of her reproductive system. The results were astounding. A marble had been placed in her cervix, the opening to the uterus, effectively closing it permanently, ensuring that the mare would have no estrus cycles at the track, which can be disruptive to training and racing. Vet magic, it seems, knows no bounds.

━7━

THE VETS

A shiny new Mercedes pulls up at an intersection in Elmont, New York, and stops in front of a man on the curb holding a bag. The driver pops the trunk, and the man gets in, bag and all. A few blocks later the Mercedes is waved through the main gate at Belmont Park and makes its way to the barn of a famous trainer, where the trunk is popped again and the cargo hops out with the athleticism of a middleweight contender.

Nothing unusual about this, right? Just the world's most famous veterinarian, Dr. Alex Harthill, arriving from Kentucky to do his regular routine work—surreptitiously of course, because the pioneering methods of such a legendary racetrack magician were not welcome at the time in New York. Being ruled off the track in the late 1970s and early '80s was merely a travel inconvenience to the man most responsible for the veterinarian culture that dominates horse racing today.

There was no way to know precisely what "the Doc" had come to administer to horses in those days because Harthill was always well ahead of his time in the field of equine medication. But whatever it was, the odds are 1 to 9 it was not yet in the bag of any legal New York vet. Even if it was, the other vets could not match his skill in administering it.

Dr. Harthill died of pneumonia in 2005 at age eighty, taking with him a treasure trove of secrets concerning the history of medication in thoroughbred racing. But the legacy he left behind is now one of the most controversial aspects of an ailing sport trying to find an antidote to demise.

Harthill's skill at nursing a horse through injury and enhancing its ability to compete unquestionably was once considered an advantage to any trainer who could command and trust his services. By his own count, he treated at least twenty-six Kentucky Derby winners, from Citation in 1948 to Northern Dancer in 1964 and Sunday Silence in 1989. A lot of losers were in his care during the week before the Derby as well, supporting a belief in some quarters that his presence at Churchill Downs could have been the most important factor in countless outcomes of the world's greatest race in the modern era. By his own admission, he was certainly a factor in some of them.

Born in his father's veterinary clinic and a lifelong pioneer of liberal medication policies, Harthill was in his prime not only the most highly skilled and important track veterinarian in the world but one of the most powerful men in the sport. The veterinarian of choice at historic Calumet Farm, he was also a close personal friend of the influential Louisville breeder Warner Jones, who eventually became the chairman of Churchill Downs.

In an insight into the closeness of their friendship and the nature of both men, Harthill once recalled. "We'd go to Warner's place on Sunday afternoons, way before there was Sunday racing. We'd drink whisky and have bare-knuckle fights, just for the fun of it."

Also quick with a punch to the face of a loudmouth heckler or an irritating journalist, he was known for carrying a pistol and once allegedly had a hit contract put out on a Kentucky trainer. This combination of success, prominence, and hellcat volatility led him repeatedly to high-drama controversy and collisions with the law.

The only public drug scandal in the history of the Derby, the disqualification of first-place finisher Dancer's Image in 1968, who tested positive for an anti-inflammatory painkiller that was then illegal, was laid at his feet. Harthill acknowledged giving the horse four grams of phenylbutazone, or "bute," 152 hours before the race—twice the amount of time normally required for it to clear. On the very night the positive became known, Harthill was driving a Louisville reporter through the tunnel that connects the backside of Churchill to the grandstand. He gave the reporter a clue not only to how the drug may have gotten into the horse's system but perhaps to the tools that make skilled track veterinarians an "edge" in the competition.

"You know where they went wrong, don't you?" Harthill said. "They gave the horse the stuff in tablet form. Use a syringe and it doesn't stay in the system nearly as long."

Discovering racetrack applications of new drugs and how they worked long before anyone else was as vital to Harthill's success as his superiority at diagnosing, treating, and suturing. Dropping that knowledge to a reporter at the height of the Dancer's Image controversy was later considered by many to be part of a scheme to cover his own tracks by blaming the positive test on a less knowledgeable saboteur.

The Kentucky journalist Billy Reed, who covered the Kentucky Derby for years as a reporter for the *Louisville Courier-Journal* and later *Sports Illustrated*, went to Churchill Downs the night the disqualification became known to talk to Harthill, whom he encountered outside his barn.

"I'm Billy Reed of the *Courier-Journal*," was all he had time to say before Harthill grabbed his right hand and decked him with a left hook to the head.

Reed has gathered mounds of circumstantial evidence that indicates that Harthill meddled with the Derby for more than fifty years, protected only by "the outrageous boldness and audacity of the possibility." Trainers who were around Harthill over the years and still revere him are certain that he did, stopping favorites when it suited him and helping pals achieve the stardom that accompanied the upsets he had engineered. None wanted their names attached to their beliefs, however, out of loyalty to their relationships or fear that "the Godfather," as some called him, might somehow get even from the grave.

In many quarters he was as beloved as he was feared and loathed in others. Over the years he performed dozens of surgeries for struggling trainers and owners that were never billed. He would stop at a barn, look over an ailing animal, and dispense an antibiotic or topical ointment without leaving an invoice. A onetime trainer, now deceased, remembered using his last few dollars to enter a horse in a cheap claiming race at Keeneland three decades ago and lamenting about it to Harthill, who had stopped by just to ask how things were going.

"Okay, Doc. But I just put one in and God, I really need to win that race."

"When you in?" Harthill wanted to know. "I might come by."

On the morning of the race, Harthill showed up with a syringe. "Just give him this before you go over. It'll help him finish."

The horse won by six lengths. The trainer never got a bill.

One of Harthill's loyalists at Churchill, now in another line of work, said that when he was a trainer in bad need of a win, the Doc would tell him to look for him at a certain spot between his barn and the gap in the track rail through which horses are led from the barn area over to the saddling paddock.

"Doc would have a shot of something in his coat, called it B-12 sometimes, and by the time I got my horse to the paddock he'd be jumping out of his skin," he said. "Hell, every now and then we'd win by twelve."

Harthill's most lasting contribution to racing came four years before the Dancer's Image scandal and remains today one of its most controversial and incendiary features: furosemide, or Lasix, the antibleeder medication then illegal and unknown as an equine medication but now a legal race-day application in every U.S. racing jurisdiction and used by 95 percent of all starters.

In 1990, Harthill told the California veterinarian Rick Arthur, "It started with me. I used it on Northern Dancer in 1964."

And who knows how many other horses, including those in New York, which refused for the next twenty years to legalize its use, finally relenting in 1985.

That someone would attempt to manipulate the world's greatest and most heavily bet upon horse race is still a taboo subject in Kentucky racing circles, even among those who believe it happened. Yet Harthill, toward the end of his life, was bold enough to tell Jay Hovdey of the *Daily Racing Form* how he was able to give Northern Dancer the illegal Lasix.

"Security was following me, though," Harthill told Hovdey, "so I got a vet I know from out of town to come along with me. I told him I was going to turn to the right, and he would go that way and take this little syringe down to Barn 24, stall 23, and give this to that horse. There would be a guy there named Will. He'd be waiting. So he did it, while the gendarmes followed me. They were following the mystique."

Could Lasix have made the difference in Northern Dancer's victory? You bet. In one of the best Derby stretch battles ever, he beat Hill Rise by a nose and became the first Derby winner to complete the mile-and-a-quarter distance in two minutes flat, a record that Secretariat broke in 1973.

A longtime confidant with whom Harthill had fallen out before his death believes that the veterinarian tampered with

Derby outcomes not for the money he could make by betting against the Derby favorite but simply because he could. And that the ultimate beneficiaries of the subterfuges likely had no knowledge of them, Harthill being too shrewd to risk getting them involved.

Over the years Harthill repeatedly placed himself in positions where close friendships and conflicts of interest raised questions about his involvement in Derby outcomes. He was a close friend of Lynn Whiting, for example, whose 1992 Derby champion Lil E. Tee was among the unlikeliest of winners and ridden by the Kentucky jockey Pat Day, a Harthill favorite. "It helps to have Dr. Harthill on your team," Whiting told Billy Reed. "He's the best there is. If a problem develops that he can't solve, he knows somebody that can fix it."

And the night before the Derby in which Dancer's Image was disqualified, Harthill's overnight guest at his home was Milo Valenzuela, the jockey on Forward Pass, the horse who would finish second to Dancer's Image and inherit the crown.

Another of Harthill's buddies was the trainer Charlie Wittingham, who won the Derby twice, with Ferdinand in 1986 and Arthur Hancock's Sunday Silence in 1989. Harthill was a fixture in Wittingham's barn whenever he was running under the Twin Spires.

The "mystique" Harthill was talking about did not always require an enhanced performance on the part of the winner. For the first seventy-one years in which the Kentucky Derby was waged under the pari-mutuel betting system, the favorite won thirty times. But between 1980 and 1999, not a single favorite won the roses.

Sometimes, horses widely believed to be the best didn't get to the gate. The year Lil E. Tee won, the leading contender A.P. Indy scratched on Derby morning with a sore hoof. The 1996 Derby went to Grindstone, one of five entries by D. Wayne

Lukas but the only one owned by the popular Kentucky businessman W. T. Young, then seventy-seven years old and perhaps taking his final chance at a Derby win. The prerace favorite, Unbridled's Song, had foot problems all week and appeared rank and unhappy in the post parade.

All the favorites folded in one way or another in 1993, when the 13-to-1 longshot Sea Hero won what turned out to be a retirement present for eighty-six-year-old Paul Mellon and his seventy-one-year-old trainer MacKenzie Miller. There is no hint of veterinary intervention in any of these races, other than the looming presence of Harthill around all of them and his close ties with their connections.

The trainer Jimmy Croll went to his grave in 2008 convinced that somebody had "stopped" his 6-to-5 Derby favorite Holy Bull, who ran the worst race of his career at the 1994 Derby and finished a dull twelfth to Go for Gin, who had gone off 9 to 1.

"They got to my horse," Croll said. "I know more than ever that Holy Bull was drugged."

Croll never publicly accused Harthill but privately told friends that he believed someone had given Holy Bull some Halcion, a strong sedative prescribed for heart patients. Croll's belief as to the source of the medication became public knowledge when two years later the U.S. Drug Enforcement Administration filed 102 charges against Harthill for keeping in his pharmacy without a prescription large quantities of amphetamines, painkillers, and sleeping pills. Among them were four thousand Halcion tablets. The case was settled out of court.

The owner of Dancer's Image, Peter Fuller, ultimately came to believe that Harthill's involvement in the disqualification was actually part of a conspiracy to make sure Forward Pass rather than his horse won the Derby.

Dancer's Image had been housed in a barn where Harthill maintained a laboratory. Before the positive was announced,

Harthill not only leaked his "pill" theory to the *Louisville Times*, but participated in a bizarre "salting" incident in which he and the trainer Doug Davis were caught putting powder from "crushed" pills in Dancer's Image's feed tub, presumably reenacting what had occurred in an effort to make sure that Lou Cavalaris, the trainer of Dancer's Image, got the rap for the offense.

Their explanation was that the powder was only aspirin being used to test the veracity of Lou Cavalaris, who passed by and reported them to authorities. Both got minor fines.

That scheme, old-timers insist, was vintage Harthill. One of the lawyers pushing for the truth in the Dancer's Image case was Edward "Ned" Bonnie, a dedicated antidrug activist and industry reformer who is now a member of the Kentucky Horse Racing Commission. Back then he was also an accomplished steeplechase jockey.

With the case still fresh in everybody's mind, Harthill hired Bonnie to ride one of his horses in a steeplechase event. At the last minute, a family emergency prevented him from fulfilling the obligation, so he had to get a substitute. Following the race, the horse that Harthill had asked Bonnie to ride tested positive for phenylbutazone, just like Dancer's Image.

Performance-enhancing medications and the ability to mask them from the routine but often inadequate, erratic, and unfair testing procedures now used in horse racing are inseparable. So the quest for new drugs and combinations of drugs that can improve an animal's performance and not be detected in post-race testing has been ongoing for decades.

As Harthill told Hovdey toward the end of his life, "Everything [drugs] went through a transition period of being detected. The thing everyone wanted to find out was what didn't show at the time. It was just part of the game, ever since I can remember. Everybody was looking for an edge. I don't care who it was.

A trainer would say, 'Don't get me caught, but keep me worried.' "

In those days veterinarians were a scarce commodity at Churchill Downs and other racetracks.

"For a long time there was just Alex and a couple of others, one of whom was starving and had to leave town," said one of Harthill's longtime clients under the Twin Spires of Churchill Downs. "That's how he had the run of the place, his office and own barn right on the track. There was only one Alex Harthill. And there will never be another like him. But today, the veterinarians are everywhere . . . like a swarm of locusts around here now."

The nefarious genius of Alex Harthill has never been matched since, but not because people haven't tried. Despite an unreliable and virtually ineffective system of testing, offenders are regularly nailed for possessing and using a wide range of illegal pharmaceuticals in an effort to gain an edge, everything from simple marijuana and cocaine to ecstasy and designer drugs and exotics such as etorphine, or "elephant juice," an opiate eighty thousand times more powerful than morphine that can tranquilize elephants but in smaller doses can act as an equine stimulant.

Not long before his death, Harthill himself began to rail openly about the activities of the new generation of vets swarming over the tracks. He was infuriated by the best-known practitioner of the controversial screws-and-wires procedure, the renowned orthopedic surgeon Larry Bramlage, who he said "would put a screw in your eye if you would stand still for it." The Doc was particularly and specifically critical of Steve Allday, a controversial but highly successful veterinarian thirty years his junior whose reputation as a racetrack magician began to rival Harthill's own.

Allday's ability in the 1990s to give a trainer an edge rose to near mythical levels when he served as the racing manager for the late Allen Paulson, whose thoroughbred champion Cigar tied Citation's record of sixteen consecutive victories, and later for the Canadian auto parts magnate and racetrack owner Frank Stronach. Both men won Eclipse Awards as owners and breeders while Allday was in their employ. In 1997, the Kentucky trainer Patrick Byrne, who conditioned some horses for Stronach, won two Eclipse Awards in the same year while Allday was his vet, for the Horse of the Year, Favorite Trick, and Countess Diana, the two-year-old filly champion.

Soon Allday was advising the biggest and most important training stables in the country, simultaneously working for Todd Pletcher, Bobby Frankel, Steve Asmussen, and Dale Romans. Big Brown's trainer, the admitted doper Rick Dutrow, said his decision to administer steroids to every horse in his barn was made on Allday's advice. His critics believe him guilty of some magic on behalf of the 2000 Kentucky Derby winner Fusaichi Pegasus, who never ran so well before or after that race and has yet to live up to expectations of a sire reportedly valued at more than $50 million.

Now a vocal advocate for abolishing all race-day medications, Allday, in an interview with the *Blood-Horse* in 2008, said that there is nothing "sinister or unsavory" about his work and blamed his departure from conventional veterinary approaches as the reason for people's misconceptions. "If anybody really wanted to come and work with me, spend time with me, work with the outfits I work with, and see the care and trouble I take with medication and things of that nature," he said, "I think they would understand that it is a prime example of people wanting to believe the fantasy more than the reality."

He said he had not administered a prerace workup on a horse for more than a decade and had been concentrating primarily on lameness, where his ability for diagnosis and reha- bilitation is equally highly regarded. Even his sternest critics who believe him a "pharmacist" in the tradition of Harthill can- not cite specifics regarding his methods or his activities. But their contention is that whatever miracle was at work in these extraordinarily successful barns never occurred on race day and was most likely masked from inept testing.

Many of the trainers who availed themselves of Allday's ser- vices have served suspensions for the same drug positive but not for the kind of exotic concoctions linked to enhancing perfor- mance by competing veterinarians and knowledgeable specula- tors of Allday's perceived genius. The common denominator among them is actually the "caines"—lidocaine and mepiva- caine, nerve-deadening agents injected to relieve pain. But there is at least one anonymous blogger who believes that mepiva- caine injected into a horse's breathing apparatus will do the trick. Who knows? If Harthill were still around, he could tell us.

If Allday had a single "silver bullet," he masterfully kept it a secret from his associates and the plethora of assistant trainers who were usually around the horse when he was. And it obvi- ously had to be used sparingly, producing superhorses here and there for clients who were in fact competing with each other at the top of the game. And in every case, the glory and earnings that accompanied the successes have been cheapened in the eyes of many.

But like Harthill in his time, Allday—guilty or not—is still the poster boy for a wave of suspected cheaters, not all of them licensed veterinarians, who have tried one trick after another in the past twenty years to gain an edge, starting with simple nar- cotics. One former veterinarian actually quit his job and became a pharmaceutical company representative after being asked by a New York owner to administer etorphine to his horse.

Narcotics were followed closely by an epidemic of

"milkshaking"—funneling to the stomach by tube a concoction of bicarbonates, primarily sodium—designed to neutralize the buildup of lactic acid in the muscles, thereby increasing stamina. Believed to have originated with standardbred racing in Australia, the practice quickly spread to New Jersey and other racing jurisdictions until regulators began outlawing it.

In some jurisdictions the mere presence of the tubing used in the process was illegal on the racetrack grounds before the race. One trainer even hired a private detective to photograph a tube-carrying veterinarian climbing aboard a competitor's horse van while stopped on a Florida interstate en route to a track. In New York stakes horses have to be moved to a monitored quarantine barn six hours before a race. California periodically orders all the horses of suspected trainers to undergo the same monitoring.

Most scientists and veteran drug reformers believe that in recent years the "edge" has been shrewd combinations of legal steroids and bronchodilators such as clenbuterol that kept thresholds below the legal trace limits of a particular state. A horse can pass a test one day in one state but be tripped up on another by a "spike" caused most likely when an illegal substance leaks from the tissue where it has been entrapped.

Although some trainers allow regular doses of Ventipulmin Syrup—the most popular oral brand of clenbuterol—to appear as a specific item on vet bills (thirty-seven dollars a dose), many medications, such as regular doses of a steroid like Winstrol, are seldom if ever even acknowledged to owners.

A cheater with a shrewd chemical adviser, in an effort to leave no trace of a steroid or bronchodilator, might use inhalant versions that disappear more quickly from the horse's system. When used regularly, the "puffed" version will maintain a constant threshold lower than the oral elixir.

Instead of a painkiller injected into the bloodstream, the same drug used topically can be harder to detect. And the more exotic the painkiller, the less likely it will be picked up at all. One of the nation's leading trainers, Patrick Biancone, and his veterinarian were ruled off the track in 2007 after cobra venom was found in his barn at Keeneland. The same year, a Florida veterinarian was awarded a $100,000 grant to develop a test for "conotoxins," which signal the presence of venom from the cone sea snail, a pain reliever.

No doubt to avoid blood pressure spikes among owners who find cobra venom or cone snail venom listed on their bills, such items are never listed. And the cost can be hidden as easily from them as the drugs are from tests. Since antibleeder medication became routine, costly prerace medication regimens, sometimes costing as much as five hundred dollars, have become a staple of veterinary income.

In reality, the "edge" will continue to be whatever can escape the particular testing procedure being used by authorities at the time. Human athletes cheated by using steroids and other substances that would increase red blood cells and stamina such as erythopoetin, a drug prescribed for human cancer patients or those needing dialysis. Because specific tests are needed for these substances, cyclists have gotten away with using them for years due to the difficulty in distinguishing "EPO cells" from red blood cells produced naturally. The same problem exists with steroid testing, which must distinguish between synthetic testosterone and the athlete's own product.

Until the steroid controversy arose last year, furosemide, still illegal in Europe and many other horse-racing jurisdictions around the world, stood alone as the symbol of the sport's drug controversy. The argument over its use is emblematic: does its obvious therapeutic value as a diuretic that prevents exercise-induced pulmonary hemorrhage outweigh its potential for enhancing performance and for masking other illegal substances hidden in legal prerace medication regimens?

The most fervent proponents of drug reform want all antibleeder medications outlawed along with the body- and strength-building steroids and the anti-inflammatory corticosteroids such as the infamous phenylbutazone that Harthill gave Dancer's Image. Arthur Hancock, for instance, says run them on hay, oats, and water or send them home to be treated. Widespread opposition to Hancock's notion is couched in the inevitable and serious economic consequences of doing that.

Therapeutic medications such as furosemide, clenbuterol, and anti-inflammatory corticosteroids are to horses what aspirin, antihistamines, and antibiotics are to humans. They make horses more comfortable when they are sick, cure their diseases, and get them going again. The mepivacaine injected so an eye banged on a starting gate can be sutured cannot be distinguished from that injected into a knee so a crippled claiming horse at the bottom of a racing food chain can make one more start.

True drug reform affects the small-time trainer and the claiming horses far more dramatically than it does the Dinnies and their global competitors that dominate the weekend stakes, the Triple Crown classics, and the Breeders' Cup program. If a top trainer such as Todd Pletcher or Larry Jones has to send a horse home to be rehabilitated on drugs, another is ready and waiting to occupy his stall, and his spot in the starting gate.

What happens to the claiming horse trainer, however, whether he has ten horses in his barn or fifty, and to the racetrack operator is a different story. The trainer's income is reduced. So is the pool of entries that racetracks count on to fill the fields and attract bets. Claiming horses fill 70 percent of all races, so the economic impact of meaningful drug reform is a terrifying prospect.

Most local horsemen's organizations, which under the 1978 law authorizing interstate pari-mutuel gambling are entitled to approve off-track simulcast agreements, are dominated by trainers and veterinarians who make their living off claiming horses. Any proposed uniform or model drug rules that threaten their revenue stream soon run into massive political opposition—rational behavior by the trainers and the tracks but not necessarily good for the horses, jockey safety, or the image of the sport.

For generations the private trainers for the thoroughbred establishment maintained at least a veneer of integrity. As shepherds of the sport and guardians of its treasury, the Hancocks, the Phippses, the Whitneys, and the Farishes would not risk having their reputations or that of their breeding stock sullied by drug positives and suspensions. Their long-standing global competitors—the Europeans and the Arabs—have managed to avoid scandal as well.

But in the past decade their racing dominance in North America has been diminished by the stream of big-spending owners who turned their auction prizes over to the new-breed trainers who maintain huge public stables with divisions all over the country. These purveyors of change and their horses began to dominate the classic races and the coveted Eclipse Awards given annually for leading horses, trainers, owners, and breeders.

The awards themselves often had to be bestowed in an atmosphere of skepticism under clouds of drug-related controversy. The former claiming trainer Bobby Frankel set consecutive winning and earnings records, dominated the big stakes races, and won four straight Eclipse Awards while somehow successfully arguing that a morphine positive on one of his horses was due to "poppy" seeds—maybe from a groom's breakfast roll.

Frankel's earnings record was almost immediately broken by Todd Pletcher, who accepted one of his three consecutive

Eclipse Awards while serving a forty-five-day suspension for a mepivacaine positive. The all-time record for wins in a season was broken by Scott Lake, who had just been nailed for two drug violations in the mid-Atlantic region. And the 2005 Horse of the Year, Saint Liam, had to be shifted in midyear to Frankel's barn so his regular trainer, Rick Dutrow, could begin serving a suspension for his thirteenth drug-related citation.

In 2005, after years of neglecting the problem, the Dinnies and the organizations under their control coughed up $3 million to fund the Equine Drug Research Institute, which quietly began developing tests to catch the cheaters stealing their races and winning their awards. As evidence of sincerity, they recruited to head it Dr. Don Catlin, the distinguished researcher responsible for developing drug tests for Olympic athletes, and built him an equine lab at the University of California at Davis, adjacent to his human test research facility. Now they don't like his public admonitions that simply trying to regulate four testosterone-based steroids and set threshold limits on bronchodilators and antibleeding medications is not a serious effort to rid racing of drugs.

So despite all the ballyhoo about model uniform drug rules, the authority and tests necessary to enforce them were only good intentions in the hearts of reformers and brouhaha in press releases until Larry Jones's filly broke down on racing's most important day before racing's biggest audience. Then the tragic death of Eight Belles became both a blessing and a curse.

PART THREE

THE RECKONING

8

RIVER OF STONES

Ed Musselman is a gadfly who bites the thoroughbred horse industry for fun and profit—or maybe just fun. Under the nom de plume "Indian Charlie," Musselman appears to somehow make a living distributing a free, randomly published single-sheet newsletter around the important sales and race meets. Its value as the only medium in existence that even tries to jar the business out of its complacency is diminished by the accuracy of the slogan atop the masthead: "We never let the truth get in the way of a good story."

With ads on one side and barb-laced satire on the other, it is sometimes pithy, often pitiable, and usually harmless. Nonetheless it is widely read and every now and then even funny, especially to those privy to inside jokes. Its most effective harpoons are usually aimed at friendly targets with clownish reputations unlikely to retaliate or to hapless characters without the means to do so.

The funniest thing Indian Charlie ever wrote was—like most of his stuff—fed to him by someone else. It was about Maryjean Wall, for years the horse-racing writer for the *Lexington*

Herald-Leader. A few years ago when Wall fell off a ladder in her living room and broke both of her ankles, Indian Charlie reported that she was treated at Rood & Riddle Equine Hospital, the area's largest, where her ankles were repaired with "two screws taken from her head."

One of the meanest, most humorless items he ever published was about me. Minutes before the kidney stones ambushed me at the Fasig-Tipton July sale, I had been weighing the pros and cons of punching Indian Charlie in the face, which reflects my state of mind that day and perhaps even some yet-to-be-discovered physiological phenomenon that makes kidneys manufacture stones.

Earlier that day, someone had given me a copy of Indian Charlie's July 13 newsletter, which contained as mean-spirited and unfair a political cartoon as any I ever published in thirteen years as a newspaper editor. And that is saying something. The *Chicago Tribune*'s political cartoonist during my tenure was the late and great Jeff McNelly, who tried his best to offend the pope and the Catholic Church at least once a week.

The largest graphic on Indian Charlie's satire page on a day when the Fasig-Tipton sale paddocks were jammed with buyers from all over the world was hardly McNelly quality. It was a crude but unmistakable two-headed cartoon likeness of me, my facial features lifted from a photograph and captioned "Two Faces Is Too Many for Jim (Two Bucks) Squires." One of my faces delivered the bubbled message "Hay, Oats & Water . . . Hang the Cheaters . . . Zero tolerance," and the other said, "We were sabotaged and framed . . . Hey, what's a nanogram or two of clenbuterol among friends?"

I didn't need my two decades of experience avoiding and fighting libel suits to know that my reputation had been unfairly and irreparably damaged but that I had no legal recourse. Due to recent events I had clearly become a *public figure*—the Supreme Court definition of that term basically makes it impossible for someone in public life to successfully sue for libel damages.

Every insider on the sale grounds knew that a horse owned by Two Bucks Farm and trained by Larry Jones had tested positive the month before for clenbuterol, the performance-enhancing drug I had written about in the *New York Times* and which Jones and I contended needed stricter regulation. We had announced the test results ourselves and were convinced the horse had been tampered with in a deliberate effort to damage our credibility.

An investigation had been launched, but neither DNA testing nor the confirming test of a second half—or split—of the urine sample had been completed. As yet there was no real evidence the sample tested had actually come from our horse, and certainly none that I had personally administered the drug or approved its use. But for some inexplicable reason, Indian Charlie, with whom I had been friendly for years, had made the judgment that I was guilty of doping and hypocrisy.

Now that the shoe was on the other foot, it hurt like hell. Whenever in the past I had published something mean and unfair, I'd faced the distinct possibility that the target might appear in my office the next day and punch me in the nose. When you're barred from collecting libel damages, what more satisfying way is there to properly avenge such a grievance? And punching is emotionally—if not physically—healthier than carrying a grudge.

A violent course of action had been foremost in my mind much of the morning. There was precedent for it. Having gone to grammar school in a rough part of Nashville, I had grown up fighting in the streets. One of my grandfathers was a navy boxer who taught me the manly art of self-defense at a young age. My other grandfather was a cop who had taught me every dirty, street-fighting tactic he had learned in a lifetime of arresting unruly drunks and armed bullies.

My younger brother Tommy would fight a buzz saw, and the two of us were often recruited for score settling of one kind or another. Although Indian Charlie was probably twenty years younger than me, I figured to do him a lot of damage in the five minutes before I ran out of breath. But just in case he was tougher than he looked or I got arrested in the process, I prudently decided to postpone the assault until after my unsold yearlings were safely back to Two Bucks. In retrospect, the kidney stone encounter was a lucky break for us both.

When I was lying on the gurney in the emergency room later that day, all the fight had gone out of me. But the sense of injustice from a cheap, amateurish, and personal sneak attack was as persistently disturbing as the pain in my abdomen. For the first time I understood how Cindy Jones could have suddenly wanted to quit the horse life she loved for twenty years. I wanted to quit it, too. What the hell was the use trying to improve an industry that not only defied improvement but also defiled those who sought it? The rhino skin I had grown while a big-city newspaper editor had turned to tissue paper. At that moment I would have given away all my horses and spared the future cost and humiliation of commercial horse sales by a witless dunce who made his living making fun of people. At some point later that afternoon, a rush of delicious irony washed away all the bitterness and self-pity of my self-absorption. When the ER doctor read the CAT scan of my kidneys, he found more than one stone.

"It's the big one blocking the ureter that is causing the trouble," he said, "but you've got a few more coming down the river."

A River of Stones. You can't make this stuff up. My horse in the Jones stable with the drug positive was named Stones River, after a stream outside Nashville along which an important Civil War battle had been fought. It serves as a dividing line between a neighborhood called Madison, where I was born, and another called Donelson, where Frank Woods, my good friend of forty-four years and a co-owner of Stones River, grew up. Woods was also a co-owner of Morava, the first horse ever raced by Two Bucks Farm, and was at Churchill Downs the day his half brother Monarchos won the Kentucky Derby.

Stones River was our hope for a second lightning strike. And on the afternoon of July 14, sandwiched between the muggings by Indian Charlie and the kidney stones, he had won his third consecutive race handily at Delaware Park. Barring injury, he was headed to the Pennsylvania Derby and its $1 million purse.

A late-maturing three-year-old son of Monarchos, the lanky gray had missed the Triple Crown competition due to chronically sore shins and a disastrous beginning in another racing stable from which he emerged looking like a refugee from a concentration camp. The first time Larry Jones saw Stones River as a skinny two-year-old, the trainer looked him in the eye and said, "If you are going to be the successor to Hard Spun, you're going to have to gain some weight and muscle so you can carry my big ass around the track."

In the past year, Stones River had gotten considerably bigger and stronger. But in his first three races in 2008, he played around like he was frolicking with friends in the pasture, never taking a deep breath and finishing fifth each time. After his third lackluster race, an uninspired effort at Keeneland in April in which he never broke a sweat, Jones said, "Don't worry, I'll wake him up when we get to Delaware Park." I later learned that meant that the trainer planned to start riding Stones River in the morning himself.

The wake-up process did not take long. A week after the

Kentucky Derby, the colt was entered in a maiden race at Delaware Park, a track where his half sister Unbridled Belle had won the $1 million Delaware Handicap the year before. Never quick out of the gate, he got an even slower start because the assistant starter, trying to calm him in his chute, still had hold of his bridle when his gate opened.

Stones River got away last of ten horses and spent the first half mile ten lengths behind the leaders being pelted by slop from the rain-drenched track. Running directly ahead of him most of the way was another Jones trainee, a promising Maria's Mon colt named Zipped, also a gray and owned by Hard Spun's owner Richard Porter and ridden by Jones's go-to jockey, the now infamous Gabriel Saez.

When a trainer has two horses in the same race, owners can tell where they are in the stable pecking order by which mount gets the more celebrated jockey. An able jockey, Abel Castellano, was atop Stones River, but there was little doubt—at least in my mind—which horse the Joneses expected to win. Adding to my pessimism was Unbridled Belle's lack of success on sloppy tracks. She'd won $1.3 million in her career but not a dime on a wet track. I figured Stones River would take after his half sister. Of course, what's in my mind is often at odds with reality. Jones seldom if ever runs two horses in the same race unless he considers them relatively equal in ability.

As I watched the race on simulcast at Keeneland with another of Stones River's co-owners, the gloom hovering over the Jones stable settled comfortably on me. Stones River was loping leisurely along in eighth place as usual like a carousel horse bolted down in place behind Zipped and the clearly more eager bunch ahead of them. My breeder's pride was further wounded by my equally pessimistic co-owner, Glenn Bromagen, who had served with me on the Kentucky Racing Commission and who was describing the progress of the race by cell phone to one of his family members.

"He's running way behind again," Bromagen said, "not even trying . . . just like the other times."

Three quarters through the race, when Saez moved the mud-splattered Zipped out of line and began quickly picking off the leaders, I thought it was Stones River. But when he took the lead, I recognized my error and disappointment set in again. Then Saez began repeatedly looking back under his elbow for challengers.

It quickly became apparent who he was looking for. Stones River, his white bridle completely obliterated, had followed Zipped out of the crowd and was on his heels like a runaway freight train. Saez only got his head out from under his arm in time to see the backs of Castellano and Stones River through a spray of slop as they went by. Stones River had broken his maiden by four and a half lengths and was still pulling away from the field an eighth of a mile past the finish line.

The following morning the atmosphere in the Jones barn had changed dramatically.

"You can't believe what Stoney has done for us," Cindy Jones told me over the phone. "It's like this heavy cloud has lifted off of us for the first time. We needed this win more than anything. It has really picked us up."

The win set Jones off on another hot streak toward the training title at Delaware Park and the top echelon of trainers nation-wide. But the respite from trouble and controversy was short-lived. A month after Stones River's victory, he went to the post again in an allowance race against other winners. With Gabriel Saez aboard this time, the colt's performance was even more impressive, winning by nine and a quarter lengths. A week later came the stunning news that Stones River had tested positive for clenbuterol, the very drug his owner and trainer had been complaining about and wanted more strenuously regulated.

When Jones told me of the positive, I didn't know whether to laugh or cry, only that we were not guilty. Either our horse or our test had been tampered with. And we had no choice but to fight the charges. No matter the outcome or how loud and resolute our protest, Stones River and our reputation had been besmirched, our important victory negated, and our purse held in abeyance pending resolution of the matter. It was the first drug positive ever for Jones and the only one in the brief history of Two Bucks Farm. But that did nothing to alleviate the pain of our embarrassment.

Delaware had obviously seen the storm over steroids coming a full year before. Following the lead of neighboring Pennsylvania, it became the second racing jurisdiction to make them illegal in 2008. Over the years racing jurisdictions have differed dramatically in regulations concerning how close to race time a steroid can be administered and what test levels constitute illegality. The withdrawal times ranged from as long as five days in California down to twenty-four hours in Louisiana. Delaware's tolerance level is zero, so detection of the very presence of the drug in a horse's blood or urine is a violation punishable by a $5,000 fine and a two-week suspension for the first offense.

Based on their experience, Delaware Park trainers had arrived at the consensus opinion that administering the drug no closer than ninety-six hours to race time would produce a zero-level, negative test, an interval Jones had observed religiously. By the time Stones River failed, more than forty winners from his stable had tested clean in 2008, fifty-five more the year before. That Jones would change his routine on a horse belonging to the only owner in his barn as vocal as he about the need for stricter regulation was far-fetched. Some horses retain clenbuterol traces in their system longer than others, but Stones

River had tested negative after his first race at Delaware back in May.

That somebody was out to nail Jones with a positive was far more likely. Stones River had been a clear favorite to win his race, and therefore certain to be tested. And sabotage in Jones's barn was nothing new. The previous October, a promising two-year-old stakes filly named Maren's Meadow went off as an 8-to-9 favorite to win her race at Delaware Park against obviously outclassed competitors. When she ran third and later came up with a persistent mucus discharge from her nose, Jones sent her to a Kentucky veterinary hospital, where surgeons, suspecting a tumor, discovered she had been the victim of an old race-fixing trick called *sponging*.

Someone had shoved a round section of sponge about two by three inches up her nose in a successful effort to block her air passages. The sponging, which requires at least two people, is believed to have taken place two nights before the race when the barn night watchman was distracted by a fire that had been deliberately set nearby. No one has ever been charged in the incident.

Chances are neither the sponging nor the tampering with Stones River would have occurred had the cowboy trainer not rocketed out of Ellis Park obscurity to the top of his profession. As in many other competitive arenas, success by newcomers in horse racing almost always breeds envy and contempt. Both D. Wayne Lukas and Bob Baffert faced this when they loped onto the scene. The racing game is so tough that winning often ends up being attributed to blind luck or deliberate cheating. When Monarchos won the Derby, I quickly lost half my four friends. And two years after moving his ready smile, big hat, and well-conditioned horses into the forefront of East Coast racing, the Kentucky cowboy was forced to conclude, "We are obviously not the most popular people in Delaware."

That both Jones and I had been running our mouths for drug reform of a business more comfortable keeping its mouth shut probably had a lot to do with it. As fans of country music, we had heard the outlaw singer Willie Nelson's wisdom that "the turkey with the longest neck is the one that gets shot at."

In my case, I couldn't say I hadn't been warned. How right my late mother was when she told me repeatedly, "Son, your mouth is going to keep you in trouble all your life."

And it was hardly a surprise that the dominant female at Two Bucks weighed in with an even higher-brow diagnosis of the situation: "Looks like you and Larry are hoist by your own petard."

At the risk of offending the two distinguished American universities where I got my formal education, I must admit I had to look up *petard* in my copy of *Webster's* dictionary. I don't think Willie ever used the word in a song, so I didn't bother asking the cowboy how he felt about being "hoist" by one.

For years, a savvy Jack Russell terrier named Two Bucks Al was the only financial adviser to our horse business. His nanosecond attention span was perfectly suited for the shifting yearling market, and the truth is we haven't done as well since he wandered under the rear wheel of the family car several years ago.

Al's place as a companion in the truck has been taken by his son, "Little A," a liberal arts major preoccupied with eating whatever I am eating. So now our only financial advice came from my banker brother who is afraid of horses and an old college friend who specializes in estate management for a successful and respected Nashville trust company. But the fact that both are investors in Two Bucks Farm suggests questionable judgment on their part and demands that both remain anonymous to protect their own reputations. However, the estate planner is quite good at finding cash in my account to help me keep the farm afloat and patiently listens to my whining after disastrous sale experiences, which is exactly what I was doing during my delirium days following the Fasig-Tipton July sale. In the horse business making financial decisions while you are out of your mind is as good a time as any.

Having known me for forty-six years, my old college fraternity brother detected the weakness in my voice and inquired about my health.

"Kidney stones," I whimpered. "Hit me at the sale."

"You still having them?" he asked.

"What do you mean, 'still having them'?"

"Hell, you had kidney stones forty years ago."

"The hell you say."

"You sure did. I remember when it happened. After we both got married. We were about twenty-five."

He was right. It all came back, even the name of the doctor who had treated me.

"Shale in your urine," Dr. Bill Card had told me. "Probably from too much vitamin C."

Vitamin C? That's healthy stuff, which meant the family diagnostician was as wrong about me as she was about the Green Mountain maple tree and the yellow-bellied sapsucker. If I was having kidney stones forty years ago, they could not have been the result of years of hedonistic eating. At twenty-five I was barely a hedonist. So now why was I being denied all the foods that made life worth living: milk, ice cream, cheese, biscuits and gravy, donuts, even chocolate? Strength cannot be recovered on three gallons of water a day, lettuce, and cantaloupe. Ask Little A. He was starving.

This welcome revelation came on my first day strong

enough to do anything but shuffle to the bathroom. So was I out taking care of horses? Recruiting new owners? Trying to sell privately the sale yearlings nobody wanted?

No, I was doing something that actually had a chance of being accomplished. I was sitting on my tractor in a large pasture, having shut it down to take the call from the planner of my diminishing estate. At 4:30 p.m., it was still ninety degrees in the shade, and I had been mowing for hours. Not the lovely, lush bluegrass-laced meadows for which Kentucky is famous, but the inevitable and infernal consequences of the devastating drought of 2007. According to the diagnostician's Internet research, more trees die and weeds flourish most not during the drought but the year following. She must have been right because the only things green on Two Bucks Farm were my John Deere batwing mower, the damn ragweed, and my complexion.

With a half acre of pollen yet to inhale, I watched the two remaining stars from my tiny, aging broodmare band and their 2008 foals being led into the pasture. Along with six other mares and babies, they had spent the afternoon under fans in a cool barn shielded from the July sun and were being turned out for the night to search for grass among the weeds.

The minute they were released from their shanks, For Dixie, the dam of two multiple graded stakes winners, plopped down in the dirt just inside the gate. Newly turned-out horses often do this to roll and scratch their back. Then they get up, shake off the dust, and move off to exercise or graze. But For Dixie, nineteen years old and our most productive broodmare ever, didn't get back up, which was not a good sign.

The handler who turned her out, Bruce Hammond, who has worked with me for the entire twenty years we have owned a farm in Kentucky, realized that, too. He got to her about when I did. But she got up, walked off a hundred yards, and began grazing.

By the time I got back on my tractor, she had gone down again, a clear indication of distress. For Dixie was one of the three mares by the stallion Dixieland Band that I had bought in 1995, shortly after we started raising thoroughbreds. Since then the stallion had established himself as one of the truly great broodmare sires of modern times. One of his earliest successes was Regal Band—the dam of Monarchos—who was buried fifty yards outside the pasture where we were.

For Dixie had been an even better producer. She was the dam of Vicarage, the only Two Bucks–bred horse to ever win a graded stakes at Keeneland, and of Cotton Blossom, a multiple graded stakes winner of nearly $1 million, who had brought the farm $210,000 in revenue as a sale yearling and was resold by her new owners in November 2007 for $1.9 million. Cotton Blossom's full brother was now pawing at his mother, presumably trying to get her up so he could nurse.

To the practiced eye, this did not look all that serious. Bruce said that For Dixie had cleaned up her afternoon grain and that there was fresh manure in her stall, both encouraging signs. Still, before getting down from the tractor again, I called our regular veterinarian, Dr. Michael Beyer, whose expertise had saved Little Bold Belle. He was only twenty minutes away.

Colic often results from indigestion or bowel impaction, but it can be caused by a myriad of other factors. That it is a prolific killer of horses is evidenced by equine insurance company rates that make coverage virtually unaffordable for animals more than fifteen years old. And it is the bane of a horse owner's existence because it can strike in the middle of the night when the horses are out of view. Even quick detection and response can be too late.

To experienced horse people, the signs of colic are unmistakable: sweating, increased heart rate, pawing, tail ringing, violent rolling on the ground. So far For Dixie had exhibited none of these. But when we got her into the closest barn, a training facility with a walking ring and round pen, all the deadly signs showed up simultaneously. And they were unallayed by a shot of flunixin, a mild painkiller that relaxes muscles and often provides temporary relief.

Together Bruce and I had dealt successfully with dozens of serious colic cases over the years. But by the time Dr. Beyer arrived, we were having trouble keeping For Dixie on her feet and moving, which is about all you can do other than administer mild sedatives. When a horse goes down on its side, it has to be rolled over to an upright position before it can stand. For Dixie was a big mare, even for a thoroughbred, standing sixteen hands, two inches, and weighing well over a thousand pounds. Weak as I was, we couldn't even roll her. Only with the help of Dr. Beyer and his assistant and a cruel-sounding but effective technique of pouring water in the mare's ear were we able to right her and load her into our horse van for the trip to Rood & Riddle thirty minutes away.

Over the years Two Bucks had lost only one thoroughbred mare to colic, a twenty-six-year-old daughter of Damascus just a few months earlier. But the emergency run to Rood had been made dozens of times before with suspected colic cases, mares having foaling difficulty, and most memorably when Regal Band died of liver failure. Sometimes just the trip itself bouncing the horse around in the trailer is a remedy. Other horses go down and flail around in agony on the trailer floor and appear doomed when unloaded, only to recover after a few hours of hospital care or within a few days after surgery. Twisted intestines can be manually straightened and damaged membrane tissue removed if necessary.

But there is an unmistakable distress sign horsemen come to fear. When a horse suddenly grows cold and begins to tremble, it often means a toxin from a bacteria cell wall has been released into the circulatory system and ignited a massive but futile immune system response likely to be deadly. For Dixie was standing calmly in the trailer when we arrived and walked into the surgery reception area without assistance. But she was ice cold and shaking everywhere. I knew then she was a goner.

After an ultrasound examination, the surgeon was so certain For Dixie had ruptured internally that he offered immediate euthanasia, which would save the $3,000 expense of exploratory surgery. But there was no way to be positive that she could not survive. A few months earlier, facing the same choice with the long-retired and then valueless Damascus daughter, we had spent the money. Due to chronic age-related reproduction problems, For Dixie had not been bred back for 2009, and Michelle LeBlanc, Rood's world-renowned equine reproduction expert, believed her unlikely to ever carry another foal full-term.

But the horse was the pride of the farm, a truly dominant female so intimidating she went unchallenged throughout her lifetime, even by the stubbornly aggressive Regal Band. That every effort should be made to save her life was never in question. For Dixie died on the operating table not from colic but from endotoxemia caused by a tiny leak in a worn-out stomach membrane, which explained the suddenness of her decline.

LeBlanc, who was out of the country at the time, had once called For Dixie her "favorite" and the "classiest mare" she'd ever treated. And the mare had always been the favorite of LeBlanc's pal, the Two Bucks diagnostician and dietary expert who had witnessed the horrible scene in the training barn and had stayed behind to watch over the newly orphaned foal. Somebody else might tell these two women he had authorized euthanasia without knowing the precise cause of death in order to save $3,000, but not me. I'd rather have passed another kidney stone—which I did the following day.

As it turned out, my death had only been wishful thinking

on my part. Gastroenterologists, urologists, and my home-based personal diagnostician all agreed that bankruptcy was still alive for me as an option because so was I.

It took some convincing. Five days without food and normal bodily functions had left me a mere shadow of my former self. The only thing weaker than my body and my mind was my cash flow.

9

THE RIGHTEOUS BROTHERS

In the Sport of Kings the only thing as constant over the years as the Dinnies is the stream of rich men eager to sit beside them. They come as regular as the sales, from the worlds of investment banking, digital innovation, pyramid schemes, automotive sales, inheritance, and lottery luck. Austrian auto parts magnates, Canadian pharmaceutical tycoons, Egyptian merchants, and high-rolling predatory lenders—many of them not knowing which end of a horse to feed and which end to clean up after.

Anxiously awaiting to explain the difference is a legion of middlemen (and -women) flashing the look and business cards of experts who make their living off such naïveté, marking up the bloodstock as it passes from hands they know well into those they have just shaken for the first time. Though unlicensed by any authority, these horse brokers represent themselves as "agents," and indeed they are. But agents of what?

Many bloodstock agents are among the most knowledgeable horsemen anywhere, others as ignorant of horses as the newcomers themselves, their credentials as phony as their costumes.

Some are lifelong horsemen who make safe, competent guides into a complex world of lovely animals and interesting people. Others are merely predators. The livestock they transfer is often as fraudulent as their own smiling demeanor and the exotic paper instruments of Wall Street wizards. Recognizing the difference demands the primary prerequisite for success in the horse business: luck.

Even the shrewdest and most competent business moguls, fresh from clever endeavors and ingenious schemes that made them rich, are easy marks. Partly because nobody can outsmart them, right? But mostly because the horses themselves are like the fragrant lilies fronting the corpse in the funeral home, their natural aura an aroma of sweet opium that overwhelms the natural stench of greed and struggle that roils in the underbelly of exciting commerce.

At first blush, everything passes the "smell test" of the supremely confident. Anxious "stargazers" envision themselves in the winners' circles, holding their lovely treasures prancing high-headed on the other end of the lead shanks, a Dinny waiting to hand them a gleaming trophy.

It is behind the backs of the starry-eyed that easy money changes hands most facilely. Many of the fleeced never admit it. They become disenchanted and depart quietly, their wallets a lighter load. Others, lessons learned, recover and persist, their passion for the game overcoming their humiliation.

In an understatement untypical of lawyers, the opening sentence of a recent *Brooklyn Law Review* examination of thoroughbred horse auction ethics warned, "In today's thoroughbred racing world, sometimes what you see is not at all what you get."

Perhaps never in the history of the game was this ever more true than with the two most prominent new auction-goers in recent years: Satish Sanan, the Indian computer whiz whose software helped the world avoid the fearsome "millennium bug," and Jess Jackson, the California billionaire winery magnate. As early victims, what they saw was not at all what they got. But then, to the chagrin of their victimizers, they were not all what they appeared to be either.

No one ever exhibited more vulnerability to vultures than Satish Sanan. In the movies, he would be the unwitting Easterner who wanders into the saloon wearing a stuffed money belt in full view of the outlaw bullies. Pat Forde, an ESPN sportswriter chronicling Sanan's first horse auction experience, likened him to a Pentagon bureaucrat negotiating a defense contract: "One thousand dollars for a wrench? Great, I'll take six."

In the interest of taste and possibly in observance of FCC obscenity regulations, ESPN described him as so much a fall guy he might as well have had PIGEON stamped across his forehead. To insiders, Forde was obviously cleaning up a widely quoted comment allegedly made by one of several infamous horse evaluators that Sanan ultimately employed: "When I first met Sanan," the trainer said, "he had FUCK ME written on his forehead, so I did." Apocryphal maybe, but undoubtedly a greater truth.

Short, untaut, and looking every bit the quintessential computer geek, Sanan landed on the thoroughbred table like a feast. Small-time hustlers eyed him from afar, awaiting a chance to approach like hungry dogs hoping for any crumbs that might fall. There was no chance. The wolves already had him surrounded, ready to feed and then leave the fresh kill for others.

At his first sale, the July sale at Keeneland in 1997, Sanan dropped a couple million bucks, buying three or four horses. Then he came back in September, now with the supertrainer D. Wayne Lukas in his entourage, and spent $14 million, including $2.5 million for a Mr. Prospector colt that ended up winning only one race.

"By this time we were hooked," Sanan told ESPN. "We were back at every sale."

By his own tabulation, over the next ten years Sanan blew $150 million on thoroughbred horses with only a couple of slow Kentucky Derby starters to show for it. Both finished up the track, as he watched inexpensive colts like Bob Baffert's $17,000 Real Quiet take the roses.

The one memorable time that Sanan got outbid on a horse he badly wanted was in 1998 when he let the Japanese business-man Fusao Sekiguchi buy the eventual 2000 Kentucky Derby winner Fusaichi Pegasus for $4 million. But by 2001, when Sanan had settled into his new seven-hundred-acre training facility in Florida, named Padua, he had figured out that he had not squandered all that money unassisted.

In April 2004, the *Blood-Horse*, the industry-subsidized magazine controlled by the Dinnies, took a rare veer off the straight and narrow, finally suggesting in print what every experienced horseman already knew: that the sales companies were turning a blind eye to behind-the-scenes "deals" at thoroughbred sales, including some of the huge headline makers.

In a column titled "Buyer Beware," Ray Paulick did not use names or give specifics. The conspiracy of secrecy pervasive in the industry culture and the lack of transparency surrounding indi-vidual transactions prevent the kind of documentation necessary to defend against libel. Yet even without specifics Paulick was waving a red flag at bulls. Unhappy sales company executives, among the magazine's most important advertisers, descended on the editor in protest. But there was an uprising of support, too.

One of the calls of support was from Sanan, candidly acknowledging that he had gotten the short end in some of those "deals." Sanan followed it up with a supporting letter to the editor. And he didn't stop there. Paulick had suggested that "it's about time someone stood up on behalf of the industry's biggest investors, the owners." And someone did—Sanan, who turned out to be tougher than he looked.

Surprisingly, Sanan knew a lot more about the horse business than anyone suspected. Hooked on racing while a college student in England, he had been active in the European horse market during the mid-1980s before founding his software company in Florida at the end of the decade. There, he had been similarly unsuccessful, paying $1.5 million for a French Oaks champion filly that never won another race. But a guy who was once down to his last twenty-five dollars but worked his way through college and built a company worth $1.6 billion should not be underestimated. As Lukas once said of him, Sanan had "the balls of a gorilla." By this time Sanan had dispatched Lukas and replaced him as his primary trainer with Bob Baffert.

After being besieged by callers who had suffered similar indignities, Sanan announced the formation of the Alliance for Industry Reform in an open letter in the *Blood-Horse*, just in time for the fall yearling sale season. To the dismay of the sale companies that had been the major beneficiaries of his largesse, Sanan began rallying everyone else who'd had similar experiences. By year's end, the Thoroughbred Owners and Breeders Association, which had been in existence for nearly fifty years without once publicly addressing the problem of auction fraud, had launched the Sales Integrity Task Force, ostensibly to clean up the industry's act. Sanan was appointed, along with a few other known reformers, although its membership was carefully stacked as usual.

Once again the Dinnies had been prodded into action by a newcomer, and this time by a billionaire who had been shamed and ridiculed by saloon bullies before rising up and punching them in the face. And soon he would no longer be standing alone. Big old Jess Jackson, an ally with a stubborn streak longer than Sanan was tall, was ready to take up his cause.

The resident dominant female, who'd once made her living by evaluating and selling high-quality farms in the Barrington Hills horse country outside Chicago, was euphoric with the biggest news since the late 1990s, when Texans with a pyramid edifice telephone fortune began paying $20,000 an acre to assemble their sprawling WinStar Farm just a few miles from Two Bucks.

Now "some big wine guy from California" was trying to buy Woodford County all at once. Jess Jackson, the owner of Kendall-Jackson Winery, had just paid nearly $30,000 an acre for Frank Stronach's pristine Adena Springs Farm about six miles north and was looking for more.

"Are we ready to sell?" I asked.

"No, but we've probably peaked," she declared. "We'll [meaning our land] never go any higher in our lifetime."

"Or his either," I said. "He's nearly eighty."

That Jess Jackson's arrival in Kentucky had caused me to "probably peak" was the good news. The bad news was that on one of his farms, fabled Buckram Oak, which he had renamed Stonestreet, our new neighbor had installed an electronic security system so potent it blocked out the satellite signal of the county's main broadband provider, shutting down half the computers in Woodford County, including mine.

When Jess Jackson arrived in Kentucky, he bought horses by the herd, two hundred at least, valued at more than $75 million; and fenced real estate by the mile, more than 1,100 acres of already manicured, turnkey farms fronting the showcase avenues of the Bluegrass, for $32 million; and two more of Adena's satellite farms in Ocala, Florida, totaling 1,000 acres for $25 million.

And he had not come alone. A wealth of wild rumors had traveled with him, first that he was gay and that the younger men with him constituted a "harem" of sorts, and then that he was terminally ill and the men were doctors shepherding him on a final spending spree.

Once Jackson began striding manfully through the sales with a lovely, younger wife at his side and Kentucky got a closer look at the entourage, it turned out to be a bevy of California-based bloodstock agents familiar with the territory, trailed here and there by a local jackal or two disguised as real estate and bloodstock agents.

In the spring of 2005, shortly after Sanan started kicking sand back into the faces of the bullies, Tom Bachman, the general manager of Jackson's California operation, was contacted by John Silvertand, the breeder of Afleet Alex, the winner of the Preakness and the Belmont Stakes that year. Among the horses Jackson had purchased was Afleet Alex's dam, Maggy Hawk, for $750,000. Silvertand told Bachman that he had sold the mare to Jackson's celebrity bloodstock agent, Emmanuel de Seroux, the owner of Narvick International, for $600,000—not $750,000.

Jackson's response to being cheated was more direct than Sanan's had been. The computer whiz had simply written a new program for his operation. He terminated his initial horse business relationships, began evaluating his own purchases himself, and named his first acquisition Vindication—appropriately, it turned out, as the $2.1 million yearling colt went on to become the two-year-old champion.

But Jackson's training was as a lawyer. Before becoming a billionaire winemaker, he had worked as a police officer while in law school in Berkeley, then as an investigator, and eventually a lawyer in the California attorney general's office. He believed he knew a kickback when he saw one.

Jackson terminated his relationship with de Seroux and started backtracking the purchases of other horses in which Narvick and the California trainer Bruce Headley had been involved as middlemen. The investigation entailed trips to Chile and Argentina. Meanwhile, Jackson's attorney, Richard A. Getty, was dispatched to Europe on a similar mission to investigate the background of horses that had originated there. Getty said he traced some of their ownership through shell companies belonging to the Irish, and came back reporting how unwelcome they had made him feel.

Ultimately Jackson concluded that for thirty suspect horses he had paid at least $3.2 million more than the sellers said they had received. Among them was an $850,000 colt named Rhythm Mad for which the owner said he received only $675,000 and a number of other horses bought at public auction on the advice of Headley, whose eye for a horse and a good deal is equally respected among Kentucky horsemen. Headley once paid $160,000 for a horse raised at Two Bucks that a respected surgeon had said was worthless and should be euthanized. The horse went on to win over $200,000 out of Headley's barn.

In a response rare for unhappy horse buyers, Jackson filed suit in California Superior Court charging that de Seroux, Headley, and an associate named Brad Martin had defrauded him, accusing de Seroux of inflating the price of private acquisitions and Headley and Martin of conspiring to "artificially increase the level of bidding on horses."

The suit claimed that all three had "obtained secret commissions, payments, or profits or other things of value from consignors, sellers, or other secret agents in return for assuring that

Jackson would purchase their horses or interests in horses at inflated prices." In the same filing, Jackson accused the three men of conspiring with another agent to commit similar fraud, causing him to overpay in his $17.5 million purchase of Buckram Oaks Farm. The California court struck that section of the lawsuit for lack of jurisdiction, and it was refiled in federal court in Kentucky.

California had a law on the books prohibiting "double agency," which is precisely the process Jackson had described: a single agent collecting commissions from both sides simultaneously and surreptitiously. Kentucky had no such law, and none of the defendants were Kentucky residents. But by naming specific horses on which he believed he had been bilked, Jackson pointed fingers at a broad range of well-known figures in the thoroughbred establishment, including some big consignors.

In the horse business there was no way a drama such as this could take place without Texas getting involved. Before Jackson's suit could be heard, another character leaped onto the stage, the prominent Houston racehorse owner James McIngvale, the founder of Gallery Furniture.

Known in his television commercials as "Mattress Mac," McIngvale filed a federal lawsuit in Galveston accusing Bob Baffert and two sidekicks, Floridians J. B. and Kevin McKathan, of fleecing him in identical fashion on a $950,000 colt he had purchased from Murray Smith, the Florida pinhooker who had bought Monarchos from Two Bucks back in 1999.

The filing included a canceled check for $95,000 that Smith wrote to a company affiliated with the McKathans, who pick out horses for Baffert. The trainer quickly threw the McKathans under the bus. "I just trained the horses," Baffert said. "J.B. was in charge of the sales."

Jackson and McIngvale eventually got what they wanted:

their money back. In a settlement, Jackson recovered $3.5 million from de Seroux, $900,000 from Headley, and $250,000 from Martin. McIngvale got money back, too, but the amount was "confidential." Accompanying the Jackson settlement was a statement accusing the wine billionaire of a "well-funded effort to destroy Emmanuel de Seroux" and labeling the settlement a "ransom." However, it also said, "There is no admission of any fault or wrongdoing by either party. There is a negotiated peace."

The big wind heard at that moment was the sigh of relief by the thoroughbred establishment, having been spared the airing of a load of dirty laundry that might have embarrassed many witnesses not named as defendants. The only deposition ever made public—that of former Kentucky governor Brereton Jones, the owner of Airdrie Stud—made it patently clear what was at stake.

Among the horses on which Jackson claimed to have been bilked was a weanling filly sired by the Airdrie stallion Deputy Commander and bought from an Airdrie consignment by Narvick International in the 2004 Keeneland November sale for $170,000. Another was a yearling filly by another Airdrie stallion, Yankee Victor, which Jones sold to Headley for $270,000.

In deposing the former governor, Jackson's lawyer asked him about two specific checks made out to Headley, one for $17,000 and a second for $86,687.50, and their relationship to a line item on an Airdrie accounting sheet denoting a $27,000 "consulting fee" to Headley on the Yankee Victor yearling. Jones said the $86,687.50 check would have also included "consultant" fees paid to Headley "on a number of things" including the $650,000 sale of another filly to a prominent California buyer, the late Bob Lewis, a transaction signed for by their agent, D. Wayne Lukas.

Why was Headley being paid a "consulting fee" on a horse

bought by Lukas? Jones said it was part of the trainer's compensation for "identifying horses" that might be of interest to other trainers. Due to the settlement, Headley never had to answer such highly personal questions as how much of Jones's commission payment was actually reported as Headley's taxable income. Yet another court document in the California case included a copy of a check clearly suggesting how commission systems work.

One of the horses on Jackson's alleged fraud list was a Brahms filly bought for him by de Seroux in the same Keeneland sale for $450,000. She was purchased from Eaton Sales, one of the industry's largest consignors, a company co-owned by a prominent industry leader named Tom VanMeter. A copy of the receipt portion of the check—from the account of VanMeter's farm—indicates it was a $22,500 commission for the Brahms filly, and an accompanying handwritten note reads, "Narvick 7,500, Martin 7,500, Headley 7,500."

Jones's public defense of his dealings, in which he readily acknowledged making the payments, provides the remainder of insight needed to understand how the game has worked all these years and why nobody ever did anything about it.

"That is the beauty of the free enterprise system, that you have the right to reward people who do business with you," Jones told the *Lexington Herald-Leader*. "I have done it on a few occasions. Quite frankly, I will continue to do it."

Virtually all the transactions alleged in the lawsuits could be verified by checks, for the simple reason that the commissions being paid would end up as "cost of sales" deductions on income tax returns. Because they were not illegal, no one involved believed the practices anything other than routine business. Everybody seems to remember that back in the 1980s when Nelson Bunker Hunt and Warner Jones were the leading consignors at Keeneland sales, each made it a practice to send "thanks" in the form of commission checks to everybody who bought a horse from them. But nobody seems to recall at what point consignors starting sending checks to people who had bid against the winning bidder with no intention of buying the horse. One former employee of a major consignor told me one of his jobs after a sale was to deliver checks to a list of people who routinely bid up specific horses in their consignment.

There is one aspect of all this on which there is no dispute. Not one of the Dinnies or their hand puppets had greeted Satish Sanan and Jess Jackson when they walked through the door of the sale arena and warned them what they might be getting into—that the very agent at their side might be one of those known for prearranging sales, recruiting buddies to bid horses up to whatever limits his client was willing to spend, and that even some big-name sellers routinely kicked back the excess for distribution to conspirators who routinely target naive new-comers.

It took two bold rich guys willing to swallow their pride, stand up, and yell publicly what a thoughtful Samaritan confided to me the day I took a seat on the Kentucky Racing Commission in 1993. "Never forget," he said, "that we are only as honest as our business allows."

It is all becoming clear to me now. In trying to raise racehorses for a living, I am merely a bit player in a Shakespearean tragic comedy, having been just so enlightened by the woman next to me before she dozed off. Her understanding of the Bard's work being second only to her knowledge of biochemistry and diet appropriate for husbands suffering kidney stones, I think she might be on to something.

Indian Charlie is just the *anomalous* character in the drama, she explained, forcing me—an English major and former newspaper editor—once again to get out the *Webster's* and look up the word. No, it is not synonymous with *harmless moron* as I suspected, but instead means "unusual" or "irregular"—which certainly fits. When applied to Shakespearean theater, it refers to a character difficult to figure out, which might not be so hard in Charlie's case.

Whatever Indian Charlie's role, he obviously dislikes the troublemaking Jess Jackson even more than he does me. Jackson has been excoriated regularly in the sheet, always referred to as "the white Jesse Jackson" as opposed to "the black Jesse Jackson," who once tried to get himself hired as head of the jockey's union.

The "white Jesse" was always depicted in the cartoons with a bottle of spirits—marked WHINE—protruding from his pocket. Indian Charlie ridiculed him for forming his Horseowners' Protective Association (HOPA), into which Sanan had folded his Alliance for Industry Reform. Together the two pressed their case all the way to the Kentucky General Assembly, where they lobbied through a bill prohibiting "dual agency" modeled on the law in California. Indian Charlie scalped them at every turn along the way.

The *Wall Street Journal* provided insight into the root of such unflattering characterizations in its report of Jackson's lawsuit settlement with Emmanuel de Seroux. The bloodstock agent's wife told the newspaper that Jackson is seen as "a pariah" in horse circles. "Pretty much everyone in Kentucky hates him," she said, obviously oblivious to the way pretty much everybody in Kentucky feels about her and her husband and the way at least some people feel about bloodstock agents ripping off new owners.

But Ray Paulick, who should know, told the *Washington Post* that de Seroux was right. While Jackson's penchant for rubbing "almost everybody the wrong way" was part of the problem, Paulick said, his open challenge of the system had set the old guard against him. "There are people who say, 'if Jess Jackson is for this, then I'm against it,' " he observed.

The industry's official response, first to Sanan's call for reform and later to Jackson's successful effort to pass the Kentucky law against dual agency that took effect in 2006, was to appoint its own broader-based Sales Integrity Task Force under the auspices of TOBA and to direct it to work with Kentucky lawmakers in hopes of preempting more interference.

By then the task force had evolved into an industry-wide giant that included both Jackson and Sanan among its members as well as Robert Clay, the owner of Three Chimneys Farm, and the bloodstock agent Reynolds Bell, both of whom were Jockey Club members with aboveboard reputations for ethics—the same tactic used to neutralize previous reform efforts.

The reliable D. G. Van Clief, Jockey Club member, chairman of Fasig-Tipton Sales, and an old hand experienced with mastering task forces and committees, was named the task force's chairman. And Keeneland's influential lawyer, the late William T. (Buddy) Bishop, authored a dense legal critique for *Bench and Bar* contending that Jackson's dual agency law was both unnecessary and harmful.

Predictably, when the Sales Integrity Task Force reported its recommendations at a public meeting at Keeneland in October 2007, serious reformers were disappointed. In its assessment of the final Code of Ethics proposed by the task force, the *Brooklyn Law Review* concluded (in an article titled "Cart Before the Horse") that the code lacked the one element necessary to be effective: teeth.

The task force recommended that the sale companies be compelled to include as a new condition of sale their compliance with Jackson's new state law, which made it a crime for an agent to represent both seller and buyer without the written consent of both. But virtually no other recommendation carried with it any meaningful punishment to compel compliance.

For example, a vital element in many scams is the lack of transparency of ownership. Horses are almost always sold in the name of the Jockey Club registration papers turned in weeks before the actual auction day. But horses were often sold in the interim on handshakes or contracts with no change on the papers, instead with the specific and secret condition that the ownership on the papers not be changed before sale time. The task force dealt with this problem by establishing a "voluntary" ownership registry that can be accessed only by a buyer interested in a specific animal, a provision absolutely valueless because there is no requirement or penalty for secret ownership.

Asked publicly why anyone would want to keep their ownership secret, Van Clief's explanations were offered seriously but received by many as comical: (1) people involved in divorces might not want their spouses to know that racehorses were among their assets; (2) people might not want business associates or coworkers to know they have such an expensive hobby; (3) public knowledge of horse-racing involvement might embarrass those whose churches disapproved of gambling.

Oh, okay, and maybe identifying the owner might violate the privacy of the horse or shame him among his friends.

For all the talk about drug-free sales and races, the best the task force could come up with was to recommend that "horses not be sold under the influence" of anabolic steroids, that none be given within forty-five days of sale, and that sellers be warned that if a buyer requests a test, the presence of exogenous anabolic steroids "may result" in its return.

This forty-five-day abstinence rule quickly became the industry's answer to the steroid problem, something for the organizations to brag about. Naturally, it sent some prominent sale consignors off in frantic search of medical and chemical advice on the last possible moment a yearling or a two-year-old in training can be given a steroid that will not be detected. Detection, not the impact on the animal, became the focus. Of course, steroids can often be detected sixty days later, or in the case of some steroids for months. And their effect can last a lifetime. In other words, it is okay to go ahead and raise and train your horse on steroids, just don't administer any too close to a sale or a race, or you might get caught if our testing procedures are good enough.

The task force did recommend adding to the list of "prohibited practices" injecting the horse behind the knee to conceal its true conformation, but it did not deal with human drugs such as Valium and Dantrium that are commonly injected to disguise a horse's temperament or movement.

Although a step in the right direction, the *Brooklyn Law Review* concluded, the task force's Code of Ethics amounted to "little more than discretionary guidelines." Unlike a similar code undertaken by the British Jockey Club as a result of a bribery scandal in the United Kingdom, the Americans empowered no authority to identify and punish offenders. As the ultimate authority over racing in the United Kingdom, the British Jockey Club created a separate Horse Racing Authority with the means and power to catch and fine offenders and even ban them for life.

Sanan complimented the TOBA task force work as a reasonable step forward toward reform, and he appeared to have signed on to the industry proposals. After all, he reasoned, this apple is so big it must be eaten one bite at a time. Jackson applauded the efforts, too, but made it clear he was not satisfied.

A statement reshuffling HOPA's board of directors and outlining a new mission declared: "From the dialog of the Sales Integrity Task Force, it has become apparent that larger, national level solutions are needed to address some of the larger problems affecting the horse industry. A unified and cooperative national model for both the rules and production of the Thoroughbred racing product as well as sales and horse transactions is needed.

"Accordingly, HOPA will be specifically working towards the national standardization of medical regulation . . . In addition HOPA hopes to take a leading role in uniting race tracks with state thoroughbred organizations to form a united Thoroughbred racing league, implementing its marketing and lobbying efforts at the state and national level."

Jackson's defiant pursuit of government intervention sent two less strident pro-establishment reformers, Jockey Club member Robert Clay and Bill Castner, one of WinStar Farm's principal owners, scurrying off the HOPA board. Two inveterate disturbers of the peace—"Mattress Mac" McIngvale and Frank Stronach, the longtime Dinny tormentor from whom Jackson had bought farms and who owns eleven racetracks—immediately filled their abandoned spots.

This development landed Jackson, Castner, and Clay (whose Three Chimneys Farm stands at stud a stallion from Sanan's Padua training facility in Florida) in a series of Indian Charlie cartoons depicting them as a broken family in a custody fight with Clay as the baby.

Its caption read, "It looks Hopaless for the white Jesse Jackson . . . Bill Castner files for Divorce . . . But the question everyone is asking is Will the white Jesse Jackson sue to keep custody of Robert (Baby Head) Clay."

Whatever respect and gratitude might be due Jackson and Sanan for their public battle against corruption, their struggle with the old guard had already slipped from the stature of a Shakespearean morality play into an episode of *The Three Stooges*.

For all the bumps and bruises and money lost from trying to buy their way into the winner's circle, Sanan and Jackson remained so vulnerable to the smell of roses they were still willing to take the calls and trust the judgment of bloodstock agents.

On February 3, 2007, a $57,000 yearling with a suspect ankle, which hardly anybody but the trainer Kenny McPeek wanted to buy at the 2005 Keeneland September sale, made his racing debut. Now trained by McPeek's former assistant Helen Pitts and named Curlin after an African American slave who fought in the Civil War for the South, the colt won by twelve and three quarter lengths at Gulfstream Park in Florida.

As is normal after such an impressive beginning in the Triple Crown season, bloodstock agents smell the sap rising in wealthy Kentucky Derby aspirants and simultaneously the green aroma of a fat commission. The Kentucky bloodstock agent John Moynihan, whose ability to corral big spenders rivals that of even Emmanuel de Seroux, was lucky enough to reach Jackson, who then telephoned Sanan. Both men had seen the race.

Within hours Moynihan had put together a $3.5 million deal for an 80 percent ownership stake in Curlin, with the original owners, Midnight Cry Stables, keeping 20 percent. Jackson said later that at the time he had no idea who the principals in Midnight Cry Stables were. He does now.

When Curlin won the Preakness the following May, the first Grade 1 victory of many to come, Jackson found himself in the winner's circle with the most notorious of his new partners, the disbarred Lexington lawyers Shirley Cunningham and William Gallion. Along with a third lawyer, they had been charged with stealing $65 million from a $200 million damage settlement they won for four hundred clients who had taken the diet drug fen-phen.

The next morning, every newspaper in America showed the rascals of Midnight Cry trying to peek over Jackson's massive shoulders to get their faces in the win picture with the wine-maker and his wife.

No one was quicker on the draw to satirize the irony of the new Curlin ownership team than the "anomalous" character himself, Indian Charlie. His take on the two industry reformers and their scurrilous partners was a cartoon trio gathered around a microphone captioned "The Righteous Brothers and Fen-Phen Man." In an industry that loves nicknames and play-on-word monikers for horses, Jackson and Sanan will never be viewed as anything other.

Cunningham was already in trouble in Florida, where federal prosecutors claimed he had donated $1 million of the $21 million he'd paid himself out of the fen-phen money to Florida A&M University, which in turn was paying him back $100,000 a year for sitting in the chair he had endowed without doing anything to earn it. As the inquiring press soon learned, Curlin's namesake was Cunningham's great-grandfather, a western Kentucky slave who had fought for the Confederate army.

By August 2007, a Kentucky judge had termed Cunningham and Gallion "flight risks" and ordered them held without bond in the Boone County jail in northern Kentucky until they could be tried the following January.

Later in the fall, the travail of all concerned was alleviated—at least temporarily and financially—when Curlin, who had lost the Belmont Stakes by a head-bob, romped home in the mud at Monmouth to win the $5 million Breeders' Cup. A few days later a trial judge in the civil suit resulting from the fen-phen scam ruled that the 20 percent of Curlin owned by defendants Gallion and Cunningham should be turned over to the four hundred plaintiffs. (In April 2009, the two would be convicted of eight counts of wire fraud and one count of conspiracy to commit wire fraud.)

This was obviously enough vindication and too many owners for Sanan, who then sold out his 29 percent interest to Jackson and George Bolton, a third but less controversial and press-worthy partner who had been part of the original deal put together by Moynihan. Bolton bolted as well the following month, selling his 20 percent stake to Jackson.

In between owner changes, there was a return cameo appearance by the trainer Kenny McPeek, belatedly suing Midnight Cry Stables for payment of a 5 percent commission he claimed he was due when Curlin was sold to Jackson and Sanan.

Somewhere in most melodramas with as many unlikely victims, villains, perpetrators, corruption fighters, and anomalous characters as the story of Curlin, there lurks at least a quest for justice, if not the attainment. So far in this tale the righting of wrong has occurred in small bits and pieces, each veiled in conflict.

If there is one morsel to savor, it is the lack of television access in the Boone County jail. When Curlin won the Breeders' Cup Classic in 2007, it is said that while Jackson and Sanan were cavorting in the glory of victory and vindication, the incarcerated owners of Midnight Cry Stable, Cunningham and Gallion, were gathered around a single cell phone getting a secondhand race call from a kindhearted waitress who used to serve them drinks at the Thoroughbred Club in Lexington.

Sadly, the Curlin saga is as schizophrenic as his ownership—the Righteous Brothers and the Fen-Phen Man, vindicated victims and imprisoned victimizers. Each rich sweet irony comes with a bitter aftertaste: Curlin, the inexpensive, classically bred horse discounted by silly repository issues, becomes the richest racehorse in history. Then named for a black man who fought in defense of his own enslavement, he passes from rich owner to rich owner enriching each as he runs on strength and endurance perhaps chemically induced.

Whatever his place in the sport's history, Curlin was at his peak a four-legged, fire-breathing emblem of the sport's moral dilemma and the reckoning that was upon it.

10

THE SWEET POTATO DEFENSE

There was something unnerving about my lawyer reading a John Grisham novel on our way to a judicial proceeding. Did he really need remedial education to convince the Delaware Board of Stewards not to take away our $25,000 share of the purse and to clear Larry Jones of a hokey drug-positive violation that would ruin his pristine record as a trainer?

Finally I determined that he was reading *The Broker*. Maybe the guy was preparing for a second career helping bring down the economy, having just casually dropped the news that he's leaving his prestigious Lexington law firm—whose meter was now running at $250 an hour—and had not decided what to do next.

Sitting only a couple of rows away with his own meter running was our star witness, who wrote the book on the drug in question—the bronchodilator clenbuterol—and who—unless I had misheard his thick Irish brogue back at Blue Grass Airport—may have just recanted the testimony his e-mail said he would offer in our defense. Also on the tab and waiting in Wilmington to meet us for dinner were two Delaware lawyers—$350 and $300 an hour respectively—to fulfill state law requirements that a local law firm must be employed in order for my Kentucky lawyer to present our case before the stewards. Dinner for three lawyers, an expert witness, and two defendants, and guess in whose plate the check lands.

This could have been the beginning of another Grisham yarn headed for the silver screen. But it was just another day in the life of the "pygmy" horse breeder learning how to make $1 million in the horse business by squandering $5 million. That investment grew a few hundred more at dinner and again at breakfast when the star witness bypassed Hilton's perfectly adequate—and free—continental cereal and fruit buffet in favor of a sit-down eggs benedict version in the elegant dining room. This was obviously not the first rodeo for Dr. Thomas Tobin, veterinarian, pharmacologist, toxicologist, and resident guru at the University of Kentucky's Gluck Equine Research Center. He had been an expert witness before.

At least the dining room was quieter than an airline cabin, and to my relief came the realization that indeed I had misheard what Dr. Tobin was prepared to tell the stewards. M.A. is right about my hearing. My ears do mumble what others are saying clearly. No recant. The defense we had decided to present was on course.

Once our $1,500 test of the blood taken from Stones River the day he won his allowance race confirmed the presence of clenbuterol that had been picked up in Delaware's three-dollar urine test sample, there had been no choice but to argue that Larry Jones had not violated any rules when he gave Stones River the medication outside the seventy-two-hour withdrawal time frame regularly observed by all Delaware trainers, nor was his negligence responsible. Like most states, Delaware has a trainer responsibility rule that in the absence of "mitigating circumstances" holds a trainer responsible for any rule violation from his stable.

In our search for mitigating circumstances, our options had quickly narrowed to the only plausible one: that someone out to damage Larry Jones's reputation as an advocate of drug reform in horse racing and his perfect record of compliance had given Stones River an extra shot of clenbuterol closer to race time.

The other possibilities—that Jones had deliberately defied the rules for the first time in his life, or that Stones River somehow became the lone aberration in over 120 Jones-trained Delaware Park winners tested over the preceding two years (all on the same clenbuterol regimen)—made no more sense than the facetious explanations we'd seized upon to make us laugh rather than cry: that Stones River, an escape artist known for getting out of his stall, had gotten loose, found the jug, and sucked it dry on his own; or that his regular race-day dose of sweet potato wedges before going to the track had somehow caused the mysterious "spike" in trace levels that Dr. Tobin's research had confirmed occurs infrequently.

The stewards' proceeding took place at the Delaware Racing Commission's racetrack office, an enhanced doublewide in a room so small the court reporter could even understand Dr. Tobin, who sometimes delivers complicated scientific findings in heavily accented whispers.

Tobin's testimony was as impeccable as he is eminent in his field, having done most of the important research on clenbuterol in the late 1990s, when its suspected use became a problem on racetracks, including in some surprising Kentucky Derby outcomes. A valuable therapeutic remedy for respiratory congestion in humans and equines, the medication given as a regular regimen can have steroidal effects such as converting fat to muscle and raising metabolism.

Clenbuterol is not considered performance enhancing, Dr. Tobin told the stewards, in that it cannot make a horse run faster.

It can, however, remain in a horse's system so long that threshold levels higher than those found in Stones River are tolerable in many states. Any zero-tolerance rule, he testified, would disqualify a helpful drug valuable in keeping horses in training.

In a polite and academic way, he was telling them that their urine test for clenbuterol is worthless and that trainers should not be wrongly punished simply for trying to keep their horses healthy and filling race cards. Tobin said his research proved that once in a great while urine analysis will detect a spike in clenbuterol presence long after it should have cleared the horse. But the odds against Stones River being that rare horse were astronomical.

Our lawyer, Brent Caldwell, an old friend who had been attorney for the Kentucky Racing Commission during my six years as a member, then led Larry Jones through a recent history of obvious sabotage directed at his horses over the previous twelve months. These included the effort to fix a Delaware Park race in the fall of 2007 by placing a sponge in the nose of a filly known to be a heavy favorite. More recently two horses in Jones's care had been deliberately set free during the night, and one of them, his big yellow escort pony, was discovered to have had a blistering agent injected into his mouth. Whoever did that, Caldwell told the stewards, was certainly capable of slipping a syringe of clenbuterol into the mouth of Stones River while the security guard was making his rounds elsewhere.

My sole contribution was to point out that the Stones River incident had occurred only a few days before the House Commerce subcommittee hearings that would take the industry to task for lax drug policies and other horse safety issues in the wake of Eight Belles's death. I also reminded the stewards that prior to the hearing Jones and I had been among the most visible, vocal, and controversial proponents of reform.

The three stewards listened politely and asked questions that suggested they had been listening carefully. Then they took only three minutes to find no mitigating circumstances and slapped Jones with a five-hundred-dollar fine and a seven-day suspension. Realistically, this was no surprise. Though the Delaware trio was cordial, perhaps even sympathetic, most stewards' hearings resemble kangaroo courts with the outcome predetermined.

Five years ago in a case like ours—involving a first offender and a once-in-a-lifetime set of circumstances—stewards in most jurisdictions would have dismissed it as inconsequential, with a warning and no second thoughts, but no more. In recent years the mid-Atlantic region of racing had been embarrassed by dangerous blood-doping cases in New Jersey harness races, and a high percentage of suspected and proven drug violations on thoroughbred tracks had involved clenbuterol. In 2007 the legislatures in the region, particularly those of Pennsylvania and Delaware, reacted with stronger regulations and stepped-up enforcement. Shortly after the death of Eight Belles, the Delaware thoroughbred racing board, reflecting the new attitude, hammered the respected jockey Jeremy Rose with a six-month suspension for striking his mount on the head with his whip, in an incident many observers believed could easily have been an accident, as Rose claimed.

In the wake of that ruling and the nationwide public outcry over drug abuse and unsafe conditions at racetracks, the Delaware stewards, knowing Jones would automatically be granted an appeal, simply followed the strictest interpretation of the trainer responsibility rule. The Stones River case took the leap over justice from which kangaroo courts got their name and into the lap of political appointees on the racing board even less likely to take the heat.

Having been in their position, I realized how difficult board members would find it to overrule their stewards on a case involving one of the highest-profile and now controversial trainers in the business. Appeal or not, we had lost and so had the industry—again.

What clearly was either an aberrant result of routine therapeutic medication or at worst outright criminal sabotage would be recorded as cheating by a trainer who does not cheat and owners who not only don't condone it, but campaign publicly against it. The ruling validated the branding of us as hypocrites and Stones River as another soldier in Jack Van Berg's "chemical war."

We could have thrown in the towel that day, but Jones's suspension would have kicked in immediately. Still ahead in late October was the Breeders' Cup, to which at least two of his most important owners still had hopes of going. The Pennsylvania Derby, in which Stones River had been entered, was just a week off, on Labor Day. We decided to take the appeal before the Delaware Racing Commission, which would in effect postpone any penalty until the end of the Delaware Park race meet and allow Jones to delay serving any suspension until the opening of the 2009 Delaware racing season in the spring.

In the interim, the documentation of the testing methods of the original urine test, a simple form of an enzyme-linked immunosorbent assay (ELISA) performed by a small Delaware lab, was subpoenaed and turned over to Tobin for evaluation. His verdict was that the test, which uses rabbit antibodies to catalyze a biochemical reaction that marks detection of a specific protein that identifies clenbuterol, does the job for which it is intended. It signals the presence of a widely recognized therapeutic medication that might well have been administered twenty-eight days earlier to treat the kind of respiratory distress that accompanies life on a racetrack.

Not only does the subjective judgment of the lab technician become an important factor; even the varying nature of the rabbit's antibodies could result in a positive being marked one day and not the next. We argued that such vagaries deprived

Jones of equal justice under the law and resulted in his being punished for an amount of clenbuterol so small it would have been ignored in many other racing jurisdictions.

This all ultimately boiled down to whether Jones had made his first mistake after twenty-seven years of avoiding rules violations in at least 750 races in which his horses had been tested, or whether Stones River was the one horse in a thousand that might retain the drug in a tissue beyond normal intervals and expel it at precisely the time he had won a race.

After thirty years in the press and national politics, I found either explanation too much coincidence. But under the strict interpretation of the commission's trainer responsibility rule, to which it seemed wedded, our contention that someone could have deliberately and easily given Stones River an extra shot of the oral elixir without being detected could not be considered an "extenuating circumstance."

Despite our repeated entreaties that upholding the stewards' ruling would only benefit the cheaters and the opponents of drug reform, the commissioners ruled unanimously against us, while heaping praise on Jones and claiming that it would not reflect on our credibility as drug reformers.

Our appeal had put the commission in a tough spot, a consequence not necessarily unintended. State racing commissions are filled with political cronies of elected officials, very often lobbyists for one special interest or the other. Like the Delaware authority, which is buried in the state's Agriculture Department, these boards generally have inadequate funding for expensive tests that can establish tolerable threshold levels for therapeutic medications. Nor can they afford the security capabilities or investigative resources necessary to protect horses housed on the backside.

Even the clear evidence of repeated sabotage in Jones's barn, including an incident in which someone was able to free a two-year-old thoroughbred from its stall in the middle of the night, then find and release his stable pony, Pal, in a barn nearby, could not move the commissioners toward common sense. Instead they only compounded an injustice already done. One of them even told us what we already suspected: that had we produced the saboteur, it would not have relieved Jones of his responsibility under their rule.

But in a half dozen other important racing jurisdictions that have established thresholds for therapeutic medications, the level of clenbuterol detected by our expensive split sample test of Stones River's blood would never have triggered a positive in the first place.

Back in July in the same week that Jones was notified of Stones River's positive, Rick Dutrow, the trainer of Big Brown, was nailed in Kentucky for a similar offense. One of the horses he had raced in Kentucky during Derby week had tested positive for a level of clenbuterol above the legal limits allowed in Kentucky.

Two weeks before Jones's appeal hearing in Delaware, Dutrow's appeal was heard in Kentucky by a former colleague of mine on the Kentucky Racing Commission, now sitting as a special hearing officer. He threw the case out because one sample was tested in plasma, and the other in serum, and he had no hard evidence that allowed him to compare the two and confirm a level higher than allowed.

Virtually every testing lab has its own method of finding and measuring drug levels. Some are competent. Some are not. Almost none operate the same way. So the mishmash of disparate rules and regulations lets the repeat offender off on a technicality—at least temporarily while Kentucky tried to figure out what to do next—and in Delaware the poster boy for clean living gets it in the neck.

By filling Delaware Park's race cards daily with by far the highest-quality string of horses on the grounds and setting a sterling example of rule compliance for twenty-seven years, one of racing's best people is rewarded with cheap punishment and expensive embarrassment.

The entire episode was such a farce I rechecked to see if the King of the Fairies and his mischievous servant Puck were on the agenda that day, too. They were, of course. Us.

As predicted by the sage scientist of Two Bucks in her Shakespearean vernacular, Larry Jones and I had indeed been "hoist by our own petard," a phrase more clearly understood after translated into our native hillbilly: "blown up by a bomb of our own gases." It was more painful for some of us than others. Our $25,000 purse loss was doubled by an equal amount of attorneys' fees for Two Bucks Stable—ultimately a $50,000 debit for the business.

Costs such as these discourage contesting even unfair or erroneous test results. Racing commissions everywhere face the same obstacle in prosecuting them. It cost the Kentucky Racing Authority $125,000 to pursue charges against the Frenchman Patrick Biancone after cobra venom was found in his barn at Keeneland. Neither the owners nor the regulators can afford it.

When all was said and done, we should have stuck with the sweet potato defense.

At Two Bucks when there is no sale revenue, filling the void falls to our tiny fledgling racing stable, which anyone who knows anything about racehorses will tell you is a sign of complete desperation.

But hope springs eternal in the community of optimists and fools, ours riding on the fleet feet of the now clenbuterol-free Stones River. Having already earned more than $150,000 for the year, he was entered in the $1-million Pennsylvania Derby where a lot of smart handicappers liked his chances.

The size of the purse, however, had attracted some of the best three-year-olds in the country, including former Kentucky Derby contenders Anak Nakal and Smooth Air, who had later won the Ohio Derby, and the West Virginia Derby winner Ready Set, a $700,000 colt owned by Roy and Gretchen Jackson and trained by Michael Matz, the "connections" of Barbaro, the ill-fated Derby winner from 2006.

Also among the entries was a Dogwood Stable horse named Atoned, a hard-knocking competitor with a penchant for finishing second, partially owned by our New Jersey friends Carl and Cathleen Myers.

For years we had rooted side by side with them for the Two Bucks–bred filly Cotton Blossom, the Dogwood runner that upon retirement the preceding November had sold for $1.9 million as a broodmare prospect. Carl Myers had been in on her half brother Vicarage, another graded stakes winner for Dogwood, so he had already made enough money off Two Bucks horses. Now it was our turn.

If all the people who come to racetracks in America were treated like the owners of stakes horses at Philadelphia Park, one of the many tracks owned and operated by the casino company Penn National Gaming, racing might not have such a shortage of fans. The "connections" of the Derby entrants were hosted on Labor Day afternoon in the manner of high-stakes gamblers in Las Vegas—a superb lunch comped in a luxurious restaurant overlooking the track, box seats at the finish line, and classy souvenir VIP credentials in your own stable colors—all delivered by lovely smiling women.

On the strength of his Ohio Derby win and a second-place finish in the Florida Derby, the speedy Smooth Air was made the favorite at 7 to 2, followed at 4 to 1 by Tiz Now Tiz Then, who had run second in the Jim Dandy Stakes at Saratoga only a month before, and the Jacksons' horse Ready Set at 5 to 1.

The morning line had Stones River at 8 to 1, but by race time his odds had dropped to 6 to 1. The new odds reflected his having been picked to win by a *Daily Racing Form* scribe and as a long-shot victor by a couple of local handicappers.

The track oddsmaker had set the Myerses' hard-luck colt Atoned at 15 to 1, but bettors had dropped him to nearly 30 to 1 by race time, which both his owners and I knew to be a joke. In the end, the rascal cost Stones River the race and Two Bucks a great deal of money.

Both horses are "closers"—horses that run faster at the end of the race than at any other time. They were running side by side, ninth and tenth in the thirteen-horse field, when Stones River made his first move on the turn toward home. But Atoned's jockey Jose Lezcano got the jump on Stones River's rider, the embattled youngster Gabriel Saez, and got out of the pack first.

Saez had to pull up momentarily, losing momentum and falling a length behind. He quickly made it up, but Stones River was forced another lane wide. When Saez tried to pass, Lezcano came out again, forcing him ever wider. Meanwhile, the leaders and Anak Nakal, closing down a wide-open center of the track, were sailing unimpeded to the finish line. Stones River went by Atoned just short of the wire to pick up a $62,000 payday for fourth. Take that, Carl Myers.

The week before, on the day the Delaware Board of Stewards ruled against us in the clenbuterol case, Larry Jones and I made what we considered a shrewd decision. We decided to enter Stones River in the $750,000 Jockey Club Gold Cup, a Grade 1 stakes for horses three years old and older—an invitation-only event coming up at Belmont Park in New York on September 27.

The presence in the field of Curlin, the 2007 Horse of the Year, would drive so many natural competitors away that Stones

River, on the basis of his Pennsylvania Derby performance, would surely be invited. Why not enter? Curlin might well be unbeatable by a three-year-old, but Stones River looked competitive with the rest of the field. A third-place finish would earn him another $75,000.

One of his owners, my old friend Frank Woods from Nashville, who had been disappointed that Stones River hadn't made the Triple Crown races, was ecstatic. "I won't sleep a wink from now until the Jockey Club thinking about it," he said when we were invited, the race still a week away.

The entry of Stones River in the second-oldest stakes race in America capped an extraordinary weekend for pygmy Two Bucks. His half sister Unbridled Belle, who had won the Grade 1 Beldame race on the same card in 2007 en route to her $1.3 million in winnings, was back in the race again to defend her title against her main rival among older mares, the 2007 champion Ginger Punch. On the same day a Two Bucks–bred two-year-old filly named Complicity was running in the Kentucky Cup Juvenile Filly stakes, and the following day Hyperbaric, a five-year-old grass horse from a Two Bucks mare, was in the Grade 2 Oak Tree Mile at Santa Anita in California.

Our anticipation level soared even higher when the day before the Gold Cup a two-inch downpour forced cancellation of racing at Belmont Park and left the surface a sloppy mess. Stones River had won three of his four races, including the Nick Shuk Stakes at Delaware Park, on wet tracks. "Bring on Curlin," Woods yelled, not being a bit careful what he wished for. Curlin could beat you on stones.

Upon our arrival at Belmont Park, we learned that Team Valor, the owners of Unbridled Belle, who never performed well in the slop, had disappointingly scratched her out of the Beldame in favor of a Grade 1 race during the opening week at

Keeneland in early October, ruining our chances of a sibling double G1 extravaganza. You never get too old to dream.

If the Dinnies have a place they can call their own, it is the trustees room at Belmont Park. On Belmont Stakes Day in June and when the Breeders' Cup races are scheduled there, as they are regularly, you need direct lineage validation back to old August Belmont himself just to be considered for a chair at one of its few tables. Limited seating would be an understatement.

Yet here we were, in late September, two-thirds of the ownership of the blue-collared Stones River and our luncheon guest, Atoned's owner Carl Myers, no doubt secretly atoning for the foul deeds of his horse by rooting for ours. Our other partner Frank Woods and wife, Jayne Ann, were watching the race on simulcast at Kentucky Downs near the Tennessee border along with about forty of their closest friends.

From where we sat in the corner of the trustees room, only a slight turn of the head was necessary to take in a view of all three known Dinnies—the original "Dinny," Ogden Mills Phipps, along with Will Farish and G. Watts Humphrey—and who knows how many other Dinny suspects, their proximity a perk for being invited to be one of Curlin's victims as he sought immortality as the richest racehorse ever.

I do not know Ogden Mills Phipps. Humphrey I had known as a quiet fellow hunter in the Kentucky dove fields and in the saddling paddocks as the owner of very good horses in the big stakes races. Will Farish had been cordial to me from the day I first showed up at a Kentucky thoroughbred sale.

Farish's Lane's End Farm had consigned my yearlings, and over the years Two Bucks mares had been bred to Lane's End stallions, including a foal share with A.P. Indy, which made us cobreeders of a half sister to Monarchos aptly named Miss Blue Blood.

My best mare, For Dixie, the dam of Cotton Blossom, had been booked to the court of another of Farish's world-class sires, Kingmambo, back when he cost only $42,500. Now standing to an exclusive book of top mares at $300,000 or more, Kingmambo had sired Mambo in Seattle, the only other three-year-old in the country besides Stones River willing to take on Curlin.

When we ran into each other that day at Belmont Park, Farish greeted me like I had forked over that $300,000. We discussed the pros and cons of our rooting interests being stuck next to each other on the far outside of the gate and the unlikely prospects of either of them catching Curlin if he got out front in the mud.

So pleasant had been our conversations and so satisfactory our business dealing, the fact that so many people held him responsible for so much was puzzling. Maybe he did personally kill the July Keeneland sale and maybe he was the instigator of the repository and cooks up backroom "deals" with the Irish, but you can't prove it by me. There, in his presence in the trustees room at Belmont Park, he made me feel like a Dinny myself.

That feeling was soon dissipated by the attention deficit of the wait staff, who knew damn well who was a Dinny and who was not. Finding standing and waving to no avail, my guest Carl Myers finally had to purloin his napkin and silverware from a table when they were not looking, which was always. He got no sympathy from me, however, only an expression of sorrow that Atoned was not in the race so Stones River could pass him again.

In the soggy saddling paddock, even the Dinnies got mud on their shoes. Stones River looked awesome, second only to the more awesome Curlin. Waiting to mount, our jockey Gabriel Saez was informed that no jockey from the eight preceding races had come to the winner's circle in muddy silks, which meant he needed to stay clear of the back spray for slop from the leaders.

The only favorite defeated that day, Ginger Punch, had obviously tired trying to run her usual race on the rail, which appeared much deeper than the middle of the track, where Stones River had finished in every previous race.

Inside the mind of a twenty-year-old racehorse jockey is no place to be, or for that matter inside that of the bowlegged fifty-plus trainer he's been talking to on his cell phone, or even worse inside that of the sixty-five-year-old headless horseman babbling in the saddling paddock about track conditions.

The minds of all three were as muddy as the Belmont track that day, or they would have been doing some other kind of work. Maybe shaking hands in the paddock with Carl Myers reminded Saez of how Atoned had twice pushed him too wide to win a $1 million race four weeks earlier in Pennsylvania. Or maybe the young man just reacted to the headless horseman's suggestions the same way the owner's wife and children do and took the opposite course. Or his mount could have decided to run where he damn well wanted to. For whatever reason, Stones River ran most of his race on the rail.

When he finally did move out to the outside down the stretch, he did it with his head low and nostrils stretched to their limits, directly into the back spray of the second-place finisher, Arthur Hancock's seven-year-old Wandering Boy, inhaling enough slop to shut off his wind and impair his larynx. He managed only sixth place this time, well behind Curlin, who added to his legend with a three-quarter-length victory to become the richest racehorse in history with more than $10 million in earnings.

Saez, meanwhile, had swallowed so much mud himself that he could not talk, and Stones River came down with the "thumps," a siege of heavy breathing caused by nerve and muscle malfunctions due to the blockage of his wind passage. And the headless horseman of Two Bucks went home once again with disappointed racing partners and more expense than revenue.

Indian Charlie mysteriously ridiculed me in his cartoons again, too, on consecutive days to start the September Keeneland sale, flatteringly but falsely accusing me of hanging out with prominent black people: Barack Obama, Jesse Jackson, Al Sharpton, and Oprah Winfrey. Why I don't know, because of my wife's politics maybe. Since August 2007 she had been wearing a Barack Obama bracelet and flaunting it in front of Republicans.

Maybe the Dinnies do pull his chain like some people think. But Indian Charlie doesn't look like a Republican to me. He smiles too much. It could have something to do with Chicago. My wife, Obama, and Oprah are all from there.

This time, my natural instinct to punch him in the face was replaced by another act of violence of which I also had intimate knowledge: the letter to the editor.

"Dear Indian," I wrote, "I have been looking for you at the sales to thank you for featuring me in your sheet with my old friends. I am sure you are only trying to help me sell Two Bucks yearlings to the new target market segment of black American Community Organizers that Keeneland has assured me will show up by Book Eight, Week Sixteen of the sale where all my yearlings have been catalogued.

"If you see them before I do, please tell them my yearlings sell with a free jug of clenbuterol."

Of course, he did not print it, out of fear either that my satire was better than his or that Keeneland would not like the implied criticism. Not only did my fictitious new market not show up; no market showed up at all for any seller in the last third of the sale where three Two Bucks yearlings were cataloged.

Four had originally been entered, each needing a five-hundred-dollar set of radiographs, now fifty dollars more expensive than in the past due to the new digital X-ray machines that are more precise and therefore more likely to find disqualifying issues. The veterinarian manning this modern tool was a good judge of horseflesh, who immediately singled out a chestnut filly in the foursome. "Boy, that's the one I'd buy," he said.

Naturally, of the 128 superb-quality images of the joints on the sixteen legs radiographed that morning, the only one exposing a "Goddam OCD" was in a critical spot on the hock of the only one he'd buy. She had to be withdrawn from the sale and became the only one that would have to undergo surgery at his clinic.

The other three were perfect specimens, all cataloged at the end of the sale where cheap horses are bunched. Two of the three garnered a single bid of $2,000, failing to meet their modest $20,000 reserves, and the third, a crackerjack colt, was withdrawn before he could be embarrassed, too. The tab on this fiasco: $2,000 in worthless radiographs that no one ever saw but the veterinarian and myself; $7,600 in sale costs for Keeneland and my consignor showing my horses to no one; and a $1,500 bill for surgical removal of an OCD in the medial condyle of a lovely filly who has never taken a lame step in her life.

A few days after the sale ended—mercifully—a routine pregnancy check of the eight Two Bucks mares bred for next year thumped us again. Uncharacteristically, three mares whose pregnancies had previously checked healthy had reabsorbed their embryos. For the first time ever, we would be feeding more barren than pregnant broodmares over the winter.

Convinced that things could get no worse, I went to Wyoming for two days of mountain riding in the Teton wilderness on a twenty-four-year-old paint horse named Sam, a trip that had been planned for a year.

The wisdom of my going, particularly the timing, was subjected to scrutiny by the more rational thinker at Two Bucks, who sees the bigger picture. After checking airline flights, she said, "The planes are all full coming back. It looks like everybody else is coming home from vacation at Jackson Hole when you are going."

"Why is that?" I asked, ignoring the implied criticism soon to be verbalized.

"The world economy is crashing—that's all."

"What can I do about that?" I asked. "I can't even stop my own economy from crashing."

Her look said there was no disputing that.

If truth be told, my trip was an elk hunt that became the longest trail ride since Lewis and Clark—fourteen hours in the saddle without seeing a single elk in the mile-high meadows where there are usually thousands.

"I believe the elk are dead," said forlorn Carl the guide. "They must all be dead."

"No," I said. "It's just the Bush economy."

11

COLLAPSE

Horse racing should have known another self-mortification was near when Wall Street came calling again.

It had happened before during the 1980s when the auction sales mania reached the executive suites of Merrill Lynch and Prudential Securities. The idea of a single breeding to Seattle Slew being worth $710,000 was all it took. Leslie Combs's public offering of 650 shares in Spendthrift Farm raised $160 million on paper, and one Merrill Lynch broker alone sold $60 million worth of breeding partnerships.

Then the savings and loan scandal hit, depressing the country's real estate market, and it all wrecked on the rock of flawed expectations. Horse investments inevitably rest on the critical factor of revenue projection, an art comparable to guessing how often the ball will land on red.

A quarter of a century later, only a few months ahead of another real estate debacle, the Street was back again, this time riding the back of a lightly raced, tender-footed horse named Big Brown, in honor of a Brooklyn trucking company owner's affinity for UPS stock.

His front man, a young Wall Streeter named Michael Iavarone, was peddling a $100 million hedge fund based on the upside of buying racehorses, for which his high-flying horse had become a living, breathing cold call. Iavarone claimed to have been able to raise $40 million for his International Equine Acquisitions Holdings (IEAH) from eighty investors, which seemed remarkable until ten months later, when the world found out what other folly Wall Street investors had been up to.

The bulk of Iavarone's fund, it turned out, came from a $25 million loan of sorts from a single St. Thomas–based company called TAG Virgin Islands, whose principal, James Tagliaferri, had tired of "vanilla" investments and wanted something more exciting. Admitting to little knowledge of the sport, he had quickly figured it out.

"Very risky," he said, "much like Wall Street."

Iavarone might as well have been selling default drafts on subprime mortgages, not because Big Brown was not valuable— he was—but because the upside of racehorses is as tenuous as their next bad step on the track, or the next goofy decision by his trainer or jockey, or the next trend wind blowing through the breeding sector. Based on their early success, Tagliaferri and Iavarone could never have discerned the debacle around the next turn. But then Wall Street didn't see its own crash coming either.

To anyone with years of horse manure stain on his boots, it should have been clear that Iavarone had already had all the good luck anyone in the horse business had a right to expect. Two modestly bred stakes winners he had purchased off minor tracks in Texas and Iowa for around $1.5 million had already won nearly four times that in purses. Then he bought a controlling interest in Big Brown for a reported $2.5 million and had already gotten his money back plus another million.

Big Brown had been as lucky as Iavarone: sold for $60,000 in the October Fasig-Tipton sale in 2006—traditionally the bottom of the food chain of Kentucky yearling auctions—he had survived the rigors of the drug-laced two-year-old training sales and ended up as the favorite in the 2008 Kentucky Derby on the strength of three races, all won easily against soft competition.

The sordid drug history of Big Brown's trainer, Rick Dutrow, was common knowledge. Buying a good horse out of the boondocks and placing it with a top trainer with good exercise riders and a state-of-art drug regimen was a proven formula for success. No doubt Big Brown was talented, but there was nothing in the horse's breeding to suggest that without pharmaceutical help he could run as fast and as far as it would take to win the Kentucky Derby.

Predictably, his eventual Derby winning time of 2:01.8 was slow considering that Secretariat, in setting the Derby track record of 1:59.4 in 1973, would have beaten him by a dozen lengths. Still, the hero-thirsty racing world embraced him like the reincarnation of Big Red himself, certain to demolish a class of mediocre three-year-olds and win the exalted Triple Crown.

With Iavarone and Dutrow extolling his ability as perhaps the greatest racehorse ever—or at least another Man o' War—Big Brown was pulled from the "hedge fund," and his breeding rights were put up for sale. For a Kentucky Derby winner well on the way to being hyped to immortality, the auction was rather puny.

When a Triple Crown threat is not snapped up by either Coolmore or Sheikh Mohammed, who spend whatever it takes to get whatever they want, it means that either the horse is not that good or his owners are impossible to deal with. Whatever their reasons, the two most obvious and desirable potential buyers made quick U-turns and left Big Brown to the Kentuckians. At the top of the list of the farms that wanted him was Robert Clay's Three Chimneys, where Seattle Slew stood for years and where Smarty Jones, the last "certain" but failed Triple Crown winner, had ended up.

A direct descendant of Henry Clay, Kentucky's most famous politician, Robert Clay is as politically astute as he is nimble and quick as a businessman. For years he kept one leg anchored in the rock of the industry establishment and the other in the vanguard of every sensible effort to improve its image, which he realized was its greatest drawback. This has made him an important liaison between the Dinnies and reform movements such as those started by Satish Sanan and Jess Jackson.

Clay has a sterling reputation of being even more honest than his business allows. The harsh and persistent judge of character whose unerring moral compass keeps Two Bucks straight holds him beyond repute. As Clay's former travel agent and regular customer as a breeder at Three Chimneys for years, she has nothing but praise for the way he does business. And until 2008 the manager and president of Three Chimneys was Dan Rosenberg, a paragon of class and good horsemanship.

The suggestion by the misguided acting chairwoman at the congressional hearing that Eight Belles was "a genetic disaster waiting to happen" was a gross injustice and hard evidence why such hearings are often public policy disasters rooted in the genetic deficiencies of the people running them.

The success of Three Chimneys, however, was not built on missed opportunities. Projecting the revenue of a popular new stallion during his first two years at stud is the closest any equine business planner can come to making a reasonable business model, a far better bet than those Iavarone had been making that a racehorse will get more valuable after his next start. Rational business behavior dictated that if Clay bought Big Brown, who then became the first Triple Crown winner since Affirmed in 1978, he would have the hottest stallion property of the past thirty years—and probably at a bargain price.

Although specifics were never publicly disclosed—transparency being such an aversion in horse sales—rumor had it that Big Brown was valued at $50 million, with Three Chimneys putting up 10 percent and IEAH agreeing to peddle or keep the rest. Reportedly, it was IEAH's insistence on retaining a portion of ownership that drove Coolmore and Sheikh Mohammed to the sidelines.

So on the eve of the Preakness Stakes, which Big Brown seemed certain to win, Clay sent his son Case, who had recently succeeded Rosenberg as farm president, to do his first stallion syndication deal with a Wall Street horse hustler of his own generation. Young Case Clay was at the New York Stock Exchange on May 28, helping IEAH executives ring the opening bell; the next day Bloomberg News and the *New York Times* publicly shattered Iavarone's self-projected image as a "high-profile" investment banker on Wall Street.

The news organizations reported that Iavarone had been even luckier than anyone thought. He'd previously escaped from a penny-stock selling swindle with a censure, a $7,500 fine, and a suspension, and out from under judgments against him by the IRS for $130,000 in unpaid taxes and by Keeneland for failing to pay for $554,000 worth of horses bought at auction.

That he had picked Dutrow to train his horses was now better understood as well. IEAH's first trainer, Greg Martin, had been charged with a felony for juicing one of his horses and ruled off the track, suggesting that Iavarone obviously knew more about horse racing than anyone thought.

In his blog, Ray Paulick, now the new conscience of the industry, questioned why Clay would risk his Mr. Clean image by dealing with a character like Iavarone. He cited the drug violations of Martin and Dutrow and claimed that Steve Allday, the "silver bullet" veterinarian that Dutrow said had put his horses on steroids, had quit Dutrow because of undisclosed things the trainer had asked him to do.

Paulick's "Odd Couple" characterization of the Big Brown–Three Chimneys relationship clearly put Robert Clay on the defensive. "My mother taught me to take people as they come," Clay told Paulick. "They have done nothing but what they said they would do and more, and have been totally straightforward in their business dealings with me."

He declined to defend Dutrow, however, separating the trainer and the owners as "two kettles of fish." But Dutrow's admission that Big Brown ran on a regular regimen of Winstrol was a bigger image problem, even for the nimble Clay, his having been a longtime proponent of ridding the sport of performance-enhancing drugs.

He was left with the sadly accurate generalization that Big Brown was only one among many race champions on steroids. "You can't find a trainer who doesn't use it," he said, which, of course, is not literally true. A lot of really good horsemen don't use steroids. They are just more likely not to have multiple barn stables or drive a Mercedes.

Prior to the Belmont Stakes, after Dutrow's candor had damaged the horse's reputation, IEAH declared that all its horses would soon be steroid-free. Then Dutrow candidly admitted that he was putting Big Brown back on the drugs until he quit racing. When or if Big Brown came off steroids cannot be verified. Certainly his best performance, a sizzling show of speed and endurance at the Preakness two weeks after the Derby, suggests he was still on whatever he had been on all year. But his miserable showing at the Belmont three weeks later, in which he was pulled up in obvious distress, would have been consistent with a horse coming down off a steroid regimen.

The other possible explanation is equally illustrative of the embarrassing state of the sport. In an effort to curb drug use, especially the "milkshaking" of horses prior to a race, the New York Racing Association had instituted a highly unpopular policy of requiring all horses to spend the final six hours prior to the race in a monitored detention barn.

Many horses, particularly young stallions, react negatively and sometimes violently to changes in their environment. Going from the barn where they live to the track to run becomes a familiar routine. Stopping along the way in an unfamiliar barn full of other strange and disturbed horses can be a recipe for disaster. Many come apart emotionally, sweating profusely, exhausting adrenaline, and depleting the electrolytes needed for endurance—just as Big Brown was reported to have done on Belmont day. He was a victim of either drug abuse or the misguided rules written to prevent it.

As a sport whose image is seen mostly through society's rearview mirror, racing was understandably disappointed that Big Brown failed to deliver the Triple Crown in June or that he failed to show up at the Breeders' Cup for a kind of Curlin versus Big Brown October slapdown. It would truly have been billed as the match race of the new millennium, a sort of showdown between champions of the steroid era not unlike the home-run contests between baseball's muscled sluggers.

That it might have been the last battle in Jack Van Berg's "chemical war" on the track, however, is only one thread of the silver lining in Big Brown's short reign as a racing icon. Another is that rather than another exaggerated stud fee of $100,000 or more and 120 of the best mares in the world as his court, Big Brown will have to settle for $65,000 and a slightly less royal harem, and IEAH investors will have to wait longer for a return on their investment. What Wall Street gives quickly, it can take away even quicker.

The stallion Big Brown will have to prove his worth in the breeding shed by validating Robert Clay's reasoning for putting what Indian Charlie would term his "Babyhead" on the line. "If I were to speculate, I'd say steroids don't have anything to do with their genes," Clay said after acquiring what he acknowledged might be the most famous steroid stallion. "If we are being fooled, then we are taking the wrong genes to the breeding shed. I'm not smart enough to know the answer to that."

Arthur Hancock, for one, is certain of the answer: "When you breed to horses running on drug-induced abilities as opposed to natural abilities, you are going to be breeding more unsoundness."

The conflicting opinions of these two industry stalwarts is a line in the sand that divides the industry over the issue of drugs in horse racing, which cannot be separated from the safety and welfare issues that shape public opinion or the economics of a business that depends on the support of fans and professional gamblers.

If on the basis of their racing prowess Curlin and Big Brown become the most popular stallions during their first two years at stud, as they are likely to be, together they would attract three hundred of the best-bred mares in the world each year. Their offspring then would dominate the select portions of the elite sales two years hence and attract the lion's share of investment capital available to the industry the same way the intricate financial instruments of Wall Street did to the housing market.

Just as those financial instruments did for investment bank executives, both horses produced extravagant bonuses for their owners on the front end of the transaction, transferring the risk to breeders two years later. If it turns out that they cannot pass on in their genes their chemically enhanced racing prowess, they will have been just as fraudulent an investment as Wall Street perpetrated with the subprime mortgage package. The industry will have repeated precisely what Hancock says is responsible for the unsoundness and decline in quality of the American thoroughbred.

Publicly, the stature of the sport had been victimized, too, by the nature of Big Brown's ownership, the mindless boasting and erratic behavior of his trainer, and the eagerness of the embattled racing establishment to reach for anything—even a suspect Triple Crown champion—that might divert fan and bettor attention away from the death of Eight Belles and the forced government reforms that might result. In reality the main force driving the impending reckoning for horse racing—public outrage over track surfaces, drugs, and bad breeding practices causing the repeated breakdowns of horses in televised races—was misplaced.

A postrace necropsy showed Eight Belles to be drug-free. The 2006 Kentucky Derby winner Barbaro, who broke down while trying to win the Preakness Stakes, was in the hands of the former Olympian Michael Matz, a highly respected horseman. He was owned by the knowledgeable breeders Roy and Gretchen Jackson and raised on the hallowed ground of Mill Ridge, among the best Kentucky farms.

The filly Pine Island, who broke down in the 2006 Breeders' Cup at Churchill Downs, was also under the care of a first-rate trainer, Shug McGaughey. She was a product of the Phipps breeding program at historic Claiborne Farm, like Three Chimneys known for raising horses naturally and as drug-free as possible.

If there was one area of horse safety where industry investment and progress had been notable, it was safer track surfaces. Years earlier, Keeneland had led the way developing and installing its own artificial Polytrack, after a successful experiment with it at Turfway in Florence, Kentucky, south of Cincinnati, in which Keeneland owned an interest.

In the wake of a rash of tragic track deaths, California had mandated that all tracks switch to artificial surfaces by 2008. Though meaningful statistics are not yet available, early indications were that daily training on the synthetics would significantly reduce the number of fatal breakdowns.

The realization that American thoroughbreds had become more fragile and more susceptible to injury than their global competitors was also atop the list of industry concerns. Study after study, most of them financed by the Dinnies in one way or another, had shown conclusively that each year horses were running far less often and leaving competition at a younger age than their predecessors. But horses prepared and pushed like Big Brown—not Eight Belles or Pine Island—were the more appropriate and logical focus for attention.

The problem was not so much the breeding of horses or the nature of the ground beneath them, but rather how they were being raised, prepared for sale, and trained: first overfed and raised on steroids to enhance their size and appearance at sales, then pushed to early two-year-old sales where their value depended on speed and their speed on pharmaceuticals.

The lack of effective regulation had allowed track cheaters to become dependent on veterinarians and chemists to keep their horses in the winners' circles and their barns full of expensive horses. The policies of sales companies and consignors had led to vast overproduction of drug-disguised, often fraudulent animals that could not run a classic distance on their own.

Such rational bad behavior in the short-term interest of quick profit—and to the long-term detriment of the breed—was consistent with what had happened a quarter of a century earlier to the horse industry and with what would happen to Wall Street and the rest of the financial world by the end of the year.

The word for it was right there on the title of my Two Bucks co-owner's favorite and most often consulted book: *Collapse.*

Every fall the most irrelevant of horse racing's so-called leadership organizations—the Thoroughbred Owners and Breeders Association—hands out awards to the leading breeders in each state in a seemingly endless ceremony at one of the elite Kentucky breeding farms. It is an entertainment-laced, business-attire version of the Jockey Club's summer black-tie dinner at Saratoga, only this event has actual laughter and is attended mostly by friends of those being honored and the employees of those who are not.

Its highlight is an uplifting forward-looking speech by the current TOBA chairman and the presentation of the Industry Service Award for outstanding contributions by some individual. Dr. Dean W. Richardson, the surgeon who struggled so valiantly but unsuccessfully to save Barbaro from his breakdown injuries, was the 2007 recipient.

In 2008, perhaps the most tumultuous and difficult year in the sport's modern history, TOBA gave the Industry Service Award to itself—actually to the thirty-five-plus members of its Sales Integrity Task Force for producing the Code of Ethics termed a toothless step in the right direction by the *Brooklyn Law Review*.

While the task force included many of the most respected and ethical people in the industry who worked hard at the task, the timing of the award was emblematic of what was wrong with the sport. Every crisis or problem is answered with hyped, often lame window dressing designed to preempt whatever more serious remedy it finds threatening.

After successive televised breakdowns on dirt surfaces in 2006 and 2007 at Churchill Downs and the Barbaro nightmare at Pimlico Race Course in Baltimore, the marketing-minded decision makers made sure the next televised extravaganzas would be held in 2008 and 2009 on the new artificial surfaces not even yet in place at Santa Anita, the site of the elite Oak Tree race meets.

There were more good reasons to do so, among them the reality that negotiating revenue sharing with the enlightened

Californians, fearful that the historic Santa Anita site might soon become a real estate development, would be easier than to deal with Churchill Downs management. And where the Dinnies are concerned, it is always about the money and who controls it. But in light of horse and jockey welfare being the trigger of public support for federal government regulation, the safety issue was clearly the factor to be emphasized.

Less than two weeks before the 2008 Breeders' Cup at Santa Anita and any more possible embarrassment, the National Thoroughbred Racing Association held a New York press conference to unveil its Safety and Integrity Initiative that basically amounted to a pledge by the NTRA to help fund implementation of "reforms identified as necessary in the aftermath" of the Eight Belles breakdown. Having learned the hard way that its most formidable critics are best addressed through East Coast media, the NTRA boasted in a press release of a now suddenly united effort to have uniform medication rules, to rid racing of steroids, and to provide safer and more secure racetracks. "Every horseman's group has signed on, and every major Thoroughbred track is on board," said the NTRA spokesman, CEO Alex Waldrop.

Not a single specific reform with which they were "on board" and to which they had "signed on" was mentioned, nor did the NTRA explain how it planned to accomplish what it had never before been able to do. To mask that glaring inadequacy, Waldrop announced the hiring of Tommy Thompson, a former governor of Wisconsin and secretary of health and human services under George W. Bush, to serve as "independent counsel" and provide annual public reports to detail compliance with an entirely vague set of goals. This was another page from a very old book of defense by diversion and bombast.

Five years earlier, after the 2003 Breeders' Cup at Arlington Park outside Chicago, it was discovered that an employee of the company in charge of computing wagering totals in New York had been able to place a "pick-6" bet after the first four races had been run. It would have produced a $3 million win ticket—basically an outright robbery of other bettors made possible by an outmoded, low-tech wagering system that is still vulnerable today to late wagering by high-tech robot bettors known as the "whales."

Despite all the hoopla about attendance and fan base building, keeping the whales in the betting pool is crucial because their bets are so large. But so is keeping them from becoming sharks, natural behavior when $15.2 billion in pari-mutuel wagering is floating around annually in poorly protected waters.

The NTRA's response to the 2003 scandal, a virtual invitation for the government to monkey with the pari-mutuel gambling's interstate gambling exemption, was to hire the security firm of former New York mayor Rudy Giuliani, then riding high as a national hero of the 9/11 attack on the World Trade Center. Giuliani was paid at least $1.5 million to investigate the scandal and produce a report of security recommendations, most of which have yet to be implemented.

The hiring of Thompson in 2008 was just another instance of turning to a well-connected, well-regarded Republican politician the industry can count on to lobby against more government involvement in the sport. Without any means of enforcement, the Safety and Integrity Initiative was another statement of good intentions, a paper-and-flesh Potemkin village constructed well out in front of what was feared might be looming on the horizon. And indeed something was.

Simultaneous with NTRA's public declarations, a group of determined and dedicated reformers was working quietly on the language of federal legislation designed to shake up and restructure the sport's leadership and revamp its failing economic model, a move they considered the only hope for effective uniform drug testing and the eventual improvement of the breed. Led by Arthur Hancock and the longtime reformer Fred Pope, the group planned to draft and deliver to Congress proposed legislation amending the Interstate Horse Racing Act of 1978 that allows and regulates pari-mutuel gambling. Although specific provisions were yet to be agreed upon, the goal of the legislation was to establish a national organization of racing, complete with an antitrust exemption, similar to the governing structure of Major League Baseball. By changing the rules that now determine how tracks divide pari-mutuel wagering revenue with horsemen, a new economic model would be forced on the sport, along with the effective drug and safety regulation enforcement that is now nonexistent.

Already, an even stronger force for change—the failure of the old and long-flawed business model—had the fragmented industry's leadership on the ropes. The steadily falling racing revenues dropped like a stone during the failing economy toward the end of 2008—declining by more than a billion dollars from the year before—and an outmoded formula for purse distribution plus the host/parasite relationships with the Internet-based betting sites had racetracks by the throat.

Frank Stronach's Magna Entertainment Company, which owned eleven tracks and had been hemorrhaging money for years, had finally acknowledged impending disaster and now made an effort to sell real estate in an ultimately unsuccessful attempt to avoid bankruptcy. The threatened properties included Gulfstream Park in Florida and Santa Anita in California, two of the sport's most important venues.

Churchill Downs, the jewel of the traditional racing establishment, had cut purses across the board as a result of a dispute with horsemen's groups over the split of revenue from betting on the Internet-based betting parlors such as Youbet.com and TVG to which the tracks had been selling its simulcast racing product for peanuts. At the same time Churchill was buying some of these wagering platforms and fighting with others in an effort to recover a bigger share of the betting revenue it foolishly let slip away in previous contract dealings.

Privately, the new Churchill Downs management, led by Robert L. Evans, an interloper from the world of high tech, was peddling a terrifying vision of the future that not only united all the horsemen's groups in a way that no one had ever been able to do, but might eventually bring the Dinnies, owners, breeders, and reformers to the same table.

After spending hundreds of millions in marketing schemes to turn horse racing into a television-driven, fan-based sport like NASCAR, the embattled leader of the nation's most important racetrack company was saying the future of the sport—if it had one—rested with Internet-based wagering by a small group of big bettors. And what if the whales keep feeding in the Web waters and offshore betting parlors and not the track pools?

As supporting evidence, Evans produced a study basically showing that racing in North America could retain its annual $3 billion takeout of wagering revenue with 7,500 full-field, high-quality races a year. Currently the industry relies on 54,000 races of mostly inferior quality to produce the same level of gambling revenue.

Evans's idea did not include strategies on how to attract new owners—which had been the mantra of the Dinnies and their marketing gurus—or what to do with the thirty-five thousand horses being bred annually, or the veterinarians, trainers, bloodstock agents, and sale company personnel whose living depended on them. Why should he? They would not be needed. And the Wall Street analysts who graded Churchill Downs stock would never even ask about them. Besides, the future of all those horses and people was already being addressed—brutally—at the fall yearling sales.

For the first time in anyone's memory, a Keeneland sale official actually uttered the dreaded term *overproduction* while publicly explaining why its September yearling sale had tanked unmercifully. Every indicator used in the past to cover up the growing number of unprofitable horses going under the hammer was no longer viable. Gross revenue, average price, and median price were all down in double digits.

Even the formidable Keeneland spin machine ran slowly from day one of the fifteen-day sale. "We are an optimistic industry, so we have to be optimistic," said sales director Geoffrey Russell. "The world is a lot different than this time last year. You have the credit crunch, you have lack of easy financing." With that redundancy he ran out of excuses, but he did manage to find one high note: the median price for the first five hundred or so cream-of-the-crop yearlings offered during the first two days of the sale that normally drives up indicators.

"But on the positive side our median is $300,000," Russell said, "which I think is a spectacular median."

Equally spectacular were the numbers that resulted from the overproduction of yearlings in general and the overbreeding of popular high-priced stallions that finally began to throttle the wrong throats. Of the 493 choice yearlings cataloged on the usually red-hot first two "select" sale days, only 217 sold profitably.

More than a hundred yearlings by horses with stud fees of $100,000 or more failed to earn a dollar, many of them by the world's leading sires: Storm Cat, A.P. Indy, and Giant's Causeway. Some yearlings did not even return their stud fees, of $300,000 or higher. More than 30 percent of the yearlings were bought back by their owners. And it got worse from there.

A third of the 5,555 horses cataloged—1,841—were to pass through the ring the last weekend of the sale and the following

Monday and Tuesday. On the fifth day out, a Friday, 43 of those horses sold profitably, then 20 on Saturday, 19 on Sunday, 10 on Monday, and on the last day only 4.

One month later, as Wall Street stock markets and their global counterparts imploded, so did the livestock market. The Fasig-Tipton October sale—normally the last hope for marketing Kentucky yearlings—had cataloged 1,090 horses. When it was concluded three days later, half of them had been recorded as sold but only 38 at a price that could be considered profitable.

For the first time, Fasig-Tipton set aside a parking lot for horse trailers that could be accessed only through a monitored gate. Many sale attendees simply attributed the change to the sale company's acquisition earlier in the year by Dubai associates of Sheikh Mohammed, who might be more security conscious than the old owners.

Perhaps. But trailers are seldom burglarized at Fasig-Tipton horse sales. Tires and hubcaps are usually safe. Consignors don't often ramble through strangers' trailers in search of hay, feed, and equipment. But in addition to the owners, another aspect of the sale was clearly new.

With so many horses failing to garner even a single bid and with new antislaughter regulations preventing owners from hauling them off to slaughterhouses, there was the distinct possibility a buyer or seller might return to his trailer to find it holding unidentified abandoned animals. The precedent had been established at another sale of a different breed just a few weeks earlier.

That this particular sale—which two years earlier had produced the reigning Kentucky Derby champion Big Brown— would become such an exclamation point to the decline in the value of a Kentucky thoroughbred was perfectly in keeping with the dramatic irony that permeates the saga from start to finish. From 1996 to 2005, the Fasig-Tipton October sale had produced

145 stakes winners. All but 17 horses had sold for less than $50,000 and nearly half—72—for less than $10,000.

When the massive Keeneland November breeding stock sales rolled around, buybacks and withdrawals together were doubling the number of horses actually sold, and Wall Street hedge fund managers were using the results as a barometer of further world economic decline.

That such a day would come was inevitable. And it can hardly be blamed entirely on the Bush economy. It could have been envisioned when the farms started increasing stallion books to two hundred mares in a season and fraudulently running up the yearling prices to further increase their popularity; when the radiograph repository and other sales company policies began rendering nearly half the horses unprofitable; and when incessant misrepresentation of reality kept enticing new players into the game and encouraging them to breed as many horses as possible.

We all should have known that the time was coming when there would be so many horses we couldn't give them away.

12

ALL ABOUT THE HORSES

When Big Brown's big-mouth connections succeeded in taunting Jess Jackson into sending Curlin out to California to defend his status as the world's number-one racehorse in the 2008 Breeders' Cup Classic, they constructed a likely template for the sport's future.

Back in the spring, at the height of the Big Brown hype, when his trainer Rick Dutrow was sure his horse would win the Triple Crown, he started taking verbal pot shots at Curlin, who as a three-year-old had been beaten in the 2007 Kentucky Derby by Street Sense, and in the Belmont Stakes by the filly Rags to Riches. "We ain't been beat by no filly," Dutrow said.

Out of the other side of their mouths, IEAH spokesmen were building up Curlin as a great champion and raising as the ultimate goal for Big Brown a showdown with Curlin in the 2008 Breeders' Cup Classic at Santa Anita, just as the Breeders' Cup was hoping for.

Even after Big Brown fizzled in the Belmont, his backers kept offering his participation in multimillion-dollar match races at this track or that, if Curlin would only show up. The truth is, the owners and trainers of the two horses dodged each other until after Curlin won the Jockey Club Gold Cup in late September and became the richest racehorse in history.

At that point his trainer, Steve Asmussen, was ready to retire him. He did not like the idea of taking Curlin all the way across the country to face Big Brown on an artificial surface that suited the three-year-old but that Curlin had never even tried. All of Curlin's honors had been earned on dirt tracks, the traditional surface for which American horses have always been bred and trained. Curlin had not run well in his only contest on grass and had never raced on synthetic.

Only a dedicated sportsman such as Jackson, who believes racing needs heroes that race until they are four and five years old, as they once did, would have even taken up the dare, which became even more persistent and irritating. Dutrow repeatedly and publicly had denigrated Curlin's ability, which trainers almost never do to another's horse, at least not in print.

It is not surprising that when the time came and Jackson overruled Asmussen and committed to the Breeders' Cup, Big Brown again failed to show up—this time literally. That the reason given was a foot injury was no shock either, considering his history.

But his absence was disappointing, not only because Big Brown did not get to meet Curlin in the flesh, but also because the lessons discernible from what was truly a "world" championship race meeting at Santa Anita would have benefited his connections.

Due to California's leadership role in drug reform, including the banning of horses on steroids, the Breeders' Cup was able to impose random drug testing at will, and the barns were persistently monitored for security. Cheating, which had been frequently reported at earlier Cup venues, was virtually impossible unless of course the magicians have already come up with undetectable "silver bullets." Corruption via modern-day medical advances such as "gene doping"—nontherapeutic modulation of gene expression—to enhance athletic performance is already on the horizon.

Sleeker, slower, and no longer on steroids, Curlin courageously defended his title as world champion but faltered in the stretch, as three horses classically bred for grass racing sprinted past him on Santa Anita's new Pro-Ride synthetic surface, for which they were better suited. He made his patented move to the lead but lacked the quality for which steroids are best known for providing: endurance.

The horse that won the $5 million classic, Raven's Pass, is a telltale template all his own. He ran on Lasix for the first time, which most experts believe moves a horse up a few lengths, which it appeared to do. He had never gone a mile and a quarter before. By doing so easily and convincingly, his victory supports the argument that furosemide is indeed performance enhancing and should be banned.

If the 2008 Breeders' Cup proved anything, it is that the Dinnies and their new generation of leaders have been right to believe that the future of horse racing—if it has one—is indeed global. Five of the nine Cup races, from which the breeding stallions emerge, were won by European-style horses, which are generally bred and built differently from the American dirt speedsters. Except for Raven's Pass, who is American-bred, all ran without Lasix, the antibleeder medication American trainers say they can't do without.

The future of Raven's Pass as an inevitable first-year star in the rapidly growing Darley stallion roster of the Maktoums is also evidence of an accompanying but perhaps more disturbing trend: the continued concentration of thoroughbred blood in the hands of foreign owners. He will stand his first year in Ireland, no doubt an outright challenge to Coolmore's supremacy there.

In his quest to compete globally with his Irish rival, Sheikh Mohammed snapped up every big-name Triple Crown horse but Curlin in 2007, adding to his formidable stallion empire the Kentucky Derby winner Street Sense, the sturdy warrior Hard Spun, and Any Given Saturday, the best son of the American-owned but aging Distorted Humor. A horse already Arab-owned, Elusive Quality, is the sire of Raven's Pass. Another young Darley stallion, E Dubai, sired Desert Code, the winner of the Turf Sprint. And Street Cry, the sheikh's onetime Kentucky Derby hopeful, sired the champion older mare Zenyatta. Americans salvaged some measure of pride in January 2009 when Curlin, despite his fourth-place finish in the Breeders' Cup, defeated Zenyatta in the balloting for the country's top Eclipse Award, winning the Horse of the Year honor for a second time. Many considered the vote a reward to Jackson by the turf writers for his sportsmanship and for sending Curlin to stud in Kentucky at Will Farish's Lane's End Farm, where he will stand his initial season for a reasonable fee of $75,000.

How the sheikh came to possess Raven's Pass, which ran in the name of his wife, Princess Haya of Jordan, adds another dose of irony to the story of Kentucky's—and thus America's—obvious shrinking presence and influence in the global competition. The horse came as part of the package when Sheikh Mohammed bought virtually all the thoroughbred holdings of Stonerside Farm and its racing stable from the disillusioned Houston billionaire Robert McNair in 2008.

In financial terms, the Dinnies' resistance to sharing leadership with McNair cost the American industry an estimated $150 million in thoroughbred equity, immeasurable blue-blooded equine genes, and one of the best business brains it had ever attracted.

McNair's Stonerside Farm had been phenomenally successful in every aspect of the business. He is reputedly the first investor since D. Wayne Lukas's client, the Californian Eugene Klein, who can claim he did not leave money behind when he departed. After Raven's Pass won the Breeders' Cup Classic, McNair said his only regret was not being able to stand in the winner's circle with the team that had made him successful, his racing manager John Adger and his Kentucky farm manager Bobby Spalding.

"I don't regret the financial aspect of it because Sheikh Mohammed paid a very substantial amount of money, and he did it to buy outstanding horses," McNair told the *Daily Racing Form*. "If they hadn't been outstanding, he wouldn't have paid that kind of money. We never try to take the last nickel off the table when we sell something. We want people to be happy with what they buy, or our policy is that if it wasn't as represented, they can bring it back."

Continually losing smart straight shooters like Robert McNair depletes the industry's most important assets. Men like McNair and his fellow rebels, the golf club maker Gary Biszantz and Richard Santulli, the founder of NetJets, who nearly brought relevance to TOBA, ought to have permanent seats in the front of the Dinnies' leadership wagon. Instead, they in effect are relegated to rented spots, from which they are supposed to kick in cash for any approved initiative but never try to drive the team.

Their brief prominence is like the promises of the Dinnies' press releases—window dressing. Once they expect a share of power back for their bucks, they are shuttled to the rear of the wagon, in many instances to make room for someone less problematic, like a new-generation bred-in-the-purple Dinny.

In the most enduring of industry traditions, it was the less radioactive and ironically more diplomatic son of American racing's most powerful individual, William S. Farish Jr., who is also Dinny Phipps's son-in-law, who emerged from the Breeders'

Cup leadership revolution as its new chairman. The election that produced him had been widely welcomed as a modest relieving of the old guard in that only Watts Humphrey among the older-generation Dinnies was elected to the thirteen-member ruling board. And for the first time in over a decade, their favorite executive chair filler, D. G. Van Clief, was no longer in a decision-making position, having been relegated along with Dinny Phipps to an honorary spot among the Cup's forty-eight-member group of trustees.

Despite a more representative board, other industry traditions endured as well; among them, the most important— control of the Breeders' Cup's $40 million reserve kitty— remained in the hands of a small investment committee chaired by Humphrey that included the younger Farish and his father-in-law. At year's end, when the Breeders' Cup calculated its receipts, it discovered that membership dues, stallion and foal nomination fees, and purse contributions from participating tracks came up $10 million short of expectations. To offset the shortfall, the board of directors voted to eliminate the $6 million it contributes to the purses of 119 stakes races in 2009, setting off yet a new revolution that included demands for mass resignations and breeder threats to boycott the Breeders' Cup program by not nominating foals. Two days later, to stem yet another uprising, the board reversed itself and decided to fund the stakes program.

Suggestions that the Breeders' Cup use the Humphrey-controlled "reserves" to subsidize the shortfall brought forth new disclosures that the fund had lost $10 million—25 percent of its value—in the fall stock market decline, as well as an old but well-kept secret that the former CEO Van Clief had gotten an $850,000-plus retirement package and that his successor, Greg Avioli, a sports marketing executive, had an annual compensation package estimated at $750,000. The Breeders' Cup salary disclosures were particularly upsetting to breeders already aggravated by the Jockey Club's top-heavy administrative costs. Although its main functions had been transferred to Lexington twenty years ago, the organization maintains a vanity headquarters in New York City, on East Fifty-second Street just off Park Avenue, and awards its chief executive, Alan Marzelli, a compensation package equal to or higher than Avioli's. With three vice presidents, each with a $250,000 salary, the club's top four executives eat up 39 percent of the organization's annual budget. Not only had the Dinnies been investing like Wall Streeters; they had been paying like them, too.

In the same news cycle, a special task force examining the future of Kentucky horse racing reported that the cradle of the sport was in danger of losing its signature industry. Without alternative sources to increase purses, fund drug testing, and strengthen regulation, the task force said, the threat of Kentucky losing its most important economic engine was both real and imminent. Not only was the industry's economic model broken, its heart was failing, and the Dinnies' wagon was again in the ditch.

Like it or not, the Irish and other Europeans, as well as Sheikh Mohammed and the other oil-rich Arabs, have their own wagons, thank you very much. And their increasing global role has so far been racing's most promising aspect. Anything the Dubai Arabs touch is almost instantly improved. The ink was barely dry on the agreement by a group of Sheikh Mohammed's associates to purchase Fasig-Tipton, when both its appearance and potential to compete with Keeneland began to improve dramatically.

With an obvious eye toward taking Fasig-Tipton global, the innovative owners immediately announced new policies of international buyer recruitment, shorter entry lead times, and faster payment of sale proceeds—all challenges to Keeneland's dominance in equine auctions. Getting sale proceeds back to the sellers in time to pay the bills due for sale preparation would be a remarkable achievement. By the time a seller gets sales proceeds now, the veterinarian's charges for useless radiographs are already overdue.

The way the Arabs do business is remarkably reminiscent of the way Japanese automakers took over the auto industry from America. With American competitors caught between labor union agreements on one side and the short-term imperatives of Wall Street on the other, Japanese car makers were able to gain market share by putting quality over profitability and establishing the brand-name superiority that had built Detroit's dominance to start with.

Like art, literature, and the press, ownership of sports has proved to be incompatible with Wall Street's growth requirements for companies whose stock is publicly held. As the American press found out too late, horse racing has a more certain future in private hands.

It would be neither surprising nor detrimental if the Maktoums expanded their American investment to racetracks, some of the country's worst-run and least-profitable enterprises. All eleven tracks owned by Stronach's debt-ridden Magna Entertainment Company are vulnerable to imminent extinction. Others not owned by casino or hotel companies are under duress. The country's most visible and important racetrack, Churchill Downs, is a prime example. Among Churchill Downs's holdings are not only the historic Twin Spires track at Louisville, but also Arlington Park just outside Chicago, Calder Race Course in South Florida, and the Fair Grounds on the edge of the French Quarter in New Orleans. As a combined asset, these properties would likely return more to the company in real estate development than they ever can in horse racing given its current state. As a publicly traded company with a stagnant stock price, all that protects Churchill Downs from takeover is the horseman-dominated makeup of its board of directors. And that defense might even be penetrable by a formidable, hostile effort.

If the Dinnies don't figure out some way to step forward and buy the tracks themselves, somebody with other ideas about their future probably will. The ultimate decision by the Churchill Downs management may be a Kentucky Derby brought to you not by Yum Brands but by MGM Mirage or Emirates Airlines, already a major sponsor of the Breeders' Cup Classic that Darley just won.

If the sheikh can't win the Derby, which he has regularly failed to do, he can probably buy it. With each new report of declining revenue from racing and each purchase of another promising stallion or mare, the sheikh will take a step closer to doing both.

Even the most committed lovers of the game and those most hopeful for its future believe the current business model of more than fifty thousand races a year with 70 percent of them filled by claiming horses—those running for an advertised sale price— is doomed. The legislation being proposed by Arthur Hancock and his rebellious band of reformers proposes an antitrust-exempted authority that would conduct both a major league and minor league of racing, much like that of organized baseball, with the highly profitable top level helping to subsidize the lower. It is the horse industry equivalent to a policy designed to preserve the middle class.

Such a radical idea has been impossible to sell to horsemen and tracks, whose race dates are mandated by legislation in every state. Like uniform drug rules, any restructuring of the sport's business model will have to come from a federal government mandate connected to the interstate gaming laws.

For years the Graded Stakes Committee of the Thoroughbred Owners and Breeders Association, which awards graded stakes status to races, has had the power to dictate random drug test-ing on animals from the minute they are nominated for a stakes race. If it is serious about drug reform, the committee could mandate that all stakes races be run without race-day medica-tion, thereby settling that dispute once and for all.

Owners, trainers, and breeders know the value of their ani-mals depends more on graded stakes performance than any-thing else. If they have to contest graded stakes races without Lasix, they would breed, own, and train animals capable of doing it. And if they are going to compete globally with the horses that won most of the 2008 Breeders' Cup races, they had better get started, because North America remains the only place where horses can run on Lasix.

Soon, the NTRA will no longer be shouting, "Go Baby Go," as its slogan. Because the name of the game is going to be "Go Global, Baby, Go Global." There will have to be a forced realiza-tion of what the reformer Fred Pope termed a refusal by horse racing to give the public what it wants. "They want only the highest level of the sport presented to them. No exceptions," he wrote in an industry newsletter. "Thoroughbred racing does not give them what they want. We give them a mix of the worst the sport has to offer and we force-feed it to them every day of the week."

One way or another, horse racing is headed—if not to its demise—at least back to its roots as the Sport of Kings, where fewer people race for less money or perhaps even only for the thrill of it. And the kings will just be of greater variety, and some of a different hue.

Racing will survive because horses are an addiction with no cure. As an organized business endeavor, the sport of horse rac-ing has been dominated by auction price shenanigans, buyer shakedowns, squabbles over simulcast revenue and purse distribution, the squandering of industry funds, and generally bad management. All too often, the response to these maladies has been that it's "all about the money." My old business, newspapers, believed it was all about the money, too, and now it is too late for them.

It is also too late for Eight Belles, but not for rectifying the wrongs spotlighted by her death. That she finished ahead of all the Kentucky Derby colts but Big Brown and was still running strong and sound after a mile and a quarter—which replays show to be clearly the case—was remarkable in itself.

There is no reason to believe that anything other than a bad step while pulling up after the race was responsible for the filly's breakdown. This happens to horses with no one on their backs every day in pastures all around the world. All that is needed for this to occur is a hole, a rock, or most often a broken stride or misstep that causes a weight shift resulting in a foot striking the ground somewhere other than intended, which appears to be what happened to Barbaro as well.

Everybody keeps looking for a target to place the blame—except the people who knew and loved her the most. Larry Jones, a religious man, is inclined to look harder for the silver lining in the tragedy that he believes is surely there.

"You don't know why some things happen in life, but they do," he told the *Blood-Horse*. "I do feel that things are coming into order and many things in the industry will be better because of Eight Belles."

If a silver lining exists, it is the impetus for real reform resulting in congressional scrutiny of the sorry aspects of a great sport that hinges on one of the most beautiful, alluring, and athletic of earth's creatures. Without the misguided allegations that Eight Belles was running on drugs, the steroid regimens of the two more prominent racehorses, Big Brown and Curlin, would have remained merely the rumors of railbirds.

Before Congress and a television audience, Arthur Hancock and Jess Jackson in effect came clean for an entire industry that needed to do so. And by refusing to testify but otherwise unable to keep his mouth shut, the trainer Rick Dutrow eventually came clean, too—not just about Big Brown, but about the lengths to which trainers and veterinarians routinely go to gain an edge on competitors.

Like much public policy good and bad, whatever happens will have been the result of unintended consequences of a decision made by Larry Jones, an extraordinary man of extremely good intentions whose life has been changed by it forever. Four months after the Derby and only minutes after an emotional public ceremony in which Eight Belles was memorialized in the garden of the Kentucky Derby Museum, Jones told me that he had decided to quit his profession of nearly thirty years at the end of 2009. It would take that long, he said, to keep the commitments he had made to me and the other owners who had sent him two-year-old horses earlier in the year. Without those commitments, which to him are as rock solid as the ethical tenets of his mythical cowboy hero counterparts, he probably would have quit that minute.

The agony of seeing Eight Belles dead on the track at Churchill Downs had just been reinflicted by the reliving of the moment. Struggling not to cry, which cowboys are not supposed to do, Jones had told the crowd, "I was the lucky one to see her come into the barn as a long-legged gangly two-year-old . . . lucky enough to see her turn into a lovely, gallant and courageous racehorse . . . She stole a piece of my heart that day, and when she fell . . . she ripped a big piece of my heart right out."

In 1978, the year Larry Jones began as a trainer, his horses earned less than $40,000, which would have meant no more than about $4,000 in income to him. By the time the Delaware Park meet ended in mid-November 2008, they had already earned nearly $6.5 million. No trainer in the business has more admirers, and few can look forward to a more solid future. Even after the loss of Eight Belles, who many people considered the best filly in the world, the Jones-trained Proud Spell was voted the Eclipse Award as the best three-year-old filly in the nation in 2008. Jones could even become a Dinny of sorts among trainers, never short of revenue or good horses.

As long as the cowboy has a racing stable, owners like me will be fighting to get their horses into it. He represents the qualities horse racing needs most to display to erase public skepticism about its value as a sport: honesty and integrity. Jones's willingness to make himself available to the press after the death of Eight Belles, to answer his telephone and face his critics, earned him one of the industry's most prized but equivocally named awards: the Big Sport of Turfdom for 2008.

"Big Sport" is hardly an accurate description of the behavior that earned him the respect of the turf writers and publicists who bestow it. And what he went through to earn it is definitely not what is being celebrated by the gaiety implied by the title. What they were recognizing, however, are the rarest commodities in the game: courage, candor, and grace under pressure. Jones's reaction to the award, calling it the "greatest achievement of his career," is all you need to know about him.

If Larry and Cindy Jones retire completely from racing—which I doubt and hope will not be the case—they will still find a way to be surrounded by horses. You have only to watch Cindy Jones being kissed delicately on the face by an otherwise rambunctious three-year-old thoroughbred stallion she pampers like a three-year-old child, or see Larry Jones swinging his long bowed legs over one member of his string after another, day after day, to realize that they were never in it for the money.

As with all of us at Two Bucks, the best they could hope for all those years was to stay in place.

For over two decades they got up at three in the morning and worked until late in the evening, seven days a week, without ever taking a vacation before they got their hands on horses good enough to win big graded stakes races in places where it mattered. For twenty-three years they never made any real money. Then the horses and the rich owners swarmed them like killer bees. And within two years, they had made enough money and endured enough pressure that came with it to consider retiring.

Other than Larry Jones, my favorite horse trainer is a young Japanese-Canadian named Michelle Nihei, who may be the only trainer in the world with a doctorate in neuroscience. She is a brilliant young woman who after four years of doing research at Johns Hopkins came to Kentucky, where she became the top exercise rider for the trainer Todd Pletcher and eventually one of his principal assistants. She was as good at developing the Eclipse Award–winning Ashado, who won $3.8 million, as she was at clinical trials.

In March 2007 a horse named The Leopard she was riding in Florida flipped over backward and crushed her knee, leaving the lower portion attached only by the patella tendon. Because of the loss of arterial blood supply, surgeons considered amputation. But Pletcher had her moved to Louisville, to the care of a prominent orthopedic surgeon, where she recovered, and after months of rehab she opened a public stable of her own.

Now, a Two Bucks three-year-old filly is regularly among the several horses in Nihei's stable that she climbs aboard and personally exercises every day—not because she has to, but because she wants to. Her father, a former Fulbright scholar, does not completely understand why his daughter does this. That I do worries me when I think about it, but not as much as the thought of people like her and Larry Jones being driven out of the business by the insanity of it.

To such people, working around horses, while physically tiring, is not really work at all. Those who regard it as such don't stay at it very long, leaving it to those of us who see it as something else entirely: a calling of sorts, like preachers and nurses and missionaries claim to have. And they are by no means all riders like Nihei and the Joneses.

Horse racing—like most endeavors involving horses—is replete with people like Gary Biszantz and Robert McNair who have money but whose horse-racing involvement has always been about the horses.

When Gary Biszantz graduated from Claremont McKenna College in 1956, he had four hundred dollars in his pocket and a job at his father's auto dealership. On the way home he stopped at a cheap horse sale and spent the whole bundle on a thoroughbred filly, which he named Affirm Miss and gave to the trainer Mel Stute, who was still training fifty-two years later at age eighty-one.

"Mel was just getting started. So was I," said Biszantz, a perpetually ebullient man who gets excited just telling the story. "I told him, I can't pay any training bills, Mel, just get her going and see what you can do. First time out she goes down the hill at Santa Anita in a minute thirty-three and wins seventeen hundred dollars. I am—" His voice halts there, and he hooks an index finger in his mouth to finish the sentence.

Hooked, like thousands and thousands of others in an addictive enterprise almost impossible to leave voluntarily. By 2008, horses owned and raced by Biszantz had started 2,100 times and won 450 races. They included 250 wins by two-year-olds, twenty graded stakes horses, $16 million in earnings, and two notable stallions made—Cobra King and Old Trieste, the first big son of A.P. Indy.

The achievements are spit out of Biszantz's mouth like machine-gun fire. If you ask him about a pimple or blemish on one of his horses, he can tell you about it, too, in detail.

But nothing he has done in the horse business gives him more pleasure to relate than establishment of the Harry A. Biszantz Memorial Center for Thoroughbred Retirement he established in 1998 at Tranquility Farm, in honor of his father and into which he has put $1 million of his Cobra Golf company fortune so far. Along with two other prominent California breeders, John Amerman and the late Robert Lewis, Biszantz has built it into a successful nonprofit rescue and rehabilitation center that constantly maintains a population of a hundred horses. Not because he had to, but because it always was just all about the horses.

Real *horse people*—and the term can cover the spectrum from the most ragged, drug-addicted, homeless, and otherwise useless but wonderful groom to the most pampered, overeducated, self-centered rich girl and her egomaniacal tycoon husband—are by genetic disposition unmitigated wackos. They have to be wired a little differently—like politicians—in order to do what they do while never really understanding why.

When I was in my late thirties I bought two horses from an Illinois man who was about seventy years old. The day we met he was sitting atop a young quarter horse stallion barely two years old, whose eyes were so wild they were frightening. He was ringing his tail and pinning his ears. I figured fire would come out of his nostrils any minute.

"This is just his second day under saddle," the man said. "Want to see him rode?"

And with that he put a boot in the colt's side and went crow hopping off in a circle inside a small muddy corral like an old-time bronco buster. I thought the guy was crazy.

Thirteen years later, after a two-year-old paint horse colt

236 | HEADLESS HORSEMEN

named Tecumseh had already warned me by dragging me around a paddock on the end of a rope, flipping over, and digging the horn of his saddle into the ground, I got on him and rode him up a hill in the back pasture. At the top we encountered a wind that blew the tail of my jacket into the air, spooking Tecumseh, who ran off bucking and veering wildly until he unloaded me. I spent the next twelve hours on a gurney with three cracked vertebrae and a bruised kidney, wondering not why he did that but why I did.

For as long as I have been around horses, there have been people in my presence asking them to do things they are too smart to do on their own—like jump over bales of rolled hay or over a rickety old rock fence so close to a creek the landing can only be in the water—"fox hunting" they call this rather than the craziness that it really is.

In the fall of 2008, after the dismal September sale, I did something just as nutty. In the Teton wilderness allegedly in search of bull elk that had already moved to the meadows below where our outfitters had no authorization to hunt, I followed a clearly dedicated but demented guide up and down slopes so steep and treacherous they would have challenged a mountain goat.

For reasons unknown to me or my mount, a twenty-four-year-old paint horse named Sam, we repeatedly scrambled straight up slippery gravel inclines, slid down muddy banks, and tightroped along traverse trails on the sides of mountains so narrow I dared not look down in search of elk tracks that were not there anyway.

Sometimes we climbed so high that the Buffalo Fork of the Snake River looked like a one-inch silver ribbon below, and the way down was so steep we had to dismount and lead the horses, fearing all the while they might slip and fall on us. And for two hours at the beginning and two hours at the end, we did this in the dark—and I mean total blackness penetrated only fleetingly by a tiny light on the cap bill of the guide.

Once safely back to camp, I was tormented by questions about my own sanity and the wisdom of my guide—but had no doubt about the greatness of my horse. A sturdy fifteen-hand black-and-white gelding with granitelike bones, Sam had perfectly shaped feet that must have had suction cups on the bottom, or my big carcass would have been left at the bottom of a ravine a dozen times.

If stalled on the way up by a horse in front trying to regain its footing or overcome an obstacle, Sam stood solid and stationary, he and I sticking off the side of the mountain like some bizarrely shaped growth anchored in the rock. On the way down, he would fall back on his haunches and pick his way to solid footing as if guided by lasers in his hooves.

There was nothing for me to do but shift my weight to his advantage and keep my seat like a passenger in a bus. At least over the years I had become horseman enough to let him take care of me, which he did magnificently. The only bad steps he took all day were on flat ground as he tried to graze on the high grass, sneaking a bite while still keeping up. He had the skill honed to an art form.

When it is all said and done, what I will cherish most about the trip is the animal that made the ride one of the most enjoyable and exhilarating experiences of my life. It is always that way with a good horse. Their nobility worms its way into your heart.

Just the mere sight of some of them will bring a wacko horse lover to tears. Lexington's premier tour company owner, the dominant female of Two Bucks, has seen it repeatedly in the clients she escorts through the great horse farms.

For some reason the old gray warrior Holy Bull, who lives among Sheikh Mohammed's Darley stallions, has a giant cult following around the world. People come to Lexington just to see him. One of the repeat clients of Kentucky Horse Tours is a bearish pediatrician heart surgeon and former Special Forces officer who has seen soldiers die beside him and infants die in his hands. At the first glimpse of his favorite racehorse, Holy Bull, he broke into tears. Upon finding out that the grave of another gray racing hero of his, Spectacular Bid, was without a monument, the sobbing surgeon paid $1,600 to have one made and delivered it himself.

In one of the more bizarre of such incidents, my favorite tour guide once took a party of a dozen business executives to see the great Cigar at Coolmore's Ashford Stud where he was to stand before he fizzled as a sire. One of the men teared up immediately and was unable to hide it. The sniffling caught on and raced through the group like a quick-moving allergy. Soon they were all coughing and wiping their eyes. The Irish groom handling Cigar looked at the tour guide and shrugged his shoulders in amazement. She couldn't believe it either.

There is just something about the horses.

It would be hypocritical of me to report the aberrant emotional behavior of others without confessing my own. Both my parents died in the same year, within six months of each other. Although both losses were heartfelt, I was especially close to my mother, whose close supervision was my salvation. But not once did I cry in public over her or my father, I guess because cowboys aren't supposed to cry.

But twice I have broken into tears in front of veterinarians and strangers over the death of a horse I had been trying to save. First was at the euthanasia of my foundered cutting horse mare Tivio, a present from my wife that became my riding horse for years.

One Christmas morning Tivio had worked four hours straight in mud and snow helping retrieve sixteen heifers that had escaped Two Bucks and melted into two hundred mother cows and calves on a farm next door. Three times she fell in the soft muck and got up without unseating me. And when without help we finally got the job done, she was caked with mud and lathered from nose to tail. I never asked her to do anything that she didn't try her heart out to do.

The second was the death of Regal Band, the dam of Monarchos, with whom I had the kind of emotional attachment Larry Jones had with Eight Belles. Unexplainably, it was a family loss unlike any other.

In the last month of her life, age and illness had robbed her of her beauty. Gone was the long grass-cutter stride and the haughty countenance befitting her name and royal blood. A combination of failing liver and pituitary, and a regimen of fish oil and antibiotics, had left her with the coat of a buffalo. Her gorgeous eyes had dulled and shrunken.

It was in fact rather a sad, shapeless sack of bones that we loaded into the van late that Easter Sunday for what turned out to be her final trip to the sprawling equine hospital she had frequented all too often over the last years of her life.

Frightened and feverish, she lurched off the van and immediately collapsed in a hospital stall, a heap that bore no resemblance to the streaking, powerful indomitable force that ruled her pasture for a dozen years. Each one of her offspring inherited her confident bearing and aloofness. Her last foal, an Empire Maker filly now named Empiress, has the same seductive runway model grace and identical unpredictable temperament.

The first minute I saw Regal Band, I believed her a queen mother in waiting, which she turned out to be. So amid scrambling veterinarians, syringes of pain-killing tranquilizers, and bags of life-extending fluids hung the inevitability of a tragic loss.

For hands-on horsemen who inspect their herds in the fields, kneel behind the mares at foaling time, and struggle to adjust the malpresented foals, for the riders who spend hours on their backs and the grooms who crouch under them in their stalls, watching your horse die is a shattering experience. It leaves a mark on your soul and, as Larry Jones said, a hole in your heart.

The trauma is particularly haunting and lasting when the horse is special to you, as Eight Belles was to Larry and Regal Band was to me. The mere presence of a horse like her was as much a gift to my life as her produce was to our income, or as her colt Monarchos was to the continued existence of Two Bucks Farm. Such a horse becomes as much a part of your life as a special family member or as a close friend for whose acquaintance you feel grateful.

The night she died, Regal Band left me a final gift. Bracing her torso on a single front leg as if about to stand, she raised her head haughtily in one final display of grandeur and, no doubt using her last drop of adrenaline, miraculously regained her youth. There again momentarily, as if to remind me of the value of my impending loss, was the glistening ebony coat and the magnificent eye, the look that once promised a wellspring of profitable thoroughbred nobility—or at least I imagined that she did all that. For she was not only the rainmaker at Two Bucks, but also its sunshine and inspiration.

The death of Eight Belles left more than a wound in Larry Jones's heart. It left the sport of horse racing with a final gift in the form of an enabling catharsis that only a tragic drama can produce, a compulsion for the industry to reform itself in hopes of never feeling the shock of her legacy again.

Larry Jones does not have to explain to everyone what the loss of Eight Belles did to his life or how its aftermath might end his career as a horse trainer. Not to me nor to a great many others who share his passion for the animals. Horse racing is replete with grooms, riders, breeders, veterinarians, Dinny wannabes—and even some of the Dinnies themselves—whose hearts rule these marvelous relationships between man and beast.

The unexplainable addiction of people to life around a horse is why horse racing has survived all these years and how it will survive the ravages of the economic downturn, the ire of its enemies, and the headless floundering of its leaders that comprised the cataclysm of 2008.

EPILOGUE

By the end of 2008, my river of stones had dried up along with my revenue stream. New Medicare-sponsored radiographs of the nemesis stone-producing organ, every bit as outrageously expensive as those for the yearling auction sale repository, showed no new issues to depreciate my worth or hasten my destined rendezvous with the reaper. Bankruptcy remained a viable option.

The tragic flaw in my character, however, first recognized by my dear departed Irish mother, was still intact. The tongue honed by constant use had become so sharp it had slit my own throat.

In search of all possible news to further depress the American economy, a journalist for Bloomberg Business News, every bit as irritating as I ever was in his profession, had finally pressed me to the point of aggravation over the financial health of the thoroughbred horse industry.

Knowing full well what he was after, I gave it to him.

"We are plagued by a vast oversupply of horses," I told him. "You can't give them away. We'll have to ride them or eat them."

The orgasmic glee this produced in the tiny psyche of the industry gossipmonger was spread all the way across his sheet on opening day of the Keeneland November sale, the third consecutive sale in which I had been the leadoff feature. This time, I had handed Indian Charlie both the bow and the arrow, and my weathered likeness was skewered to a barbecue pit basting an unsold yearling with "clenbuterol sauce."

Why is the unintelligible voice of a band of headless horsemen constantly shouting my name? Even the discoverer of the great Curlin, the trainer Kenny McPeek, wanted to know.

"What's with you and Indian Charlie?" he asked.

"Beats me. My wife says he's a anomalous character out of Shakespeare," I said.

"A what?"

"A kind of generic voice, you know, that says what he believes other people are thinking."

"Oh! No kidding. Why is he always on me? I've never done a thing to him." McPeek had often been skewered by Indian Charlie as "Kenny McPeaked."

"Me either. But maybe it's a good thing. In September he had me in a cartoon with Barack Obama, and he just got elected president."

If Indian Charlie was trying to change my luck—or anybody else's for that matter—he didn't.

The world's most prestigious offering of breeding stock fell on its face, too. The November Keeneland sale, for most breeders the last hope for revenue in 2008, always follows what has become a showpiece sale across town at Fasig-Tipton, a single Sunday night affair featuring the retiring race mares and the dams of recent champions.

Better Than Honour, the young dam of Rags to Riches (who conquered Curlin in the Belmont Stakes) and termed the "equine equivalent of the Hope Diamond," was to sell that night along with a bevy of Grade 1 winning millionaires. Among them was Stones River's half sister Unbridled Belle, who had earned $1.4 million for her owner Team Valor.

Hoping to benefit from Unbridled Belle's retirement and retire some Two Bucks debt, I decided to sell her dam, Little Bold Belle, and Little Bold Belle's 2008 foal by Strong Hope in Keeneland's second session.

The "equine Hope Diamond," whose progeny included two other graded stakes winners, set the world record price for a broodmare at $14 million. But it was a lot like that $16 million record price for the Green Monkey, in that it was not exactly as it appeared to be. Better Than Honour was being sold to dissolve a partnership, and the 30 percent shareholder was holding the feet of the 70 percent shareholder to the fire in public.

In effect, all that happened was that the minority partner, helped by Irish bidding, drove the price up, resulting in the majority partner paying $4.2 million for the minority 30 percent—or at least that's the way it looked on paper for the record—just another scene of inscrutable street theater that defies both reason and a world recession.

My decision to offer Unbridled Belle's mother for sale had been equally melodramatic.

The economy had left our future as a breeding farm and racing stable as uncertain as the training career of Larry Jones. At age fifteen, with the dams of both Monarchos and Cotton Blossom deceased, Little Bold Belle was the most valuable mare at Two Bucks Farm, carrying a foal by the highly regarded new sire Bernardini.

She was also a walking miracle, the mare who had shared a near-death experience from the vicious *Clostridium* bacteria infection with the female half of Two Bucks ownership, the dominant female herself. We still had pictures of "Belle" on the barn wall, a virtual skeleton so weak and shaky she was a danger to be around. After thousands of dollars' worth of treatment, the veterinarians at Rood & Riddle had given up and sent her home to die. The only hope, they said, was that she might rally when returned to familiar surroundings and people she knew. A friend had told us that seriously ill horses sometimes respond to human friendship, petting, soft talk, and the like.

We hung bottles of plasma from the top of her stall to feed her intravenously while we tried to coax her into eating a special concoction a neighboring equine nutritionist believed might help pull her through. For two weeks, the dominant female had gotten up twice a night for no other reason than to visit Little Bold Belle in the barn, offering soft words and caring hands.

Although she lost a valuable foal she was carrying, somehow Belle made it back, gained 250 pounds, and got pregnant on the first cover the following year. Loading her into the trailer for delivery to the sale at Keeneland left me with a sick feeling of failure. Never before had a business imperative forced us to sell our best-producing asset.

We once turned down a $1 million offer for Regal Band, which had made no sense. We'd had a good opportunity to sell For Dixie, the dam of Cotton Blossom, but had instead followed our policy of keeping mares once they got old to ensure their care until the end of their lives. The back pasture was full of pensioners who had paid our bills over the years, the results of decisions not all about the money.

After delivering Little Bold Belle and her baby to Keeneland, I drove to Fasig-Tipton to see her celebrated five-year-old daughter, Unbridled Belle. While I was standing outside her stall, my cell phone rang.

"Where are you?" the familiar voice asked.

"Visiting Unbridled Belle at Fasig-Tipton. You should see the new entrance the Arabs built overnight. Looks like a different place."

"We can't sell her mother."

"What do you mean we can't sell her? We decided months ago to do it."

"You decided. Not me. I've been thinking about it all day. All those nights getting up to go pet her and talk to her. That's what saved her, you know. Without us she'd be dead. You can't sell her."

This was no tearful plea. Dominant females don't cry to get their way. And the matter at issue was not so serious that resolution could be found only in prayer. But this was a serious entreaty from a serious source, a grandmother nonetheless.

"Let's talk about it when I get home. I'm leaving now."

No way this was going to happen. How dumb would that be? Preparing a horse all these weeks for sale, paying entry fees, and buying expensive promotional ads. Damned if I am going to bury this one in the backyard. On the day she goes to the sale we're deciding not to sell her. Bull—

Had Indian Charlie's eyes been peeled and ears pricked two hours later, he would have discerned the distinctive Two Bucks trailer pulling up to the sale barn at Keeneland. And yes, that would have been me—old clenbuterol-basting Two Bucks himself—loading Little Bold Belle to go back home, before a single buyer ever got a look at her.

"But we need the money," I had protested. "Little Bold Belle will never be any more valuable than she is today."

"This is about something a lot more important than money," the dominant female had said.

"You're a good businesswoman. Are you telling me you're willing to watch this asset depreciate in the pasture until she is too old to insure and too old to sell so we will have to take care of her the rest of her life like all those others out there?"

"I am. Are you telling me that you really want to sell the asset that regularly produces a better return than any stock we own, the one that will still leave the other mares and come to the fence every time she sees you because she knows you saved her life and trusts you more than any other human being?

"What if she can't learn to trust anybody else and just becomes another mare in some rich guy's pasture? Do you really want to sell her and make her learn to trust someone else we don't even know, after all we've been through together?"

Obviously not.

Still, there was hope for year-end revenue, inappropriately placed, however, in Little Bold Belle's handsome son by the Claiborne stallion Strong Hope. Though Strong Hope was a gorgeous, well-bred animal, his offspring had not proven to be what the market worshipped: two-year-old speed demons. So we entered the colt with a reserve of $119,000—half the value suggested by his pedigree, physical appearance, and perfect set of radiographs, which only one potential buyer even bothered to examine. Live bidding, if indeed there was any, stopped short of $110,000, and he came home with his mother.

Surely, our fortunes would be reversed when our second weanling colt went into the ring. His young sire, Orientate, had spawned a rash of fast, winning two-year-olds, just what the market wanted. Our Two Bucks baby was muscular and handsome, rendered issue-free by our five-hundred-dollar set of radiographs, without a single mark on his report in the hands of our consignor. His throat was exceptional, which three different prospective buyers had verified with their own endoscopic examinations of his wind passage.

The Orientate colt looked like a home-run horse—until a second vet showed up and took a second set of X-rays of a stifle joint. What? A tiny lesion? A minuscule OCD! Suddenly all of our buyers disappeared. He didn't bring $10,000 in the ring. Then the prospective buyers showed up again, wanting to buy him at a discount, quite willing to wait for that tiny lesion to disappear, which every veterinarian in the place knew it would, but only at a price less than his $15,000 stud fee.

The unintended consequences of rational bad behavior had claimed yet another victim, turning what should have been a profitable horse into a loser. In that same sale, the long-suspected vulnerability of the radiograph repository to be manipulated by certain consignors and unscrupulous veterinarians finally bubbled to the surface.

At least two horses in the consignment of one of the leading consignors at Keeneland and Fasig-Tipton sales were discovered to have "clean" radiograph summary reports available in the barn that did not match the actual condition of bone changes under way in the corresponding leg joints. In one case, a second set of verification radiographs found a "significant" OCD lesion not shown on either the radiograph in the repository or the barn sheet. That horse was sold but returned. Another, with a bone "issue" obvious in the radiograph filed in the repository but unmentioned in the barn report, was reported sold in the Keeneland records, but to a buyer no one has yet been able to positively identify.

When the American Association of Equine Practitioners met later in 2008 at San Diego, many of them were handed a copy of a letter written by Paul E. Thorpe, one the world's leading equine orthopedic surgeons, to Nick Nicholson, the Keeneland president, calling for an end to the policy of written radiograph reports being in the hands of sale consignors. Thorpe had long been an opponent of the practice, and his reasoning should have been shocking and embarrassing to the industry, but unfortunately it was not.

By condoning the practice of providing written reports to consignors, Thorpe wrote, sales companies "are compromising their integrities and negating the positive purposes of the repositories. Consignors are pressuring veterinarians to 'smooth over' and in some instances omit lesions from the reports . . . discouraging prospective buyers from utilizing the repositories, and facilitating the sales of damaged goods.

"Veterinarians are obliging their clients and their clients' consignors. Agents for buyers are finding it convenient and profitable to bypass the repositories. Prospective buyers are being duped into buying horses they believe have only minor issues or no issues at all. This subterfuge occurs in degrees, but few or none of us are squeaky clean. I believe this practice should cease."

A dozen years after the deed, there it was on paper, from one of the most respected veterinary voices in the land, finally out in the open for the sale companies and the consignors and the charlatans to see—as if they didn't know.

Their two most important sales had become twin exclamation points on an awful year—both rife with shameful public evidence of sale shenanigans, sale failures, and unprofitable animals—precisely what was ruining the industry.

Hardly anybody would escape the disastrous impact, certainly not Two Bucks. The name of the farm will probably have to be changed—to One Buck or Half a Buck.

Ride, headless horsemen, ride.

ACKNOWLEDGMENTS

The author's heartfelt thanks—and sympathy—to those happy, or not, to have their names mentioned in connection with this book, among them: Glenye Caine Oakford of the *Daily Racing Form*, and Ray Paulick of "The Paulick Report," on whose reporting some of its contents are based; Arthur B. Hancock, John T. Ward, Gary E. Biszantz, and Fred Pope, whose public courage in the interest of better horses and an improved sport was its inspiration; the anomalous nom de plumes—Indian Charlie (Ed Musselman) and the dominant female (Mary Anne Squires)—for their persistent monitoring of the author's public and private indignities that contributed both humor and perspective; Dr. Thomas Tobin of the Gluck Center for his expertise and good humor; my marvelous editor, friend, and savior Paul Golob of Times Books and his associate Christopher O'Connell; and my long-standing Two Bucks Farm mainstays, Sigita Budrikaite and Bruce Hammond, for their lifelong dedication to the raising of good horses.

ABOUT THE AUTHOR

JIM SQUIRES has been breeding and raising horses since 1977, thoroughbreds in Kentucky since 1990. He was the editor of the *Chicago Tribune* from 1981 to 1989 and is the author of three previous books, including *Horse of a Different Color*, an account of his wild ride as the breeder of Monarchos, the winner of the 2001 Kentucky Derby. A native of Nashville, Tennessee, Squires lives with his wife at Two Bucks Farm in Versailles, Kentucky.